POSTNATIONALISM IN CHICANA/O LITERATURE AND CULTURE

Chicana Matters Series
Deena J. González and Antonia Castañeda, editors

*Chicana Matters Series focuses on one of the largest popula-
tion groups in the United States today, documenting the
lives, values, philosophies, and artistry of contemporary Chicanas. Books in this series may be richly diverse, reflecting
the experiences of Chicanas themselves, and incorporating a
broad spectrum of topics and fields of inquiry. Cumulatively,
the books represent the leading knowledge and scholarship in
a significant and growing field of research and, along with
the literary works, art, and activism of Chicanas, underscore
their significance in the history and culture of the United
States.*

Postnationalism in Chicana/o Literature and Culture

Ellie D. Hernández

UNIVERSITY OF TEXAS PRESS
Austin

Requests for permission to reproduce material from this work should
be sent to:
    Permissions
    University of Texas Press
    P.O. Box 7819
    Austin, TX 78713-7819
    www.utexas.edu/utpress/about/bpermission.html

♾ The paper used in this book meets the minimum requirements of
ANSI/NISO Z39.48-1992 (R1997) (Permanence of Paper).

Library of Congress Cataloging-in-Publication Data

Hernández, Ellie D.
    Postnationalism in chicana(o) literature and culture / Ellie D.
Hernández.
        p.   cm. — (Chicana matters series)
    Includes bibliographical references and index.
    ISBN 978-0-292-71907-1 (cloth : alk. paper)
    1. American literature—Mexican American authors—History and
criticism.   2. Politics and literature—United States.   3. Mexican
Americans—Ethnic identity.   4. Nationalism and literature—
United States.   5. Group identity—United States.   6. Homosexuality
and literature—United States.   7. Mexican American gays—
Intellectual life.   8. Globalization—Social aspects—United States.
9. Gender identity in literature.   10. Mexican-American Border
Region—In literature.   I. Title.   II. Title: Postnationalism in chicana literature and culture.   III. Title: Postnationalism in chicano
literature and culture. IV. Series.
    PS153.M4H466   2009
    810.9'3581—dc22
                                                          2008040830

CONTENTS

ACKNOWLEDGMENTS

The writing of a book involves a host of people who participate at different levels. First I would like to thank all of the fine people at the University of California, Santa Barbara, Women's Studies Program. My colleagues Jacqueline Bobo, Eileen Boris, Grace Chang, Barbara Hawthorne, Laury Oaks, Mireille Miller-Young, Leila Rupp, Barbara Tomlinson, and Juliet Williams have been the best colleagues anyone could possibly want. Their intellect, commitment to social justice, and collegiality created a supportive environment that helped to move this project forward. I do not think that I could have done this without them. My thanks also go to Lou Anne Lockwood for her generous support.

I could not have written this book without the support of several other units at UC Santa Barbara. I appreciate the Center for Ethnic and Multicultural Archives and especially Sal Güereña for help with the research archives and the Chicana/o Studies Institute for grants to help with production costs of this book. Thanks to Carl Gutiérrez-Jones and Carlos Morton, as directors of CSI, for promoting new projects such as this study. Special thanks go to Dean of Social Sciences Melvyn Oliver for providing funding for this project. My thanks also go to the students and the director of the Resource Center for Gender and Sexual Diversity for including me in their events and welcoming me as part of the campus community.

At UCLA, special thanks go to Chon Noriega at the Chicana/o Studies Research Center for providing office space and institutional support and especially to Chicana/o studies librarian Yolanda Redder, whose dedication as a scholar provided so much as I worked there. Special thanks to *Chicana/Latina Studies: The Journal of MALCS* for permission to use a portion of my essay "Future Perfect" in Chapter Two.

I thank Lorena Vargas, Cynthia Briseño, and Daisy Velasquez for typing and technical support and Sherri Barnes for her generous work to help complete this project. I would like to thank Alma Lopez for the use of the

viii   *Postnationalism in Chicana/o Literature and Culture*

image *Lupe and Sirena in Love.* My thanks also go to Theresa May, Victoria Davis, and Megan Giller at the University of Texas Press.

Special thanks go to María "Maty" García for all the *caldo de pollo, calabazas de pollo,* and special foods she cooked for me as I was working on this project. To Morena Encina and Lupita Orantes, *doy gracias por toda la ayuda durante este tiempo de escribir un proyecto tan enorme.*

Among my close friends and family, I especially want to thank Elizabeth Dettmer, Laura Rendon and Nellie Duran for their continued friendship over the years. To Norma Cantú, Elvia Niebla, Norma Alarcón, Diana Martínez, Jorge Valadez, Nani González, Roberto Guzman, and all friends back home, my thanks for being there. I thank Harijiwan Khalsa, friend and teacher, and Erin McGeever and the kundalini yoga group in Los Angeles for their inspiration and energy work.

I thank my parents, Tony and Rosa Hernández, for being so silly, even in their old age. Thanks also go to my brothers, Tony III and Carlos, and my sisters, Rosa Isabel, Norma, and Claudia, for their inspiration and sense of humor.

But most importantly, I wish to thank Deena J. González, Antonia Castañeda, and Emma Pérez, important scholars who have influenced my thinking, for being there through it all. It is because of them that I am able to transcend the nation.

INTRODUCTION

In this book I consider postnationalism as a precursor to Chicana/o transnational culture, though some prefer the term "borderlands" or even "Latina/o globalization" to discuss the myriad dislocations of U.S. Mexican-American culture developing over the past thirty years. Throughout the book, I enumerate the processes by which Chicanas/os gain entry into transnational cultural formations. No single social, political, or disciplinary process provides a thorough answer to all facets of transnational identity. While traditional elements of nationhood or of belonging, in the case of national minorities, still exist in ethnic, race, and class structures, I conclude that gender and sexuality offer more varied responses to the idea of the dissolution of the nation than any other identity process. I thus argue that gender and sexuality are categories that arose in response to exclusion from the nation. It is from this location that gender and sexuality may help us better understand how people construct desires, produce their own social critiques, and formulate useful interpretations of the changing world.

The issues I raise in this book develop from an interdisciplinary frame of analysis; I look at the transformation of a nationalist-based identity in studying Chicanas/os living in the United States. Interdisciplinary models, rather than identity-based methods or perspectives, will be necessary in the twenty-first century to comprehend global culture's complexity and its many faces. The trajectory I track is specifically the social categories of gender and sexuality as central to the emergence of Chicana/o transnational culture. Although such other areas of interest as immigration, drug trafficking, and commerce suggest immediately a predominantly economic notion of the transnational, they do not account for more provocative social and political formations. In transnational fields of study, gender and sexuality alone do not create a basis for Chicanas/os' emergence into transnational global culture; however, the categories are critical for understanding how mechanisms of desire are figured into the nation. The gendered and sexualized body offers striking demarcations within capitalism that continually inform and transform the Chicana/o and Mexicana/o as a semiotic system of signs, enabling distinct historical and popular expression as well as eroding nationalism as the sole basis for Chicanas/os' emergence. These terms, as I use them here, reflect national cultural differences: Chicanas/os are U.S.-born residents of Mexican descent and displaced immigrants; Mexicanas/os are Mexican-born people who identify with Mexico as their homeland; and Latinas/os are those who immigrated from other Latin American countries and some parts of the Caribbean and have a different relationship to the United States than the other two groups have. "Chicana/o" also more specifically refers to the political, social, and cultural movement begun in the 1960s that intersected historically with the U.S. civil rights movement.

The transnational frame of analysis is useful because it encompasses not just a border zone but also an unmapped terrain and space for a new frontier that extends beyond the traditional geographies, whether geopolitical, cultural, social, or even physical. My use of several fields of study as well as the embedded social symbolic process serves my interdisciplinary goals for the book by adding dimensions otherwise not often considered. It is not enough to focus on close readings of literature or texts, for example, when their social context is missing. I use interpretative strategies throughout to illustrate the growing need in the academy to draw from different experiences and approaches in order to provide a reliable reading of the complex systems that we have entered as a result of transnational global culture.

For Chicanas/os, and especially within feminist discourse, this time is critical for developing the field of transnationalism. Moving beyond the cultural nationalist period has not been easy, and despite the many civil rights glories associated with the 1960s and 1970s, the fact that a new cultural logic has slowly made its way into our daily lives makes some matters (urbanization, immigration, and education) ever more pressing. Even as a critique of cultural nationalism began to emerge following its heyday in the 1960s, the limitations of cultural nationalism as a public social discourse encountered resistance from women and men alike. At the same time, the cultural and aesthetic expression built into the Chicana/o movement gave Chicanas/os the only source of expression at a time when speaking out and publishing material seemed impossible except in small presses or on older mimeograph equipment. Distribution was restricted to local populations; newsletters appeared and disappeared because mainstream media were largely inattentive.

In the many works I examine throughout this book, I engage the persistence of social discontent with nationalism as it surrounded a discomfort with Chicana/o cultural nationalism, even though it allowed a vital criticism to take shape. Briefly, Chicana/o cultural nationalism of the type I explore herein had a political arm—grassroots organizations like the Brown Berets and Chicana/o committees—and a cultural arm in artists' collectives like ASCO. In highlighting and even celebrating achievements of intellectual formation within the Chicana/o movement, it is equally important to note that Chicana/o cultural nationalism began to change in the early 1980s. The benefits of these changes have far outweighed the losses, and Chicana/o discourse gained from its engagement with a discussion about gender and sexuality because this engagement stimulated a larger and more heterogeneous arrangement of class, identity, and nation.

My own encounter with transnationalism derives from my experience in a women's studies department where I have been able to traverse the boundaries of the nation more freely than in any other academic discipline. Women's studies departments have changed significantly as well. In this frame of analysis, my focal point developed from the experience of working in the field of gender and sexuality. It has been much easier to incorporate an intersectional and interdisciplinary trajectory in teaching and researching under a women's studies model, mostly because the expectation to center gender or sexuality is already fraught with complications. But in addition to the rigors of academic life, the experience of the global and transnational condition derives from another experience of dislocation. Commuting a hundred miles each way from Los Angeles to my home institution, UC Santa Barbara, has given me firsthand experience with travel, dislocation, and the transnational condition, albeit on a much smaller scale, with home and work divided by a commute.

Within temporary spaces of dislocation, logistically speaking, I and others who share the highways or airports increasingly come to terms with economic and social displacement. Historians have commented in recent works that the example of Los Angeles International Airport alone makes this statement daily: thousands of tourists, thousands of immigrants, and thousands of others seeking to move to Los Angeles produce an image of a city where half the residents speak a language other than English in their homes and where more than two hundred distinctive languages are spoken.

These moments of dislocation led me to think about the postnational. The term "postnational" seems to capture something contemporary, moving beyond the modernism of the late twentieth century. Debates at Berkeley in the late 1990s about transnationalism lent the term diverse meanings. One arm—the drive to formulate a transnational feminism—became a leading new area of study; several attempts then to categorize Chicana/o representation by other feminists fell short because the area of transnationalism reflected more the specific interests of Third World feminism and not necessarily issues of greater concern to U.S. women of color. I was not convinced that we needed to import the issues and problems into U.S. feminism. A desire to abandon the condition of U.S. women of color who had endured hardships across the different spaces of ghettos and barrios had been suspended, too, while the focus often fell instead on women in revolutionary Latin America or in liberation struggles for indigenous rights across the hemispheres.

Was there a space, an experience that U.S. women of color could attest to in thinking about transnationalism? It appeared impossible, so like many of my fellow graduate students and junior faculty, I came to an understanding that U.S. minorities might have a different experience that required different terminology. "Postnational" characterized an effect of time similar to that in "postcolonial" and even in "postmodern," conceptually speaking, and it became a succinct way to categorize the dislocation of Chicanas/os caught or suspended between the national order and an emerging transnationalism. Because "postnationalism" sounded more like a transitory phase between the old version of nationalism with which I was familiar (1960s standard Chicano-movement rhetoric), the postcolonial and transnational areas of study seemed newer and more exciting. My definition of postnationalism thus took into account a heterogeneous arrangement of a nationally based feminism with creative and intellectual links to queer studies and sexuality.

Postnationalism characterizes many of the elements that abound within the systems and networks called "transnational global culture." Transnational feminism was only a starting point for many other matters that pertained to a global framing of U.S. people of color. The naming of a new movement or, rather, the absence of such a name led me to think about identity formations arising from this period just as Chicanas/os began their entry into transnational culture. This new time is not without its own critical crisis. I worried that a search for a new paradigm would make it seem like we were completely abandoning the historical basis for the Chicana/o movement and U.S. minority criticism when in fact the history of U.S. civil rights opened so many opportunities for us all. Historically, the U.S. civil rights movements of the nineteenth and twentieth centuries offered a public discourse on equality that was necessary to locate the material dislocation U.S. minorities had experienced under segregation, on reservations, and in barrios. Such a legacy inspired other participants in the movement to claim a sense of themselves through self-styled identity practices that became part of the revamped social movements.

Throughout the writing of this book, I naturally questioned what would become of the Chicana/o struggle in a transnational stage of capital development but, most importantly, what would become of U.S. civil rights as a model of social organization for U.S. minorities in an age of globalization. What *then* is the relationship of U.S. civil rights to transnational culture? Are these not the same civil rights that we want to compel emerging nations to espouse and follow while seemingly suspending our own rights and claims to self-representation under the rules of global culture? The importance of such civil rights histories and influence on humanism and the social fabric led me to conclude that Chicanas/os have a stake in establishing a place in transnational cultures without necessarily compromising the rights, ethics, and social power that U.S. minorities have gained in recent decades.

Cultural critic Norma Alarcón sees contradictions and critical binds inherent in the cultural experience of being Chicana/o in an age of global and transnational cultures; these contradictions surface as "real life" problems and dilemmas. Emerging from advances in civil rights, how does one account for the irony and queerness apparent in a TV show like *Ugly Betty* about a young Hispanic woman working in the world of fashion or in the packaging of celebrity "J Lo," Jennifer Lopez, as examples of a global commodification of *latinidad*? These issues seem relevant to the mixed signs and structures upon which we have relied as the nation alters its symbols and popular images, or what we might term "the symbolic."

If national discourses provide us with an endless assortment of contradictions, as Norma Alarcón, Homi K. Bhabha, and others have articulated so well over the past several decades, then do the contradictions also mean that U.S. minorities must contend with increasingly complex issues that cannot be defined or even recognized in a national or transnational discourse? Where are we, since nationalist projects no longer address the issues of identity or no longer seem relevant in academic and cultural situations— not because there is nothing more to say but because the way in which we talk about, write about, perceive, represent, and express ourselves within our own nation, culturally speaking, has dramatically changed? These are the questions that interest me most because they offer a lens of cultural matters at large, of where to locate that "we" and an "us."

Altered by movements to be closer in our relationships with peers in other nations and by what we call transnational culture and globalization, we find ourselves in a bit of a critical quandary: Chicanas/os, like other

U.S. minorities, still seem rooted in a history, legacy, memory, and dialectics of the civil rights era that cannot easily be forgotten, even as a popular television show, for example, might appear to distort minority mappings. In this study's central concern with one U.S. minority's position within transnational networks, I consider areas in which Chicana/o transnational culture became something that has yet to be fully recognized. In *Postnationalism* I suggest that an in-between state exists and links advanced capitalism with U.S. ethnic formations in a way I find intriguing to follow.

One critical thread throughout this study is the reformation of historical, spatial, and thematic reflections of culture. For example, national civil rights have been subsumed into a global movement toward human rights; an emphasis on border culture replaces a nationalistic center or core; and the rational, resident subject is substituted by the displaced or dislocated citizen. Ethnic minority, gender, and sexual identity frameworks have been developed most proficiently in strong correlation between developmental frameworks. I examine the constituting forces at work in mitigating the cultural domains I examine here not across ethnic or gender or sexual lines but rather as a conversation among them all.

Postnationalism* thus extends beyond the experience of the U.S.-Mexico borderlands and includes issues pertinent to a nation-state in apparent decline. Many of the issues I discuss here also may apply to comparative studies of ethnic, gender, and sexual minorities. I contend that gender and sexual subjectivities facilitated the emergence of a Chicana/o transnational culture as sites of identity production and as a discourse on difference, enabled but not supported by the advance of global capitalism, because of the internal mechanisms that prompted change.

Like the geographical concept of borderlands, postnationalism is a new theorization in interdisciplinary studies. Because nationalism has been replaced by far more complex world economic systems, it may seem increasingly irrelevant to many citizens. The centeredness of U.S. critical perspectives may no longer work for minorities within the United States. Or it might even be the case that identity processes beyond those with which we are familiar—race, class, gender, sexuality—are simply fabrications of our political imaginary to remain at the center of race and ethnicity globally. Other questions persist and loom: How are these processes coterminous with capitalism? Or are such facets as displacement and hybridity aligned with new democratic ideals that have the possibility of reaching far beyond our limited form of state and national governance?

We find U.S. society and communities at a peculiar juncture where macroeconomic decisions meet daily life: gasoline prices, war, terrorism, and natural catastrophe are examples. A human element has been lost because of the way people are organized in global and transnational exchange, and as people's sense of location becomes less tangible, so does the value of their lives. From undocumented workers to immigrants, including children, from migrants to sexual minorities and women, the usurpation of human-ness and humanities within global exchange can be unsettling. What re-mains as a result is a scattered organization of ethnic minorities, feminists, the diasporic, immigrants, and a loose cluster of postcolonial peoples who in turn now represent the heirs of the current U.S. national racial dis-course and the future of the global sector, economic and humanitarian. Interestingly, the same groups have different stakes in creating political al-liances and social movements or in protesting the role of the United States as guardian of the world economy. One critique I present in this work is to challenge Chicana/o intellectuals to reconsider conventional assump-tions concerning racial and ethnic formations without erasing our shared recent history. I ask that we imagine ourselves beyond the nation, beyond geographic locations, and beyond identity. We, too, are part of the global movement of capital exchange, except that even as the fastest-growing demographic group in the U.S. population, we still are cast at the lowest range of the economy and not among the nation's strongest intellectuals, poets, and writers. We are also that.

In setting forth the basis for a discourse on the historiography of cul-ture, U.S. Chicana/o cultural nationalism refers, thus, to a loose-fitted at-tempt to gain entry into national social politics and the process of eventu-ally moving beyond them. Viewed as a necessary recourse to exclusion from Anglo-American domination and nationalist discourse, cultural national-ism in today's lens fits more appropriately into the scheme of a counter-cultural movement than does a recalcitrant, postcolonial, socialist move-ment. In my theorization, however, it is not just the fact that Chicanas/os set out to redefine the national expatriation of the Mexican-American population due to broken land treaties and to the marginalization of citi-zens of Mexican descent. The emergence of Chicanas/os in rhetorical and political construction, in the Chicana/o social protest movement, and as documented in plans such as *El plan espiritual de Aztlán* and *El plan de Santa Bárbara* of 1969, for example, formalized a belief in direct action that prompted a performative discourse on citizenship. Each would ultimately reinscribe Mexican-Americans into American culture.

What motivated me to pursue this interpretation of the Chicana/o ex-perience is that inclusion into mainstream American culture has not been completed, equality has not been achieved fully, and the aesthetic processes that were created and unleashed some thirty years ago do not provide a suitable cultural "logic" for the twenty-first century. This new logic implies that the postnational frame is necessary to establish a foundation in literature, poetry, and history, and such cultural logic ultimately situates a critique of global economics from an interdisciplinary perspective.

A thoughtfully imagined cultural form of representation in the spatial imaginary, Aztlán (the mythical homeland of the ancient people in what is now Mexico), brought forth a culturally nationalist method for inscribing Mexico in North America. Along with it, the closed system of nationalism coupled with the mood of the 1960s could not continue as the contradictions of social change and cultural traditions mixed. Chicana/o literary and cultural production altered its trajectory from a cultural nationalist movement to one that openly celebrated difference; this is perhaps one of the greatest achievements in Chicana/o discourse since its inception. The creative nationhood building implied in the social symbol of Aztlán offered a response to the racism inherent in segregation. The intended goal of cultural nationalism was expressed as emancipation from an oppressive state power that created an uneven and disenfranchised culture based upon separatism. The problem, however, lies in the public and celebratory aspects of cultural nationalism, because the exuberance of national unity takes place at the level of the symbolic and is understood at the level of culture as national pride, patria, and patrimony—that is, as masculinities.

By virtue of these masculine-inscribed meanings determined by patria and nationalism, global and transnational culture appears to offer alternatives to the formed masculinity apparent in twentieth-century thinking. Its presence can be noted in organized protest movements around the world. During the massive protests that took place across the United States in spring 2006 for immigrant rights, social justice resounded as a demand for greater inclusion and protection under the national credo of equality and representation. A comprehensive examination of U.S. policy on immigration along with the shift to a global culture reveals a diminishing significance of U.S. citizens simultaneous with enhanced trade and commercialization, all without registering the toll on human life. So in writing this book I have considered the imposition of a new form of capitalism on Mexico as analogous to a steroid injection that suddenly, artificially boosts the user's illusion of strength while effectively damaging his or her body. Young women die at the El Paso–Juárez border moving northward pursuing the promise of better wages in the many manufacturing plants transplanted from the U.S. side to the Mexican side. The ill effects of transnational global capital, noted in the violent deaths of these women, call for a reassessment of the way economic development and gender play significant roles in determining border life. Missing from this equation is a humanities-based critique of the social structure.

While in this book I am not concerned with globalism of the type defined elsewhere as neoliberalism or as the advancement of capitalism around the world, the study turns to the cultural dynamics within Chicana/o production itself to make explicit how globalization will eventually intrude upon a people's sense of self. The nation-space continues to be a site for immense social and political change, even though such primary cultural practices within the nation-space run the risk of seeming reactionary, nostalgic, and essentialist in nature. Numerous inconsistencies abound in any drive to promote advanced capitalism around the world, and it is very important at this juncture to respond creatively based on what national minorities, in this case Chicanas/os, have formulated.

Postnationalism—although in process and not yet achieved—presents a new direction of intellectual, social, and economic factors in the production of Chicana/o expression. The move away from nationalism does not necessarily lead to a global, postmodern, or postcolonial perspective as it has been organized in the academy, as works I examine here will attest. Rather, the move toward postnationalism appears as a discontinuous or fragmented part of an earlier cultural nationalism, in both political and aesthetic offerings. Cherríe Moraga's and Gloria Anzaldúa's example as authors and cultural critics resulted in distinctive contributions after the publication in 1981 of the pathbreaking anthology they edited, *This Bridge Called My Back*. Now, nearly three decades later, cultural nationalism as an organizing theme for community and cultural works no longer sustains the same effect of unifying Chicanas/os. The response to Moraga and Anzaldúa's noted anthology is one example of many that suggest how coalitional forces that brought many Chicana/o thinkers together dissipated and dispersed into actual, published responses to culture after nationalism.

The postnational may bear some similarities to critiques of globalism, but the gaps and ruptures that globalism produces do not necessarily qualify Chicanas/os' participation in a global discourse as freely as one may suppose. In the 1970s Chicanas/os reflected on issues that were personal and individualistic by becoming more introspective in their writings, with a more sardonic approach that was psychological and existential in style and representation. Added to this, the influences of feminism had prompted more interest in a radical sexual politics in which American women in general, as well as women of color, looked at sexuality as a way of liberating women's personal lives. Meanwhile, AIDS nationalized the plight of gay men as they struggled to be recognized by the medical establishment, and the government and media refused to look at the crisis; after all, some forms of sexual liberation could be dangerous.

The terms of struggle obviously changed, and for Chicanas/os so did the commitment to ethnic and racial concerns. Some were well established in scholarship, but when the problem of homophobia and sexism arose at conferences, the silence over sexual rights became all too revealing and unsettling. The terms "emancipation" and "liberation," considered the indispensable rhetorical claim of America's progressive discourse in the 1960s and 1970s, now connoted a critical impasse; the divide serves as a basis for examination in this study: how did these so-called liberatory movements morph into sad commentaries of collective angst?

The dissimulations of a national identity and their bodies appear to unfold once the discussion of nationalism shifts to a postnational context. A nationalistic approach has been supplanted by feminist, performative, borderlands, and queer approaches. My argument hinges on one fundamental point: Chicana/o literary and cultural interpretations have focused intensely on embodying Chicana/o political and class subjectivity to the exclusion of all other terms, including color, sex, gender, and sexuality. This focus therefore became a problematic and critical choice in later years. Because the terms of capital production have shifted significantly enough so as to impact the cultural material space in ways that could not be effectively interpreted in the traditional Marxist empirical model upon which those early studies of Chicano nationalism relied, I argue that the locations and politics of Chicana/o representations and aesthetics have moved dramatically across the map and thus warrant a different way of reading and interpreting Chicana/o cultural production.

Today the vast scope of Chicana/o cultural production merits closer, if intersectional, examination. For one thing, and curiously the most problematic, the use of cultural nationalism as a model of resistance for many Third World nations continues to revert to a fundamentalist view of "the original" national character. Nationhood has been radically transformed by global economic forces. This dramatic reshaping of the world has been in motion for some time. The effort to globalize national economies and cultures has been a goal in the extensive propagation of late capital. In this book I am therefore also deeply concerned about the effect on cultural representation, which has taken on added significance in the face of a global economic and communications evolution through the Internet, cellular phones, and digital technology. Latina/o populations especially experience a type of assimilation process into the global scheme that will eventually reshape identities and their social spaces, and not for the better. Today the metropolitan areas of Los Angeles, Miami, Houston, Chicago, New York, and San Francisco are experiencing a migration flux of significant proportions. This strand of movement and change shapes the analysis in the ensuing chapters.

While the subject of this work is not the process of immigration, I reference global and transnational culture to elucidate Chicana/o cultural production over the past twenty-five years. Much has been written about Chicana/o nationalism as a positive and emancipatory narrative that gave rise to a new identity and political process for people of Mexican origins in the United States; cultural nationalism also has been viewed as a strategy of decolonization by ethnic minorities. Its basic tenet of resistance was to interrogate the dogmas of liberal economics in twentieth-century state formation. In the social milieu of a global framework, however, the nature of dissent, while a product of modernity, is only possible insofar as local/global, particular/universal dichotomies are established. In the main, Chicanas/os never settled and kept migrating, from rural to urban, from village to pueblo to cities and towns and toward the metropolis.

My engaged use of "postnational" rather than "transnational" or "global" mirrors the discussion of capitalism's lack of effectiveness at the local level. Critical departures from a celebrated global or transnational culture do not automatically revert to a nationalist position. I am motivated more by the contradictions of the binarism between the national and the global, as if either of those terms can account for the experiences of most people. Fredric Jameson, in his preface to *The Cultures of Globalization* (1998), finds the terminology vexing and problematic. In an apparent attempt to capture the slipperiness of global lore, he describes how

> to "define" globalization as an untotalizable totality which
> intensifies binary relations between its parts—mostly nations,
> but also regions and groups, which, however, continue to
> articulate themselves on the model of "national identities"
> (rather than in terms of social classes). (xii)

Postnationalism suggests otherwise and aptly describes a refusal or inability to enter into global modernity. Chicanas/os are global, migratory, displaced, and yet situated in an intellectual movement that possesses a cultural nationalist bent that for the most part provided a foundational logic about origins. In other words, the birth is at odds with the development that follows. From within the expansive work that has since taken hold of Chicana/o cultural production, postnationalism signals an alteration in character, rhetorical style, and thematic presentation. Stories, approaches, and the organization of knowledge no longer appeal to the emancipated male heroism or innocence in coming-of-age representation. Realistic images of plight and self-discovery have been replaced by representations of anomalous states, the marginal figures of culture, the displaced, the lost or forgotten, the dead, and the survival epics of new worldism, each of which characterizes the arduous journey into the new age. Postnationalism is neither direct resistance to global capitalism nor an unconscious drive within nationalist imperatives to maintain a tribal lineage best encapsulated as the mestizo, mixed-race Chicano. Postnationalism marks a position, to a certain extent, but is not an attempt to situate an essence or a "Chicano" character within it.

Postnationalism *should* be viewed as an adjustment phase, a period of immense progress despite its lack of origins, against the reactive political elements and degenerate aspects of capitalism that flourished during the post-1960s era. The postnationality framing of this book is a way to account for the lost nationalist aspects of the Chicana/o movement, to explore how the subtle shift to embrace various aspects of social, cultural, and sexual differences was as much a political necessity as it was an inevitable historical facet of economic development. The Chicana/o identity's traversal of the national, global, and transnational fields of study depicts a lived experience that cannot be contained by standard depictions of nationhood or of nationality. Changing social conditions made possible the sudden shift from a less nationalistic mode. The formation of cultural "difference" both as an aesthetic process and a political device are associated with the advance of late capitalism into places where difference was otherwise unintended. The conclusion is that capitalism is the source and means of expanding human rights and cultural expression. Sadly, though, the consequences of capitalism are hardly ever noted. In the midst of this realignment of culture has been the degeneration of the liberal nation-state. With its orthodoxy hinging upon definitive boundaries or Berlin Walls, drawn according to the identity of a given nation, the composition of the nation has seen better days.

Minorities within the U.S. national frame have endured the loss of freedoms such as, for some individuals, the suspension of habeas corpus in the years after 9/11 as policing of minorities intensified. The lost sense of freedom seems oddly inconsistent with the global and even transnational shift to expand labor and consumer goods until one considers the resulting limits on citizen participation in the flow. In this study, however, I hope to explain Chicana/o cultural nationalism's shift within a philosophical and rhetorical composition that once relied upon national coding and that would have had recourse to its own initiation of a heterogeneous arrangement of human life or dignity. The formation of Chicana/o literature and cultural production initially marked an entry into a form of representation that Mexico or the United States could register. Chicanas/os' mimicry of a national identity arose at a time when liberal economics were being redefined. Of course, Aztlán. It became the symbol for all that was right and all that was wrong with Chicano cultural nationalism.

The area in which the tendency is most clearly expressed is the cultural representation of the public space, the literary expression and cultural responses to hegemonic reorderings of power. In museums, comic books, novels, and scholarly writing, the reordering of power is both contested and illustrated. While the tendency to locate Chicanas/os within a global perspective still falls on the topics of immigration, drug policy, social welfare, and bilingual education, I conclude that we have at last moved out of the corner in which nationalism had us trapped. Less stylized as an organizing theme, postnationality is a series of sentiments that have altered the direction in Chicana/o production. Postnational devices are an entry point to newer ideas and are indicative of the cultural and literary influence of contemporary social movements. These are fluid and can go anywhere.

Among the issues embraced by heterogeneous Chicana/o postnationalism is the organization of knowledge produced by gays, lesbians, and feminists. The social critiques of borderland/periphery models have been the primary interlocutors of critical knowledge in the field we now call cultural studies. U.S. cultural studies can be seen as an unconscious response to the insufficiency of mainstream humanities to exact an argument for social inequity as much as a counterhegemonic response to the sexism, homophobia, and intensified capitalism that have prospered under the aegis of mainstream culture.

The observations that situate the politics of Chicana/o representations and aesthetics have changed sufficiently to warrant a different way of reading, interpreting, and criticizing Chicana/o cultural production. But such observations also serve as a basis for developing women's studies and sexuality studies. My original formulation for this book centered on nationalism as a subjugated knowledge of groups and individuals who would eventually suffer and accomplish what little they could as they endeavored to construe nationalism to suit their interests. More recent effects of the global, geopolitical economy have changed all that.

In the next six chapters I address specific issues surrounding postnationalism. The general premise resides in a notion that cultural national identity formation provided a provisional means of participation within a segregated society. Once some measure of representation in mainstream U.S. culture was achieved, the economic shift toward global society altered the dialectics—and direction—of U.S. civil rights minority movements, including those affecting Chicanas/os. In Chapter 1 I discuss the critical foundational theories in the development of postnationalist thought by looking at the formation of cultural nationalist and transnationalist aesthetics. As I developed the book's theoretical and methodological basis, the transformation from a nationalist perspective to a postnational one required that I look at several theoretical moments from the 1960s to the present. In Chapter 2 I examine Chicana feminist discourse as a unique component of postnational discourse, with its critique of exclusion from both the U.S. feminist movement and the early Chicana/o movement. Chapter 3 focuses on the excesses of border culture and the limitations of citizenship. Rather than looking at the border as an aesthetically progressive area, I find that the border zone functions as a visual and geographical site of regulation. In Chapter 4 I take up the postmodern play of fashion codes as they facilitate a more direct relationship to identity formation within consumer culture. Chapter 5 presents an examination of the autobiographical tradition in Chicana/o studies that functions as a social text with exemplary and national features such as an idealized masculinity captured in Richard Rodriguez', peformativity and ideas about citizenship. And finally, in Chapter 6 I review queer Chicana/o experiences by looking at the U.S. gay-lesbian movements; I examine the institutional and political contexts for Chicana/o aesthetics that emerge out of a Chicana/o queer experience.

In the field of transnational studies today, the traditional scholarly arrangement of study leaves Chicanas/os confined to a national perspective. In a twenty-first-century study, this problem is especially critical as new representatives of "the nation" emerge. Here we might think about the possibility that the work surrounding marginalized citizenship could occupy a central role in the academy. This book, finally, is about undoing the subjugation of citizenship, about viewing it not as a necessary outcome of an overly capitalized world; rather, humanity or human beings resisting any notion of "illegal" personhood, of being aliens upon any land, is one of its conclusions.

One   POSTNATIONALISM
              Encountering the Global

> *The hegemonic discourse of nationalism was composed out of the intertwined logics of developmental history and core-periphery topology. These logics produced the matrix for a global disposition of power which universal history mapped onto the teleological narratives out of which euroamerican nationalisms obtained their legitimating self-evidence. But such representations of nationalism as the end toward which "archaic" social formations tended substantially reduced the heterogeneous varieties and contexts of nationalism to the dimensions of an overarching evolutionary paradigm.*
> DONALD PEASE, "THE POLITICS OF POSTNATIONAL AMERICAN STUDIES," 2001

"Transnational" global culture refers to those forms of language, custom, politics, goods, and services that pertain to exchange across and beyond national borders.[1] Transnational identity formation pertains to people's national identities as they encounter the effects of transnational culture. In this study, Chicanas/os' identities take on added significance when the role of the national serves to limit the interconnectedness of their national experiences to one nation or one set of experiences. Despite any geographical separation or theorization about the colonial experience, neither globalism nor transnationalism serves the purpose of achieving the appropriate view of Chicanas/os at this moment in time. The term "postnational," as I distinguish it from "transnational" and "global," refers to those ideas, experiences, or cultural works in which the connection between two nations plays a central and vital role by offering a new critique; certainly the term refers to an important experience that is a part of the global encounter. Unlike transnationalism, Chicana/o postnationalism refers to a transition from a cultural nationalist-based critical study of U.S. Chicanas/os as the group begins its entry into transnational globalization.

Taking a cue from American critical studies, John Carlos Rowe describes postnationalism in the U.S. context in this other way: "Nationalist based studies no longer reflect the needs or challenges of the State University in the midst of transforming itself as rector of global and transnational study" (1998, 53). Urging on a new and more proficient way of challenging the terms of transnational culture, the earliest shaping of Chicana/o postnationalism began during the 1980s as the United States as a whole experienced a change in demographics, labor, immigration policy, consumer relations, and political ideologies (14). In *Global City* (2001), Saskia Sassen writes:

> The experience of the global is partial. It is not an all-encompassing umbrella. The multiple processes that constitute it inhabit and shape specific, rather than universal, structurations of the economic, the political, the cultural, and the subjective. In so doing, new spatialities and temporalities are produced, co-existing yet distinct from the master temporality and spatiality of the "national." In the interplay of their difference, strategic openings have emerged. (18)

These new openings are necessary to recategorize the focus of Chicana/o critical study as it engages with and enters into global modernity. While most discussions about transnational global culture seem to center on countries other than the United States, the impact of globalization pertains as much to the experience of U.S. minority communities and their experience as it does to the global community. It might seem natural to view the effects of an entwined world economic system as a major and perhaps destructive shift away from national culture, but such a shift also is responsible for the creation of new aesthetic expression, identity formations, and social organization that have only begun to take shape, as Sassen describes.

In a similar context, Charles Carnegie in *Postnationalism Prefigured* (2002) describes the impact of globalization of the Caribbean islands over the last two decades of the twentieth century. Globalization results in upheaval in the cultural and social life of this formerly colonized region of the globe. In his description of the Caribbean context, Carnegie notes that "postnationalism" refers to a set of economic conditions that have, in turn, resulted in a different set of cultural expressions of rights, politics, and social ordering for people native to the Caribbean. He demonstrates not only that the nation-state is an exhausted form of political organization but that in the Caribbean the ideological and political reach of the nation-state has historically been tenuous at best. Caribbean peoples, he suggests, live continually in breach of the nation-state configuration. Drawing both on his own experiences as a Jamaican-born anthropologist and on the experiences of those who consider national borders as little more than artificial administrative nuisances, Carnegie describes the native conditions as well as the colonized remnants left behind in the wake of postcolonization to delineate the social configuration of nations caught between two worldviews.

The nation has been traditionally described as the people's place of governance, as it is also a mark of citizenship, a moniker of origins, an identity, a tribal unity, a geographical space, and a site of economic and cultural exchange (Buell 1998). For ethnic minorities living in the United States, few avenues of self-expression have been as powerful as cultural nationalists' drive to formulate group solidarity and political resistance against the dominant cultural ordering of people. Unlike other postcolonial nations, its proximity binds U.S. Chicanas/os to Mexico in history, in economic relations, and in the social symbolic process. This strong identification by Chicanas/os with Mexico as the patria, the motherland of indigenous people, of mestizaje continues within the transnational inception of new colonial paradigms. Despite this tenuous history that has been well articulated in Chicana/o historiography, social and political representations have not sufficiently explained the current conditions. The experiences that developed from U.S.-Mexico transnational culture gather unique character from a highly competitive area of commercialization where the flow of people, culture, and social exchange occurs daily and is vital to each nation's existence, further illustrating the interdependent nature of the two nations. The geopolitical influences between them are viewed as necessary for the development of human and private capital to enable North America to navigate global currents, whether as industrial or immigrant corridors across the borderlands (Miyoshi 1993).

Another way to view transnational study is through the lens of material culture; this includes the circulation of goods, people, and ideas across national borders. At the same time, the conditions of material exchange within a framework of transnational study cannot be separated from colonial exploitation, since the term "transnational" is perhaps most often associated with transnational corporations, which bring images of transnational capitalism such as maquiladora factories along the U.S.-Mexico border. Masao Miyoshi, in "Borderless World?" (1993), offers an analysis of the economic exploitation practiced by transnational corporations and reminds us that this sort of transnational exchange is clearly neocolonial; critics, Miyoshi argues, should concentrate not on celebrating multiculturalism but on trying to erase unjust political and economic differences that cause migratory movements and result in the severe disruption of people's lives. One way to counter the unjust circumstances of U.S. and Mexican transnational culture is to present new terms and ideas that distinguish it from the homogeneous framing of "transnational" as a term for all to embrace.

The term "postnational" indicates a movement away from a simplistic dichotomy of colonizer and colonized and correctly labels identities and institutions that cannot be said to have just one national identity. At the same time, "postnational" suggests a time lapse or a lag and adequately reflects the struggles of the residents of two-thirds of the world against the quickening forces of global capitalism. While "transnationalism" reflects neocolonial tendencies, how transnational commerce is affecting local communities, the environment, and domestic concerns has been largely overlooked. By situating a U.S. minority experience as an important critique of transnational study, the perspective on celebrated forms of globalism calls attention to some of the ill effects of global capitalism.

Transnational mappings for Chicanas/os may not be possible as the high-tech links and highly intellectualized format take effect across social, cultural, political, and economic fields. In other words, it is not likely at this point that Chicanas/os will view transnationalism as the cultural bandwagon to join. Transition from nationalist cultural routes to transnational cultural points of reference involves shifts in thinking that have not yet materialized and will likely not materialize as Chicanas/os continue to inhabit the working-class ranks of society (Minolo 2000). The most visible movement to globalize the U.S. and Mexican economies and to make changes within the framework of culture—the passage of the North American Free Trade Agreement (NAFTA) in January 1994—signaled a new approach to the Westernization of Mexico and the rest of Latin America. However, globalization throughout the Americas has diminished people's ability to unite across borders or to lay claim to either nationalism or globalism. One must also consider how the exhaustion of the nation as a signifying model for identity and aesthetic formations is shaping a new sensibility that is changing daily.

Cultural nationalist discourses took root in U.S. countercultural movements initiated during the 1960s and 1970s that involved grassroots and community-based organizations and transformed academic discussions; later, in the mid- to late 1980s, these discourses became the basis for most multicultural education. However, the movement to occupy transnational spaces assumes a position in what Gayatri Spivak, in "Can the Subaltern Speak?" (1988), calls the "comprador elite." Spivak demonstrates a concern for the processes whereby postcolonial studies ironically reinscribe, co-opt, and rehearse neocolonial imperatives of political domination, economic exploitation, and cultural erasure. In other words, one might ask whether the postcolonial critic is unknowingly complicit in the task of sustaining imperialism. Is postcolonialism a specifically First World, male, privileged, academic, institutionalized discourse that classifies and surveys the actual modes of colonial dominance it seeks to dismantle? According to Spivak, postcolonial studies encourage "postcolonial intellectuals [to] learn that their privilege is their loss" (284). Spivak encourages but also criticizes the efforts of the subaltern studies group, a project led by Ranajit Guha that has reappropriated Gramsci's term "subaltern" (the economically dispossesed) in order to locate and reestablish a "voice" or collective locus of agency in postcolonial India (275). Although Spivak acknowledges the "epistemic violence" done upon Indian subalterns, she suggests that any attempt from the outside to ameliorate their condition by granting them collective speech invariably will encounter a dependence upon Western intellectuals to "speak for" the subaltern condition rather than allowing them to speak for themselves. Spivak argues that by speaking out and reclaiming a collective cultural identity, subalterns will in fact reinscribe their subordinate position in society.

Globalization itself often involves complex arrangements of discourse that by design exclude less-educated, working-class women and, generally speaking, any disenfranchised people from self-representation. Consequently, transnationalism, a model of material culture and exchange, is not just about material culture; the nature of its exclusionary role is epistemological and cultural. Another way in which these new ideologies have only materialized over the past twenty-five years came into focus during the 1980s, when a multicultural frame for the study of social, cultural, ethnic, and political difference played a vital role in redefining the role of the academy as heterogeneous space. These familiar organized structures of culture have often served as the historical basis for nation building and of differentiating people into diverse spheres of interaction, but the same structures also serve as group formations that find similar links to and experiences of alternate forms of creating counterresistance.

It is therefore not enough to claim Chicana/o transnationalism. The alignment of the interdisciplinary process serves as the basis for a postnational field of study despite the ongoing practice of interdisciplinary work in the academy for some time, and this alignment suggests a desire to move away from a simplistic dichotomy of colonizer and colonized.[2] The postnational discussed herein entails a heterogeneous mapping that includes feminist interventions and geopolitics within the United States and Mexico, as well as an autobiographical selfhood and a normative framing of heterosexual and homosexual.

The place of the postnational adds to the long list of dislocations initiated by either transnational or global economics in their proponents' never-ceasing desire for dominance over the formerly occupied lands and colonized peoples of the world. By producing a new set of semiotics and social codes, I suggest a closer look at the identities and institutions that can no longer be said to have just one national identity and that are in the process of either consciously responding to the effects of globalism by enlisting organized efforts to resist it or are working alongside it in a creative drive to enlist critical methods. In turn, criticism or modes of critique help people imagine more humane working conditions, political representation, and the like.

One of the salient qualifications of the postnational undertaken here is "the moving beyond" the historical conception of the nation, either by adopting identities that reach beyond the scope of citizenship or by a movement produced by a coercive global feature of displacing people from their homelands. Postnationalism, unlike transnationalism, questions the interests of colonizing conditions within the United States proper and questions the transnationalism that commerce imposes on people, such as the impact of immigration on people's lives and material needs as well as the displacement of ideas, beliefs, and traditional systems. To best understand the postnational within the U.S. context, it is important to view Chicana/o cultural nationalist formation as an anomaly of nationalism and, at the same time, a site of emancipation.

In the following segments I outline the process from national to postnational with various problems and identity concerns and movements that have led us to this point.

CULTURAL NATIONALISM

Carlos Muñoz' *Youth, Identity, and Power: The Chicano Movement* (1989) places the development of a Chicano social protest movement within a broader historical context of Mexican-Americans living in the United States. Muñoz describes the basis for the marginalization of Mexican-Americans:

> Mexican-Americans became an oppressed minority group as
> a consequence of the U.S. Empire in the nineteenth century,
> and that fact has had a profound impact on their political
> and intellectual development. The subjugation of Mexican-
> Americans, beginning with the Texas-Mexico War of 1836 and
> the U.S.-Mexico War of 1846–1848, has never been considered
> a moral or constitutional issue by the U.S. or even by liberals.
> (20)[3]

In Muñoz' explanation, Chicana/o cultural "nationalism" thus allows us to follow a much larger historical frame of thinking that recasts itself as part of social and political resistance reemerging in the U.S. counter-cultural movements of the 1960s and 1970s. Historically, though, cultural nationalist drives have been conventionally viewed as pertaining to ethnic groups and resistance stemming from resentment. Such resentment originated from the adverse effects of colonialism, leading to the "logic" of the colonizer, a colonized binary: one group took, and the other worked for the "owners." Elusive and difficult to categorize, not all cultural nationalisms work in the same way. Some forms of cultural nationalism actually serve a useful political purpose of organizing a community. Examples include St. Patrick's Day parades or gay-rights marches. But cultural nationalism varies from nation to nation, depending on the nation's internal issues of power. Chicana/o cultural nationalism resembles and imitates some versions of current Latin American cultural nationalism because it expresses revolutionary aesthetic features in its political representation.

Best described as an ideology of identity that is formed around the quality of self-determination over passivity, cultural nationalism is intended to direct people out of colonial disarray. Specifically in the 1960s and 1970s, Chicana/o cultural nationalism found its expression in the organizations of social groups and as a political ideology about race during the civil rights movements (Muñoz 1989). While the longer history of the Brown Berets varies according to different critics, all acknowledge that the group originated in East Los Angeles as Young Citizens for Community Action (YCCA). YCCA, sponsored by an interfaith religious group, was cofounded in 1967 by David Sánchez and several other young Chicanos, including Alberto Rivera, Tolin Enciso, Hank Rivera, Carlos Móntez, and Manuel Parsens.

As some of its members began wearing brown berets (berets to symbolize youth militancy, brown as a statement of identity), they came to be known as the Brown Berets not only within the community but by police as well. By 1968 the group officially took this name. Its logo or "beret patch" depicting two rifles and a cross was designed by Manuel Parsens. The Beret slogan, *La Causa*, was appropriated from the United Farm Workers Union. Initially set up to take a peaceful, mainstream approach to addressing problems facing youth such as police brutality and a lack of social activities, the group soon adopted the militant politics of Chicano Liberation (Chávez 2002). The cultural play of youth militancy and static notions of Chicana/o politics began with such organizations. Often conflated with Mexican traditionalism, many of the attitudes about gender, sexuality, and nationhood originated within these organizations (Saldívar 1990a).

However, another useful example of Chicana/o cultural nationalism can be cited in *El plan espiritual de Aztlán*, a 1969 manifesto in which discontent among Chicanas/os began to take on a social and cultural discourse. *El plan espiritual de Aztlán* sets the theme that Chicana/os (*la raza de bronce*, the Bronze Race) must use their cultural nationalism as the key or common denominator for mass mobilization and organization. Once committed to the idea and philosophy of *El plan espiritual de Aztlán*, it suggested, one must conclude that social, economic, cultural, and political independence is the only road to total liberation from oppression, exploitation, and racism. The struggle then must be for the control of barrios, campos, pueblos, lands, economy, culture, and political life. *El plan* committed all levels of Chicano society—the barrio, the campo, the rancho, the textbooks, the schools, the workplace—to La Causa.

Latin American revolutionary manifestos provided models for symbolic representation and mirroring of new community-based cultural representation. From José Martí's early writings as well as from Simón Bolívar's and Emiliano Zapata's speeches, Latin American revolutionaries' works were copied in tone and spirit. In the United States, written discourses take on added significance in that *El plan espiritual de Aztlán* served as a social platform for democratic leadership and responsibility. Included in the social critique are critiques of capitalism and U.S. imperialism and a public discourse on civil rights and class. This drive for a social critique developed in Chicana/o and Latina/o representation as a movement intended to organize communities and people for self-representation across all segments of society: the arts community, politics, social groups, and the academy (Chávez 2002, 23–35). The organizing principles that held Chicana/o cultural discourse in place still remain strong in the academy and in activist organizations. Aesthetic productions generated within this moment of Chicano cultural nationalism created new ways of thinking that provided much-needed excitement as the era of segregation started to end. "Chicana/o," as an emancipatory symbol of an identity process, was necessary.

The decades before the 1960s and 1970s saw enormous confrontations between the law and many Chicanas/os (Chávez 2002). A desire for another model of citizenship literally had to be created. The meaning of "Mexican-American" seemed overly dependent on the state as a race and class category. Developed from deep social and political desires to offer a dynamic representation of the Mexican-American, Carlota Cardenas de Dwyer, one of the first Chicana literary critics, explains in her essays that the very act of self-identifying as Chicana/o is itself a political act necessary to the formation of a definitive Chicana/o literary, cultural, and political voice. The origin of the term "Chicano," Cardenas de Dwyer explains in "Chicano Literature: An Introduction" (1975), is above all else born out of political necessity:

> Whatever the derivation of the word "Chicano," in almost
> every case, to use, to accept its use, to apply it to oneself, is a
> political act. It is an act of cultural identification with one's
> Mexican-Spanish-Indio heritage. (6)

Cardenas de Dwyer indicates that this self-identification with "Chicana/o" leads to the political and social goal of liberation from social, economic, and political disenfranchisement, suggesting further that a shift in political awareness reveals an understanding of the political act of renaming in relation to the larger process of colonization. Here the basis for a radical new identity and consciousness takes aim at pessimistic, often fatalistic, and inherently negative feelings experienced by a colonized people about their own self-representations in their formerly oppressive situations within dominant U.S. culture.

Carlota Cardenas de Dwyer describes a sense of "national cultural pride." The nationalism suggested in the term "Chicana/o" did prompt feelings of pride, premised on the belief that a "radical ideology" of the "self" would direct the decolonization of the cultural revolutionary into the space of liberation. Cardenas de Dwyer directs her use of the term not at a public political rally but in defining its use as literary. While the nexus of this radical movement did have noteworthy qualities in the ambitious project of overturning segregation and disenfranchisement, it also meant that the critical and intellectual evolution of "Chicana/o" would be necessary to make it salient on national level, and this required another sense of inclusion.

The academic sentiment had changed dramatically by the mid-1980s. This meant that the philosophical underpinning of cultural nationalism began to unravel as the U.S. academy shifted its attention toward a multicultural approach to knowledge, one taking an anti-essentialist view of race and gender. Joan Scott, in her essay "Multiculturalism and the Politics of Identity" (1992), takes to task some of the currents that shaped much of the academic debates in the late 1980s. For example, the noted historian recalls that categories were often treated as discrete analytical devices and not in relation to one another, something that developed post-1980s.

Similar contradictions followed the U.S. feminist movement as actual confrontations with inclusion and exclusion were taking shape. What this suggests is that identity production had achieved a level of materiality, and it was now time to address the deeper philosophical concerns that shaped each of these groups. These dialectical currents followed in the Black Power movement and in the Asian-American and Native American civil rights campaigns, as they all defined their own identity production according to each group's material and historical experience.

What often confronts such philosophical issues in most postcolonial movements, especially those by U.S. minorities, are the limits of Marxist analysis in shaping group identity and cultural production. Under Marxism, the internal underpinnings of sexuality and race were not thoroughly considered and did not engage shortcomings. Women's concerns were suppressed in favor of issues over wages. Over and over again, sexual politics lacked evidence of social inequity or social change, so the issues within the material or public spaces were addressed as those of structure or institution and the need for structural change.

Cultural nationalism's refusal to accept discussion on gender and sexuality in actuality reflected many of the views on sexuality that had remained in place. These attitudes about sexuality were ingrained in the traditionalism of Mexican culture, offering some form of authentic reference point for Chicana/o sexuality. Other times, the mark of cultural nationalism centralized masculinity as the only way for representation to occur, and this became evident by the 1980s as the movement to develop more elaborate and exciting perspectives on Chicana/o culture arose. Developing a sense of ethnic cultural expression based in part on Mexican revolutionary discourse (that is, dating to Zapata and Pancho Villa) characterized Chicana cultural nationalism in its insistence to cultivate a radical view of race or ethnicity but set limits on gender and sexuality. This choice may have seemed necessary for the development of the Chicana/o movement as an intellectual and aesthetic movement in some of the early years, but it became problematic as gender and sexuality became more central to grassroots as well as academic discussions. Revolutionary aesthetic styles that derive from Mexican revolutionary histories, indigenous art, and local grassroots social organizing facilitated a cultural nationalist basis that created a movement of inclusion, for men as well as women (Goldman 1990). But the male rhetoric did not match women's interests for equal working conditions, for educational access, and for an equal division of labor as well as for sexual liberation.

The self-identifying term "Mexican-American" was deemed ineffectual as a political and social category because it suggested assimilation into U.S. culture. The Brown Berets tended to reject it. College students used it, but with trepidation. The scholarly field or discipline chose "Chicana/o studies" as its name, and a national association of the same was formed in the 1970s. The ineffectiveness of "Mexican-American" resulted in the formation of "Chicana/o" as an aesthetic, political, social identity that later embraced other progressive ideas.

Representation—artistic, political, social, or economic—has been significant to Chicana/o nationalist projects because of its and their ability to garner community appeal. Art and literature represented the formation of the Chicana/o movement as critics and activists alike worked to capture "authentic" voice and experience. Among examples of such experience incorporated into the "true" Mexican-American were César Chávez and Dolores Huerta, who continue to personify favorable aspects of the Chicana/o movement. While aesthetic productions generated within Chicano cultural nationalism served social and political functions, the movement's ability to destabilize the national order from U.S. hegemony was its main achievement.

Luis Leal, one of the first critics to trace the formation of a Chicano literary canon, says, "Chicano literature, like all other literature, can give expression to the universal through the regional. Over and above the social problems with which he is at present preoccupied, the Chicano is a human being facing the concerns of all humanity. And he is giving expression to this in an original style" (1979, 4). By claiming universality for regional Chicana/o voices, Leal attempts to bring the earlier marginal Mexican-American subject into an existing American literary studies model. Leal places the Chicana/o literary voice in relation to other American ethnic canons because, he contends, a model of study could benefit from the mapping already recognized in the more established African-American literary canon. Drawing distinctions from other ethnic minorities was necessary to position Chicana/o literary expression. Cultural experience as a political act negated the tendency to draw parallel links with Latin American literature.

Some social or political progress occurred prior to the establishment of global capital, from the 1980s through 2000. Title IX and civil rights

legislation in many states assured limited but important educational access. The changes account for the discursive links that facilitated the rise
of a Chicana/o transnational culture. In mapping such a complex system,
the most viable way to conceive of it lies within an interdisciplinary frame
of analysis in which it becomes evident that a nationalist approach alone
cannot properly capture complications that have arisen as a result of an
emerging global and transnational world. After the 1980s, educational and
political advances were subsumed to global economies and the movement
of capital. In other words, short-term gains could not keep pace with long-
term movement.

This is a very different understanding from that placing transnational
and global studies in direct relationship to the Third World and thus to
their identities. While U.S. civil rights discourses served as the basis for
U.S. minorities to reflect on race, in encountering globalism and transnationalism, U.S. minorities have had to confront an odd positioning of
not having sufficient capital to engage with global capital at the level that
Western elites do. At the same time, the uneven nature of globalization
may not even qualify U.S. minorities to participate in the global economy
except as "old world" colonized people.

As I will argue, Chicanas/os are caught between the shifting terms of
globalization and the identifications of a cultural nationalism that seemed
politically necessary as well as important to the evolution of the Chicana/o
social movement as a progressive ideology and discourse. As happened with
various countercultural movements of the 1960s and 1970s, Chicanas/os
transformed traditional or nationalist ethnic and sexual ideologies into a
movement that incorporates heterogeneous framing. The Chicana/o movement reckons, for example, with nonheterosexuals as it does with women's
rights. These new ideologies came into focus during the 1980s, when a multicultural frame for the study of difference emerged in the academy and
battles over culture and identity were waged on a national scale (Saldívar
1990b).

The perspective and style of U.S. relations to Latin America tended to
romanticize political aesthetics, and Chicanas/os did not participate in the
same cultural dispositions of the Latin American experience (Leal 1979).
Even though there may have been simultaneous links with revolutionary
paradigms, it was difficult to gain recognition by the dominant culture and
especially from progressive leftists when it came to discussions about racism within the United States. Coalition-style representation among Asian-
Americans, African-Americans, and Native Americans seemed more plausible, as the experience of living in the United States could only convey the

obvious connection all of these groups had with respect to racial conditions that were part of everyday experience (Hall 2005). Only later, cultural studies, feminist and queer analysis, and postcolonial studies added new dimensions to a U.S. nationalist ethnic subject formation and furthered an understanding of gender and sexuality.[4] Postmodern and postcolonial critiques have not been successful in categorizing the global or transnational culture for U.S. minority communities. Jenny Sharpe observes, "The designation of postcolonial as an umbrella term for diasporic and minority communities is derived in part from an understanding of decolonization of an unprecedented migration from the former colonies to advanced industrial centers" (2000, 105). However, the pressing issues that confront postcolonial studies equally challenge Sharpe's preoccupation. The linkages one had hoped would be made between U.S. minority and postcolonial studies appears problematic in Sharpe's understanding of the postcolonial: "If the term *postcolonial* is to have any descriptive force at all, we need to account for the historical specificities of different national formations rather than treat 'The West' as a single and homogeneous entity" (108).

Cultural identities bound to nationalist underpinnings, whether postcolonial or U.S. minority, would best be interrogated with the proper historical terminology that positions a corrected vantage point and proves to have the most beneficial political direction. Instead, Sharpe draws a distinction between postcolonial studies and U.S. minorities in this way: "Postcolonial studies, on the other hand, did not emerge in response to student demands for racial diversity or a political activism that spilled over onto college campuses" (108). I agree with Sharpe's distinction between the categories postcolonial and U.S. minority and would add that a return to historical inquiry would have prepared us all for a transnational method more proficiently because it would account for similarities and degrees of influence but also different historical contexts.

Renaming of the self, for example, occurred in colonial and colonized communities throughout the Americas. It was one of the decolonializing strategies used by cultural nationalists to achieve a sense of emancipation. Here, however, Chicanas/os, like their counterparts in other social movements of the 1960s, used renaming as means toward *transvaluation* of culture. The Nietzschean concept of transvaluation in *The Will to Power* (1968) establishes the view that modern people within a secular worldview, absent of a totality, that is to say, without a notion of God or greater divine Truth, experience a state of nihilism. In the state of nihilism, without an absolute truth to affirm reality (representation), we can suppose an ideological wedge into the dominant discourse. Nietzsche conceptualizes, in his theory of the ideology of the "afflicted" and "suffering" or "wounding," a "slave" morality. According to Nietzsche, that "suffering," while captivating on the political stage, in actuality provides the sufferer with a false sense of triumph over the powerful. The illusion is that the "causes" of the affliction are never attended to and cannot be reconciled by satisfying the pain of the sufferer with public displays of guilt, recompense, and contrition by those in a dominant role.

Notions of radical new selfhood embedded in the logic of the nationalist tendencies result in a postnationalism that expresses a desire for a way out of nationalism, but material conditions are not sufficient to warrant it. Postnationalist desires recreate the nihilism of the national identity and its many problems; however, as a minority criticism, the "differences" become possible only after foundational or collectivized work is established. A reluctance to accept new terminology may be one of the issues at stake in postnationalism's effect of creating a new terminology. Because Chicanas/os began as a movement along with other socially progressive currents, the entire leftist project must be looked upon as a type of postnationalism that lost the trajectory of its own discourse on difference. First, it did not carry a discourse on difference; next, the one developed from global movements striving for autonomy could not link collected experiences to form a social movement worldwide.

Arguments established by such "new democratic" critics as Judith Butler, Ernesto Laclau, and Chantal Mouffe state that a "radical democracy" is possible in the contingency, multiplicity, and indeterminacy of the subject. Their arguments contrast with Marxist economic determinism and historical teleology by exposing how "power" is located in the laws of culture as opposed to the juridical and economic powers of the state. This raises a dilemma: the condition that postnationalism offers can become an orientation toward critical confinement. Butler, Laclau, and Mouffe, among others, view the contingency of the subject as a radical or new way to criticize contemporary hegemony. A question that looms in this discussion by the U.S. left on new democratic politics is this: How are U.S. minorities figuring into new democratic thinking when nationalist semistructures are providing much-needed form but no reform? The only theorist who has arrived at an answer is Butler, especially where issues of gender and sexuality are discussed and operative in the state's and U.S. culture's organization of ideology. The political apparatus advanced affirmative action, for example, but that served primarily white women.[5] Chicana/o self-identification within this postnational context is necessary because readings of power, as culturally based systems of gender and sexuality as well as class ideologies, expose the unconscious aspects of oppression; the domain of sexuality and of gender were eventually made public by Chicano gays and lesbians as well as by feminists.[6] The problems associated with a postnational identity cannot be reconciled in class or economic ideologies alone; they need to account for gender and sex, for sexuality and identity.

The transvaluation of identities also must be seen across other contexts, as other marginal groups fashioned similar terms as part of their own political and aesthetic production. Women developed a feminist critique in an effort to challenge male sexism and sexual difference and to recuperate the lost history of women's roles under patriarchy (Nicholson 1997). African-Americans in the Black Power and black arts movements reclaimed a black aesthetic and consciousness by reciting, "Black is beautiful." For gays and lesbians, a post-Stonewall generation reclaimed the "queer" as a surrogate for the modern gay and lesbian movement. Equally provocative, all of these same groups engaged the problems of self, of social identification within a given national political body politic; all of these groups experienced the same debates between identity formation and the need to deconstruct the core categories that set limits on each group's identity (Millett 1990).[7]

Against this dynamic tension between political activism and social change, lingering traces of a political group's success or failure deploys the political notion of *ressentiment*. In Nietzsche's *On Genealogy of Morals* he states that "morality" deters individuals from knowing the true nature of radicalism by soothing and assuaging their pain. Wendy Brown's *States of Injury* (1995) frames the discussion of *ressentiment* in resonance with feminist critical practices of the 1980s. "Feminism," she argues, "is implicated in *ressentiment* to the extent that it substitutes morality for politics and thus reveals its own complicity as a specific practice and ideology in power" (44). Brown paraphrases and assesses Nietzsche's argument in this respect:

> In his insistence that morality springs forth and compensates
> powerlessness, Nietzsche challenges the Marxist thesis that
> all ideology, including moral and ethical codes, issues from
> class divisions to legitimate the power of the privileged. In
> Nietzsche's account, morality emerges to account for the
> powerless to avenge their incapacity for action; it enacts
> their resentment of strengths that they cannot match or
> overthrow. Rather than a codification of domination, moral
> ideas are a critique of a certain kind of power, a complaint
> against strength, an effort to shame and discredit domina-
> tion by securing the ground of the true and the good from

which to negatively judge it. In this way, of course, morality
itself becomes a power, a weapon (which is eventually how it
triumphs), although this expression of the "will to power" is
far from the sort Nietzsche savors or respects: power born of
weakness and resentment fashions a culture whose values and
ambitions mirror the pettiness of its motivating force. (ibid.)

Brown is invested in accounting for the refusal of feminism to encounter
sexual difference in "the postmodern," citing that the "attachment" to morality precludes a discussion of the way political ideologizing creates its own
ruses and misrecognitions. I agree that a Nietzschean argument about the
specter of injury obscures and privileges the claim of injury over and above
all (radical) notions of difference that may be simultaneously taking effect.
The suggestion here is that a radical democracy may be possible within the
boundaries of the identity itself. Brown's caveat about the ensuing pettiness
of "power born of weakness and resentment" leads me to another set of issues inherent in establishing a Chicana/o identity as a political category.

Returning to Cardenas de Dwyer's simple, succinct, though enduring
political claim, I see a possibility in reading Chicana/o identifications as
transvaluative contingency. In this, an identity formed by its state of injury
can at the same time call upon a progressive generative conscience as its own
identity. We take notice of feminist tropes of "survivorship" in feminist discourses. Survivorship creates an interesting generative conscience by calling upon its own self-making and by re-creating a subject position that is
provisionally formed in a *state of injury* without absolute moral incitement
or a natural cultural identity. Here *ressentiment* must be regarded as a self-
altering contingency that changes in a historical context such as civil rights,
undoing the absolutism of nationalism and substituting it with a radical
epistemology. Chicanas/os espouse in proclamations of righteous indignation a dialogical entry into American life by resisting the terms of how one
speaks to state epistemic violence (Gutiérrez-Jones 1998).

On a similar register in postmodernist Chicana/o criticism, Rafael
Pérez-Torres, for example, sets out to demonstrate that "heterogeneity" in
the Chicana/o subject is possible if we look at the Chicana/o subject in aesthetic rather than political and economic terms:

I suggest that the notion of Aztlán, highly influential in the
articulation of Chicano identity, marks less the wholeness
than the heterogeneity evident in the subject position of the

Chicano. It is impossible, for example, to ignore the role that Chicanos and Mexican migrant workers play in the diasporic history. One can no longer assert the wholeness of a Chicano subject when the very discourses that go into identity formation are themselves contradictory. (1995, 61)

Pérez-Torres makes the determination that the Chicana/o in Aztlán gestures toward a heterogeneous concept of national identification. In Pérez-Torres'-claim that Chicana/o identity "marks less the wholeness than the heterogeneity evident in the subject position of the Chicana/o," it is evident that a contradiction exists. Pérez-Torres falls short in failing to give form to the "heterogeneous" body. He is reluctant to provide an embodiment to the heterogeneous postmodern form because, as he indicates, he does not yet believe that gender and sexuality as well as other effects have created a heterogeneous mapping. Whether it existed in early formulations of Aztlán is an important question: Could there be an Aztlán without gender and sexuality?

Chicana/o discourse flourished as it became more tenable in heterogeneous cultural expression within the postnation. Despite efforts in leftist criticism developing from the social and cultural ruptures of the 1980s and 1990s, critical works by feminists, gays, and lesbians, as well as the intensification of globalization and postmodern aesthetics, have all provided some interesting unifying themes in emancipatory discussion of a national aesthetics but also in Chicana nationalist discourse. Illustrative of these themes is the critical work by Chicana feminists in the transformation of the autobiographical center, the borderlands (as a liminal paradigm), and in postmodern aesthetics (contrasted to folkloric culture). The many works by gays and lesbians have set a salient feature of the postnational: to account for the present, the past, national shortcomings, and global critique. The project therefore resembles and is verified in the AIDS quilt, now having outgrown its venues and yet relevant to a global "village."

There is then a transitional phase from the national aesthetics model of Aztlán to a postnational aesthetic practice embodied in the AIDS Naming Project. I have discussed the ways minority nationalist literatures posit a strong moral obligation to a natural notion of a people. For Chicanas/os, to give one example, the subject of labor becomes naturalized in heterosexual terms and in racial terms to a history of cultural mestizaje. The creation of "natural body" engrains those "identificatory" emotional structures and appears in the ethnic literary model. The aesthetics of a cultural national body seems intelligible as a natural form to those who have shaped its history. Dissent from within is next to impossible without inciting displeasures from the "naturalized" group. I will elaborate examples of such ruptures later. Here I explain how a model of identification and postnationality resists the interpellative drive to form good or moral subjects and how it resists the persuasive romancing of the nation on its subjects.

One premise is that identification with the codes of a national literary and cultural aesthetics only partially accounts for the interests of a particular group identity: gendered, sexual, and antifoundationalist subjectivities and many others who escape the register are simply not seen or embodied in the reproductive model of the "nation." Many of the representations after the 1980s precisely addressed the sentiment that any attempt to identify with a nationalist minority discourse was tenuous. First, this position left open the possibility that the emancipatory goals of nationalist movements may not apply to others who are formed *differently*. Second, it was seen as necessary to employ a critical language that viewed nationalism as simply a political, rhetorical strategy. More recent critical language is better suited for a heterogeneous paradigm because it draws from various influences. The most obvious change that can be noted is the development of studies on cultural production by U.S. Chicanas/os in the 1980s. In terms of readership, this change can be viewed in the processes of identifying (as opposed to signifying), as it redirects the condition of reading in literature and culture as a political site of resistance.

Having to constantly negotiate some of these contradictions myself, in graduate school I honed specific strategies for what José Esteban Muñoz calls "disidentification," a critical strategy that informs, in his examples, queer readings in performance by queers of color. The use of "disidentification" is a rather striking way of categorizing those deep and unconscious responses to the unseemly and unidentifiable structures that our bodies and psyches naturally disavow and realign as we imagine ourselves *differently*. Muñoz' analysis of disidentification describes a facet of race-based queer performance in which "the minoritarian politics . . . is not monocausal or monothematic, but one that is calibrated to discern a multiplicity of interlocking identity components and the ways in which they affect the social" (Muñoz 1999, 5). This view of identity, or rather disidentification, promotes the idea that the concept works as a circuitry of "identifying," seeing and not seeing, recognizing and turning away. My adaptation of Muñoz' terminology frames disidentifications to read a hermeneutics of the colonized body in Chicano history as self-stylized literary and cultural performance and can therefore be mapped according to a cultural studies framework.

Examples of the new directions are explored next to link them in specific Chicana/o studies sources and as symbols of the postnational.

ARE WE BEING TRANSNATIONAL YET?

The ordering of the world still remains very much logically situated in the nation with laws, cultural codes, and interpretive apparatus allowing us to navigate the terms of this ordering. Open is the question: At what point are we being global? One of my favorite rejoinders to the issue of historicity derives from Carolyn Porter's "Are We Being Historical Yet?" (1988). She determines that the cultural play initiated by "new historicists" during the 1980s introduced a unique set of terms for encountering cultural difference by drawing upon Foucault's theorization of power. She assesses the achievements of the new historicists by contending that their practice is "becoming the newest academic orthodoxy." According to Porter, new historicists' fixation on Foucault stands between them and *effective* historicization, and she illustrates how they further erase *the other* by using Foucault's conceptualization of power.

If that failure were not enough, internal failures need to be considered. Like those employing other methods of national-based areas of study, Chicanas/os have had to confront many of the issues of their own internalized cultural nationalist histories as the movement to globalize economies and cultures alters the national character but not necessarily the economic position of "national minorities" within the new alignments. In organizing a basic format for a new national character, two primary theoretical confrontations are at work in thinking about Chicana/o postnationalism: the nationalist, with its foundationalist, nearly religious underpinnings, versus the globalist, signaling progress and technology. Postnationalism verifies the rupture in the way national cultures influence and direct a sense of legitimacy toward people poised between the shifting terms of globalization and those of colonization, that is, noncitizens working without visas, popularly known as "undocumented workers."

Recovering the national tropes and identifications that seemed politically necessary for Chicanas/os as members of a social and civil rights movement along with other countercultural movements of the 1960s and 1970s helped transform traditional ethnic and sexual ideologies from a sole source of recognition—political, social, cultural, or even personal. In theorizations of national identities amidst the rise of globalism, Mark Juergensmeyer, in "The Paradox of Nationalism in a Global World" (2002), considers the resurgence of national identities contradictory to globalism. In responding to globalism's wide sweep, Juergensmeyer considers the efficacy of globalization insufficient to reach all segments of the population: the uneven development of global economics produces varied or fractured instances of nationalist expression, whether religious, sectarian, or cultural. Juergensmeyer notes, "It should not be surprising that new sociopolitical forms are emerging at this moment in history because globalization is redefining virtually everything" (4).

Noting one of the most obvious elements of global culture, the uneven unfolding of history, thus leads to different forms of sociopolitical formation such as varied and complex identities with our own national and nationalist cultures; examples include the gay transgendered and the differently abled Olympian. The vantage point of being American obscures the structural perspective we have developed in the agencies of transnational subjectivity and in looking for a global subject outside of one's own geography. To put it another way, what it means to be global or transnational in the United States is either that one is positioned at the site of imperialism itself or one belongs to an advantaged Third World class able to maneuver Third and even First World configurations (Spivak 1988, 274).

My insistence on postnationalism originates from an understanding that the global and transnational frames are limited in helping us understand U.S. minority studies. In addition, and complicating the problem further, my insistence derives from seeing that victimhood within leftist discourses may be misused in an attempt to salvage the "decolonized" Third World from oppression, adding more dislocation from developing any agency within globalization. Unlike transnational or global studies, which situate nationalist-based study in U.S. formation of minority discourses, and unlike Third World revolutionary paradigms, the terms "global" and "transnational" are insufficient or undocumentable because they do not stem from a historical framework for U.S. minorities. Despite attempts to develop postcolonial and postmodern minority studies, which really did not go far after 9/11, postnationalism suggests that a nationalist movement does not remain static but changes. If in the beginning we understood Chicanismo narrowly and critically, after 2000 and after 9/11 we came to realize that its significance is its survival because it changed. From early MECHA (Movimiento Estudiantil Chicano de Aztlán) doctrines of "no gringos" to the mixed-race "It's my political heritage, too" that occurs on college campuses, the movement toward a redefinition is clear and necessary.

The same principles of national identity formation may have become relevant to other ethnic groups—African-Americans, Asian-Americans, and

Native Americans—in the desire to form counterdiscourses to transglobal identity productions. As these issues become clearer and more easily identifiable, terminology will shift in academic discussions of the politics of difference and identity. However, Chicana/o productions are unique and compelling for their proximity to a homeland. The relationship to Mexico as a homeland affords Chicanas/os direct ties to a transnational space. The spatial geography of land, history, materiality, and territory positions Chicanas/os within the conditions of a colonial discourse and within range of a transnational site of passage. The question then arises: Have Chicanas/os embraced transnationalism?

As with most other U.S. encounters, transnational and global experiences occur through relationships with either technology or capitalism. What is evident through the phenomenal textual production about nontraditional identity formations is that people of Mexican origin occupy a unique spatial and geographic location. With the exception of Gloria Anzaldúa's *Borderlands/La Frontera* (1987), the vast majority of publications have been focused on identity concerns within the locations of where Chicanas/os were to be found. Chicana/o gay and lesbian sexuality, feminist criticism, the transnational borderlands, and performance culture—to name a few emergent categories—did in fact materialize during the 1980s. This type of representation personifies the postnational as a progressive movement that resists the advances of global capitalism because it insists on a national recuperation of voice and representation.

A marked shift in representation occurred by the late 1970s, and this refocusing of the terms of representation departed from the masculine, Marxist aesthetics of political change toward social change. A postnational turn thus rejected that basis of representation as a segue or entry point, nonimmersion into globalism but without identity papers or cards. One of the more apparent distinctions is the level of development that cultural minorities such as Chicanas/os have achieved or not. The most visible movement has been the one to globalize economies and to make changes within the framework of cultural productivity. The ability for people to unite or lay claim to either nationalism or globalism seems to have been diminished by the effort to globalize Mexico and all of Latin America because those forces displaced Mexicans who arrived less than eager to embrace a Chicano/a past, let alone Chicana/o ways! We must also consider how the inapplicability of the idea of nationhood, as a signifying model for identity and aesthetic formations, shaped any new sensibility. Historically, the nation as frame of reference led to a static notion of Chicana/o culture; no doubt it will do the same for Mexican or Latina/o culture if left unchanged.

One can ask recent Mexican arrivals in any major metropolitan area of the country when they "stopped being Mexican" and find a look of horror. Most will respond "Never" or "Not yet." In other words, "transnational" might mean the act of emigrating, but it is *not* the experience of the immigrant (Portes and Rimbaud 1990).

THE POLITICAL AESTHETIC

In this current, advanced stage of transnational culture, many scholars are attempting to move beyond important, if simplistic, binary oppositions to achieve more nuanced understandings of both the colonizer and the colonized within a system that now lacks such binarism. Many would like as well to recognize those hybrid lives, experiences, and representations that cannot be classified in terms of a single, national lens. In modifying or replacing the term "postcolonial" with "transnational," we do not abandon the concept of political and cultural resistance. Instead, an elaboration of the national and transnational is achieved if we look for variations in this global moment. Examples include the number of women immigrating or those whose children are entering colleges and universities at rates unlike before.

Cultural nationalism can then be understood as a stage or postcolonial phase in which social and political resistance emerges in the United States. In this case, the countercultural revolution is also gendered, sexed, and classed. Its discontent involves the same efforts offered by the postcolonial movements that centered more on race and ethnicity. Historically, though, cultural nationalist drives have been conventionally viewed as pertaining to ethnic people who resist adverse colonial conditions.

Emphasis on displacement and hybridity highlights global and transnational metaphors in the Western academy. The hybrid aesthetic erases a notion of clear identity and thus diminishes the focal point of ethnic minority status or identity. While metaphors of the global can express the dynamics of change within Chicana/o culture, it is important to establish continuity with the historical identity. An example we know best is "Chicana/o" versus "Mexican"—one from 1900 to the present, the other from 1821 to 1900. Metaphors of difference adopted by the academic left replace U.S. ethnic representation, largely because nationalist forms of expression are often seen as inherently authoritarian and unable to engage in dialogics of culture or to transcend the group's narrow ideological interest. In its scope, the Chicana/o movement formed its basis and logic on the idea that exclusion from American society denied full citizens a place within the nation, especially in the post-1900 world of ethnic segregation, apartheid, and isolation.

It makes sense to adhere to the notion that our very instability as historical subjects, whether we self-identity as part of a growing diaspora or as an emergent class within minority intellectual formations, is based on some historical rupture. I mark this postnational realization and stylize it in effect to come to terms with representation, with examples of displacement, with hybridity, and as nationals (mis)recognizing any simplistic binary logic lodged along the lines of colonizer/colonized. Misreadings are inevitable in this construction of the nation, but what even they reveal is that transnational histories cannot be reconciled as easily as national minority subjects can be. Recent debates in the U.S. Congress about immigration verify the lack of reconciliation. A bill dies because the nation will not make citizen-subjects of the millions of workers its economy and infrastructure so badly require. This lack of recognition, perhaps a frustration for some, provides a dynamic way of forcing a different criticism, one that I hope will help feminist scholarship and queers of color to find recourse in a reality-based model of representation. If nation, nationality, and ethnicity are not static, how can we expect a country to come to terms with difference?

Exceeding the boundaries of self-naming outside of the national locations created both progressive and reactionary elements; such redrawing of the boundaries led me to consider cultural studies practices as interpretive models for reading anomalous and incongruous effects including current legislation or how queer voices emerged within a scholarly discipline once grounded in nationalistic practices. It is only recently that Chicana/o literary criticism has been organized along the lines of a cultural studies model, to give one more example of a shifting consciousness. At one conference, Chicana/o Cultural Productions: The Third Wave, sponsored by graduate students and professors at UC Irvine in 1999, we considered a need for alternate strategies in Chicana/o criticism and literary practices. Citing the "third wave" as a move beyond the national cultural social protest method, or a *movimiento*, this call for a new method for Chicana/o studies aimed at modeling interdisciplinary approaches, drawing from ethnic studies, feminist studies, and gay and lesbian studies, to achieve understandings about our place in an academic world of thought and reflection while not forgetting the practical, lived, and mostly impoverished worlds of those who "sent" us to study. Aware that this situated knowledge was not an either/or, that is, we are not either smart or poor, instead we sought a model allowing us to move through and beyond, in a word, the postnational.

Among the more visible issues cited throughout the conference was the need to rethink "the movement" itself, noting that this era of social protest movements had been useful for advancing civil rights claims. Chicanas/os critical studies have made numerous attempts to confront the power relations that form and construct a given minority subject position. This attempt to rethink the boundaries clearly came in the wake of many changes since the era of social protest movements. My generation's view of radical politics seems more conscious of a performance style of representation in real-world situations of late capitalism. Our legacy of radical protest activism can be summarily read within the sexual politics of ACT-Up, in Queer Nation, in the bare-breasted Lesbian Avengers, in the gender-identity politics of the Transexual Menace, and in the ecology movement in which Julia Butterfly's protest atop a redwood tree, Luna, represents a new media- and technology-savvy vanguard still evoking social protest as its preferred method of changing unjust conditions.

The vast global migrations, the crisis of the academic left, along with the future of minority studies and the proliferations of feminist and sexual identities, also have been at a historical impasse. It is a time when symptoms of less movement surface, when oppositions become flat and broken, when words regurgitate back from the body and all logic proceeds in accordance with impulses that Benedict Andersen regards as the fate of "modern developmental history" (1983).[8] I have suggested that a different model be deployed within a cultural studies format and that the problem for Chicana/o analysis now is to confront an elaborate, feminist criticism in a gendered framework led by queer theories.

ANTINOMIES OF THE NATIONAL

The politics of reading that erupted during the 1980s marked a turning point for all emergent groups in the academic setting. The politics of readership were especially valuable in the development of a theoretical canon because Chicana/o scholars began incorporating theoretical perspectives more consciously. As part of the growing discontent with academic research, theory created a new venue for the debates of the 1990s. Tey Diana Rebolledo's essay "The Politics of Poetics: What Am I, a Critic, Doing in This Text Anyhow?" (1990) represents the issue "of theory" with the changes taking place in the academy.[9] Rebolledo recounts many of the problems associated with the (mis)uses of theory in Chicana/o literary studies. Rebolledo goes so far as to say that "by appropriating mainstream theoreticians and critics we have become so involved in intellectualizing that we lose our sense of the literature and therefore our vitality" (348). The split between activism and theory could be construed as an epistemological breakdown between the interests of "the movimiento" and the academic left, where academic culture and activist cultures each developed different, even contrary, readings about the Chicana/o political body. Rebolledo makes the assumption that the "vitality" of our critical approach depends upon "certain" types of textual readings—readings that arguably represent a critical community and voice. It is obvious that the politics of authorship at about this time have shifted attention away from the individual writer to the text, decentering the author as the political agent from the social text itself. Writing was supposed to bridge worlds, that is, academic with non-academic, with "the community." But in Chicana/o studies, the academic writing in literary criticism offered two new directions: first, that Chicanas/os had a literature and had writers; second, that literature could change mainstream U.S. readers' perceptions about themselves. This was an important, if today underacknowledged, achievement in U.S. letters. Emphasis on "the author" overlapped with other concerns that some scholars regarded as necessary when they anticipated the effects of new hegemonic forms of representation, namely the rise of postmodernism in Marxist literary scholarship, of a popular-culture studies framework, and of feminist and queer methodologies. Rebolledo obviates the need to ground a discussion of Chicana/o literary studies while not diluting the political process with theoretical language. However, some Chicana/o scholars used this same argument to resist the type of change that was necessary to expand the issues of representation for women or gays in an earlier period. Some *descarados* (shameless few) were more likely to excuse the ethnocentric, heterosexist, and homophobic bias in order to secure a mythical, definitive Chicana/o textual political body that paralleled the need to define and secure Aztlán, to reconquer it figuratively.

Other academics and feminists read cultural nationalism in the Chicanas/os movement as a regressive form of essentialist authoritarianism that put aside many of its progressive ideals in order to sustain a politically "stable" subject. It begs the question: Were we ever stable enough to claim such a tradition? It seems like a false assumption to make about theoretical language, since many other issues needed immediate attention. Without the use of critical language to explain how a progressive discourse becomes entangled in its own overtones, one has to step outside of "the text" to take an observation to another level, to make it clear and understandable.

In the same decade, other trends suggested deeper, relevant changes. Alvina Quintana, in *Home Girls: Chicana Literary Voices* (1996), reads Sandra Cisneros' main character, Esperanza, in *House On Mango Street* as a complex protagonist. Quintana locates a multilayered textual process when she observes, "What I am suggesting is that a 'serious' political inquiry should consider not only the oppositional tactics of the protagonist, but also the representations of the hegemonic system through which societal boundaries and conditions for resistance are created" (58). Quintana seeks to argue against the "naive" understanding of Cisneros' young protagonist by suggesting that political naiveté should not be understood at face value as just an infantile view of Chicana writings.

Both Rebolledo and Quintana assert Chicana feminist readings, but their locations and styles of reading differ in focus. While Rebolledo would want us to believe that Cisneros' Esperanza is representative of Chicana consciousness, Quintana wants us to look at the cultural conditions that structure Esperanza's articulations, a product of dynamic forces at work in structuring her voice. These distinct views of Chicana feminist readings echo other claims made by feminist cultural studies critics and by gay-lesbian critics about voice in feminist literary studies.[10]

Articulations that prompted the self-parodying inscriptions of important anthologies—such as *Chicana Lesbians: The Girls Our Mothers Warned Us About* (1991), edited by Carla Trujillo; *The Sexuality of Latinas* (1989), edited by Norma Alarcón, Ana Castillo, and Cherríe Moraga; and *This Bridge Called My Back* (1981), created and edited by Moraga and Anzaldúa—demand a different interpretation. These anthologies were vitally important to several communities because they expressed the discontent and frustration with heterosexism and homophobia that lingered within the cultural and political movements of the 1960s and 1970s but were rarely mentioned in Chicana/o criticism. These anthologies, while offering poignant celebrations of multiple locations as Chicana lesbians, also inspired a collective view of dominant ideologies seeping through the cultural national voice of the people. In particular, *Chicana Lesbians* is a well-scripted corruption of our mothers' (cultural) admonitions about lesbian sexuality, and the meaning of those admonitions is turned inside out by returning the caveat to its proper place as narrow-minded remarks. The anthology offers a vivid example of the way transvaluation of identity formation can still be used to counter heterosexual assumptions. Is it then the case that the identificatory tensions already built into cultural nationalism itself produce another set of representational possibilities that work against a utopian vision (reclaiming the homeland) of people but as a unifying critical practice in the academy.

Some critical projects seem reticent to name the social discontinuity that exists from within because I think it implies that a political-moral identity formation is the only means toward a just or salient solution, and by implication, sexuality drains the efficacy of race and class embodiments. Structurally, at least, many of these emergent group formations found themselves locked in an academic and community bind. Organizations such as the National Association of Chicana and Chicano Studies (NACCS), Mujeres Activas en Letras y Cambio Social (MALCS), and the National Women's Studies Association (NWSA) shaped debates as they placed greater emphasis on the roles of gender and sexuality. The shifting nature of the discourse itself placed a great deal of pressure on some scholars to act as critical activists, some of whom took it upon themselves to criticize the Chicano scholarly establishment publicly.[11] The public presentation of some of these issues certainly signals a different state of mind, and they query the institutionalized practices as they influenced canonical readings.

Historian Deena González makes clear in her essay "Speaking Secrets" (1993) that the "insider" politics taking place at some of these conferences reveal the "secret" of homophobia and sexism underlying Chicana/o discourse in the academy:

> The events at MALCS and in NACCS in the 1980s and 1990s suggest an interesting development in the bumpy demarcations that map Chicana feminism as it appears on the conference scene over the last few decades; multiple issues have been raised and discussed at each juncture. No group or set of groups emerges feeling elated or at ease. Dis-ease is in fact rampant. (53)

This pervasive sense of "dis-ease" is one of the reasons I organized the texts and themes for this project in looking at them as specific examples of the ways we are discomforted by the presence of "others" as themes that destabalize national consciousness by forming a critical case for sexuality that made us realize our sense of otherness, our estrangement from ourselves and our community.

EPISTEMOLOGIES OF POWER

Just as transnationalism suggests a return to the colonizer/colonized dyad, the images and caricatures of race and ethnicity have curiously and even surreptitiously made their way back into American popular-culture advertisements. The Taco Bell Chihuahua dog draws egregiously from stereotypes of Latina/o culture. The Chihuahua, representing a subtext of the "Latin" lover, overwrites the stereotype of the hypersexualized Chicana/o and Latina/o. And in black culture, the "Whasz Up" Budweiser commercial characterizes ebonics with its vaguely audible renditions of hip-hop consumerism, a laid-back and ironic alternative to moral or positive representation. These commercials are not benign in their representations of race and ethnic culture; rather they appeal to a residual racism that exists in popular culture. I take up this question of political self-representation more extensively in Chapter 4 by discussing the fashion codes and trends that provide a new venue of circulation in a consumerist ideology or ethos.

These particular examples illustrate how material discussion of race and ethnicity in consumer culture cannot be sustained without attention to racial and ethnic injury. The caricatures themselves take effect to make the claim that we have lost all moral incitement in discussion of race and ethnicity. Many of the assumptions about pride instilled in reclaiming Chicana/o history and culture produced a series of identificatory practices that have turned away from an intended goal of inspiring decolonizing strategies in critical interpretations toward consumerism (Gil Gomez 2002). The same could be said of queer representations.

Under cultural nationalism, ethnic minorities in the United States traded off negative stereotypes for positive representations. Initially, the result may have advanced male writers and intellectuals; by the 1980s a newly reformed ideological structure made it possible for others outside of the frame of Chicana/o representation to imbibe the images, stories, and verses of Chicano/a culture. Unlike its critical counterparts—postcolonial theories of emergence rising out of Africa, Latin America, the Caribbean, and Asia that offered new models of thinking of the emancipated subject— American Marxism molded with minority claims of resistance to produce a new vanguard of American intellectualism.

These concurrent trends cannot escape another conclusion. The current global and transnational contexts are distinct from the postcolonial models because the postcolonial was still contained within the boundaries of the nation. The U.S. minority intellectual was caught in an epistemological bind as labor, immigrant, and racial compositions, as well as queer perspectives, maintained a central place in disciplinary studies. The persistent condition of disenfranchisement continued, and one could no longer assume that all minorities exist under the same rules of subjection that were initially thought of in Marxist structuralist terms; the boundaries were not clear enough to distinguish one single oppressive structure, as had been determined in decades past.

Instead, our present situation asks us to look at the proliferation of globalization that has also dramatically revised the course of nationalism. Its impact on the body politic provides, even demands, a reentering of gender and sexuality as a complex system of hegemony and counterhegemonic discussion with boundaries networked across difference and, at times, placed in ironic situations. For Chicanas/os, the state of California has to be factored into that very odd equation, since the relationship between cultural conservatism and populism has left marked effects on Chicana/o intellectual communities and more recently on Latina/o immigrant communities.

The explicit and reactionary nature of some of these measures suggests a different political dynamic, one that strategically uses historically marked perceptions of Chicanas/os and immigrants operating within the historical imaginary. Has a new subject position been created in the wake of new political and economic issues? The question involves other related issues having to do with state versus federal governance, but considering the debatable issues within the formation of a Chicana/o literary subject located across genres and representational spaces helps discern their meaning more clearly. If anything, the passage of anti-immigrant measures in the past decade forced us to think of ourselves under a different set of political terms that involve a different way of reading cultural identifications. The ugly and racist ballot initiatives will invariably help us understand the formation of new hegemonic relations. One must consider that the underlying message behind these propositions involves a dramatic reawakening of old problems that have been obscured by our reliance on earlier methodologies that faded. An example is the assimilationist model popular in the 1950s or its companion, the culturally disadvantaged or deficient model.[12]

It seems rather clear that a new hegemonic perspective was being formed in California against immigrants, one that demanded new representational forms, interpretative strategies, and critical opportunities to counter its negative implications. While some of these more recent issues and debates help locate our position within the shifting terms of U.S. political power relations, there is the temptation to make the connection between emerging global economic situations and our current political and cultural situation. The most visible of these responses has to be linked with the way ethnic and cultural identities have had to respond to economic transformations taking place outside of the national boundaries as well as those affecting the working poor (Warnock 1995).

The fluid nature of transnational economies provides one specific set of contradictory issues that cannot be sufficiently incorporated simply from a static and stable national minority critique. Some may even wish to view this moment optimistically, while others sense that changes within global economic systems lead to hostile effects in our own culture. In short, it has been easier to describe a movement in its nascent form than it has been to sustain its legacy. In surveying the political heritage of this movement, one can see various attempts to produce affirming representation. The nature of the Chicana/o movement in its own voicing of selfhood as a marginal people has invoked a complex system of identifications and counter-identifications that arose in an intensified capitalist era marked by its own terminology: NAFTA, Proposition 209, illegal alien, and criminal.

In an attempt to denaturalize "the citizen" as the normative and apparent signifier in the assimilated and hyphenated identity, Chicana/o post-nationalism as *posmovimiento* never quite achieved a level of articulation that we might say became a dominant form. Instead the agencies of articulation were rendered silent, emanating from "in the body" or, in the case of certain material discussion, rendering the excessive/transgressive as "beyond the body." From the 1980s to the present, the physical and critical discourses of the Chicana/o subject took on a completely different mode of representation. The timing is not random, but the politics of readership changed. I explore why in later chapters. For one, the production of the literary projects transformed the figurative body as well as the discourses of the Mexican-American subject into a completely different cultural sensibility, from reviled to reified.

Ernesto Laclau and Chantal Mouffe raise one of the most accurate descriptions of the problems radical or New Left programs face within a *re-visioning* of Marxist terminology. "Hegemony," they note, "will not be the majestic unfolding of an identity but the response to a crisis" (1985, 7). In thinking about the formation of hegemony as not a "majestic unfolding of an identity," and if it is, as Laclau and Mouffe suggest, "a crisis," what does this then mean for ethnicity, gender, and sexuality? Chicana/o intellectual production is based on two overlapping principles: a critique of U.S. national identification and an attempt to form a postnational aesthetic. What has long been argued as subjection for "the minority" within the Marxist frame is the embodiment of alienation, because "the laborer" is unable to be self-productive in the larger structures of cultural power. Such is evidenced when "the child" coming into consciousness in Tomás Rivera's proto-postmodern novel *Y no se lo tragó la tierra/And the Earth Did Not Part* (1990), Rudolfo Anaya's child protagonist in *Bless Me, Ultima* (1994),

or Antonio Villareal's *Pocho* (1958) is positioned as the observer of the ab-
surdity of racial ambivalence. These figures construct the epistemology of
the Chicana/o as subject along the periphery of modernity. They are not
modern as characters, but as a new generation, as children, they should be.
Rolando Hinojosa's *Estampas del Valle* (1973) and Les Blank's film *Chulas
Fronteras* (1976) similarly characterize the subtle dissonance of alienation,
a sublime nostalgia, a sense of innocence lost and returned, alongside the
residuals of everyday life that appear to generate a palatable ethnographic
view of Chicana/o life. Do these works, whether as novels or as documenta-
ries, achieve an authentic ethnography? Each tells a story, and that is clearly
one of their purposes. But do they allow for bridging cultural divisions or
improve lacking sensitivity toward immigrants? Rarely, is the answer.

Attempts to create such identificatory structures within an ostensibly
ethnic-minority culture were deemed necessary under the political context
of a segregationist society that argued for positivism and determined a subject of labor that could later claim grievances, even if unfulfilled, based on
economic and racial oppression. To really understand the implications of
race, gender, and sexuality, we must return to Spivak's "Can the Subaltern
Speak?" to make sense of any reversal of fortune. She says that "the necessary stratification of the colonial subject institution—in the first phase of
capitalist imperialism—makes color useless as an emancipatory signifier"
(1988, 273). Perhaps it is the case that segregation produced a minority subject that can voice such a claim of oppression and retribution. However,
the boundaries appear to be drawn a little differently between black and
brown. Conceivably, it may be useful to consider the same mechanisms
the police use to profile people of color that are structurally linked to homophobia and sexual harassment. Such spectacles occupy the same power
as gazing, as colonialism among disempowered subjects. Most responses
are based on an ideology of national consciousness, but the misrecognitions
that nationhood or belonging produce foreclose one's own position in relation to others.

In elaborating and investigating the terms of postnationalism in relation
to Chicanas/os, it is important to remember that cultural nationalism is
only a movement toward another location. Its temporality can be productive of culture and might even have some benefits in that postnationalism
and cultural nationalism initially exceeded the conditions of cultural production that is responsive to globalism. They can produce criticism beyond
the ethnic subject as a marginal ethnic national subject that already exists
in the canon. Benedict Andersen is at least correct to characterize nationalism as a "neurosis" that is "largely incurable" (1983), because we can see

how "the nation" can be a clearinghouse for untenable movements and ideologies left to wander incorrigibly in the subjunctive, much like Rivera's
quando lleguemos, which suggests to his reader that "liberation" is "to be"
achieved when, and if ever, "we arrive." It is the same pathway that raised
the collective consciousness once before of a nation, symbolically captured
in the saga of the Joads and the Okies.

New challenges have only recently emerged to add to the most progressive elements in Chicana/o literary criticism. As mentioned before, the
introduction of cultural studies in Chicana/o critical analysis has helped
refocus attention on specific genres. To some extent, cultural studies also
may have diverted the attention given to post-structuralism and discourse
analysis and intersected the material concern of feminist and popular culture with race- or ethnicity-based criticism. Any attempt to understand our
current critical vantage points should begin with the Chicana/o movement
as a genealogical effect of cultural transvaluation. From theater to poetry to
public art, from music to film, Chicana/o discourse has articulated a minority experience in U.S. culture that now draws international attention.[13]

Considering that there is a point of critical inquiry beyond cultural national pride and subject formation, Chicana/o cultural production has un-
dergone a series of revisionary stages that changed the course of its study
within aesthetic, political, and ethical areas. While this naming of the
"Chicana/o" as political subject has long been viewed as a contemporary
standard bearer for all Chicana/o intellectual practices, it is necessary to examine how the formation of the marginal subject outside of a national discourse can indeed provide a new sense of emancipatory significance within
the hegemonic cycle of transnational discourse.

"Dialectical" or "historical materialist" criticisms based on Marxist literary criticism, as Fredric Jameson suggests (1998), locate historical contradictory forces at odds. According to this model of developmental history, the
culture's demise or flourishing may in fact depend on whether this culture
or nation can properly synthesize contradictions without resorting to its
own massive disorganization. The gift of embodying consciousness was essential for colonial histories to end and for the formerly colonized to recuperate that which was lost to occupation or diaspora (Carnegie 2002). The
cultural memory of Chicana/o cultural national uprisings used that gift of
embodiment to form a nostalgic and utopian vision of the people. Under
a cultural nationalist voicing, however, the unifying basis for the literary
project suggests to us that radical change is necessary, perhaps logical, if
one is to achieve inclusion in American discourses.

Chicano critics, especially in the field of literary studies, initially looked at race and class as lending materialist claims to marginalization because class involves both physical and structural forms of analysis. Furthermore, cultural nationalist voices in Chicana/o studies extended the claim that cultural production could be seen as an effort to inscribe what had been temporarily lost in the cultural wars, giving us the sense that continuity can resume. In fact, the basis of Chicana/o literary subjectivity offers repeated attempts to continue recuperation.[14]

The real change takes place at the moment we turn away from structural and Marxist analysis, crediting the work of Foucault, Lyotard, Jameson, and others who discuss Marxist structuralist analysis and who provide frameworks for reconciling the "national" bind. Those of us involved in looking at Chicana/o identity formation read the role of the nation as a distilled and displaced cultural impulse borrowed from the success of past revolutionary moments, once full of promise, but also bearing its oppressive gestures.

(TRANS)NATIONAL DISCONTINUITIES

The most pressing challenge for U.S. Chicanas/os centers on the development of identity that either does not rely on nationalism or that is able to sustain a transnational identity. Mass migrations from Latin America as well as the changing demographics of central urban areas have made Chicanas/os' methodologies relevant to other emerging groups that did not experience the counterculture movements for themselves but saw their benefits because they understood the initial problems many new immigrants experience. It is important to determine the next phase. The Chicana/o literary subject has certainly shifted in cultural identification from an abject state or condition of pistol-swinging heroism toward a speaking and writing subject. A different critique of self-productivity can be achieved by drawing from cultural studies influences as media proliferate and change reception as well as artistry. Many other questions still remain about the efficacy of Chicana/o national discourse in an age of identity politics, popular culture, essentialist-based criticism of ethnicity and race, global and transnational currents, queer theories and/or gay lesbian interjections, along with postfeminist and postnationalist orientations. All of these critical perspectives presume the decline of a discernible "subject" whose embodiment in American democratic articulations appears to have receded. What we mean when we say "American" is debatable, but so is what we mean by "Chicana/o."

Cultures, like ideologies, identities, and histories, do not proceed logically, for as Baudrillard suggests, we are "bound by extremes" (1990, 143). Once thought to be an indispensable claim of the American left, ethnic and race criticisms have since taken a back seat to emerging global interests within a consumer-centered culture where postmodern cultural aesthetics seem to dominate. This raises a fundamental question: How will we be situated in all of these documents should a national context cease to provide an emancipatory signifier?

One of the more salient effects within a global and transnational context is the production of a pan-Latina/o identity in popular culture. This is most vividly represented by the excessive or glamorous production of the Chicana/o and Latina/o body in the media, in music and film. From singer Gloria Estefan's Miami Sound Machine band to *Ugly Betty*'s distortion of Latina beauty, all lend meaning to the term "extreme." The influences of popular-cultural icons under global capitalism's production form an aesthetic model of "good citizenship," one that is polished and uncritical of the political circumstances that can offer urban gang cultures, rural farmworkers, or day laborers, as if all come from the same background. Images of a clean-cut, exoticized Latina/o body are obvious in the Ricky Martin and Jennifer Lopez phenomena. Their appeal to a young "Hispanic" sensibility works in contrast to the working-class aesthetic pervasive in most Chicana/o urban hip-hop and conjunto music. Ricky Martin's radical politics of excess in "living *la vida loca*" could be read as an aesthetics of consumption, of "living on the edge" through a glamorous, thrill-seeking exercise of consumer politics, the life of "Juniors," as they are known in Mexico—young, hip, wealthy heirs who move from club to club or work in their fathers' companies. The *vida loca* naturally appeals to a younger Latina/o audience whose penchant for excess is sought by capital market industries that promise inclusion through a constituted pan-Latina/o identity.

While the success of these artists has drawn some attention to the market value of Latina/o and Chicana/o communities, their achievements mask a different political reality. At a time when U.S. Latinas/os and especially Chicanas/os experience severe state regulation in Texas, New York, Florida, and California with the reversal of affirmative action and immigration protection, the commercial production of an idealized Chicana/o and Latina/o body seems perversely at odds with popular political representations expressed in many of the advertisements promoting some of these measures. Selected positive images of Chicanas/os and Latinas/os mirror a traditionally conservative point of view and are based on a family, religion, and economic determinant. These contradictory views of the Chicana/o subject are by no means arbitrary in their effect and should be understood as complex genealogies of images and textual processes that have helped figure Chicanas/os into another ethical register of "the good minority" versus "the bad subject" minority. Chicanas/os have to rethink material issues within this capitalist intensive situation in which the transboundaries of global interests proscribe a desirable and celebrated Latina/o body in figures such as Ricky Martin and Jennifer Lopez.

The examples raise the question of whether it is at all possible to conceive of a new aesthetic practice within a postnational field that presupposes the decline of a political, national, exemplary, masculine subject. Are we left to scrutinize whether it is possible to consider a nonexemplary transcendent figure in the Chicana/o body, one that travels beyond the point of radical resistance often cited in the *movimiento* or in the utopian models of Aztlán? Can we move beyond the Brown Beret and gangbanger but not toward Ricky Martin, if that is the alternative? Or should we really be asking whether it is possible to conceive of a critical project that does not bury the need for positive self-reflection amid criticisms against cultural identification? Does the popular-culture scene provide adequate cultural representation, and can consumption really replace involvement in the political process? These are questions that should be raised and examined as we look at the "trans" effect in nationality.

The question of how Chicana/o transnationalism would proceed anticipates the very issues implicit in this first chapter. It is conceivable that representations around race, class, gender, and nation have become categorizations receiving attention over past decades because of their problematic overtones. Having realized that the politics of representation themselves produce their own issues and contradictions, I offer that Chicana/o intellectual projects, representation, and styles of reading texts have changed because they are part of the unraveling of the nation. Our present political, cultural, and intellectual situation has rendered many of our readings and assumptions about cultural identification in Chicana/o discourse ever more problematic, not because we are overtheorizing but because the postnational takes into account broad forces—global economics, drug trafficking, undocumented labor flow, and displacement. It is therefore my intention here to consider some of these effects more deeply and to test various alternative methods of interpretation.

Two

IDEALIZED PASTS
Discourses on Chicana Postnationalism

WHAT'S IN A NAME?

The ideas, activist movements, and professional groups that compose today's Chicana feminism developed from a refusal to identify with either Anglo-American feminists in the U.S. feminist movement or male counterparts in the *movimiento chicano*. This refusal to identify with and ascribe to these national social movements accounts for Chicana feminism's origins, and at the same time, this location of seeming instability creates an ambiguous outline about its own identity and trajectory within the national frame.[1] Although most feminist critical studies and commentaries about the formation of Chicana feminism attest to a variety of exclusionary practices and erasures, Chicanas attempted to create a separate and different identity process that could be productive in examining postnational discourse. Prior to any other criticism, Chicana feminism developed the first postnationalist social critique by rejecting the terms of exclusion in organized "national" movements and by offering a new set of terms.

Most comparative and comprehensive studies of the Chicana/o movement and of the U.S. feminist movement often erase and overlook the contradictions of their own development as political discourse. In the case of feminist political discourses, there are too few references to Chicana and Latina women as part of the nationalist movements. Chicana feminist discourse occupies no fixed origins except as a fiction created of developing an identity and political practice from the margins of these contradictory historical moments. Categories and coalitional directives such as U.S. women of color and lesbians of color, along with U.S. Third World feminisms and even transnational feminism, often erase the marked signs and history of each woman of color encompassed in that terminology (Galindo and González 1999).

In looking at the traces of such origins and across varied discourses that surround the emergence of Chicana feminism, several other groups and movements follow a more inclusive pattern. The U.S. women's movement and *movimiento chicano* limited the terms (or categorical participation) of "gender" and "women" within their own political articulations of ethnicity- and race-based emancipation, but doing so may have been necessary as an identity strategy that would actually later benefit Chicanas in their own self-articulation (ibid.). In this chapter I describe how the first critique against a national-based discourse began in the Chicana feminist movement. The first postnational encounter within Chicana/o discourse as an emergence into the transnational global sphere began as a critique against the limitations of nationalist movements (Aldama and Quiñonez 2002). In discussing the postnationalism of gender here I include direct and even discrete forms of criticism against nationalist-based organizations. In some respects, the nationalism of the Chicana/o movement may appear clearest in its confrontations with a chauvinistic element or as a public discourse against the notion of *women as other*. However, the same element of discontent with Chicana/o cultural nationalism appears to be in play with respect to the formation of a public discourse on feminism in naming its own emancipatory goals. In other words, some strains of dissension were contradictory even within a movement—Chicana/o, feminist, and nonfeminist. Discontent with national discussions about race and gender prompted what would be called the "women of color" movement in the United States, with its departure from a nationalist basis of study and subsequent character or identity as a coalitional style. But ultimately feminism did provide the obvious nexus from which Chicana feminism could develop its unique discourse. Its naming, as such, remains characteristically formed as a generative process in which other identities would follow (ibid., 5).

I begin with the U.S. feminist movement because within it the instability of gender and woman as a category for political activism takes shape most effectively. Most recent discussions about the foundational origins of U.S. feminism arise in many of Robyn Wiegman's essays and confrontations with the feminist movement. In one essay, "The Progress of Gender: Whither 'Women'" (2002), Wiegman questions the decision many women's studies programs have made to change (or disidentify) themselves from the project that gave women's studies a place in the institution. Such decisions are evident in the unit name change from, for example, "gender studies" to "sexuality studies" or "feminist studies." Citing a concern for a more inclusive and noncontradictory sign of the term "woman," Wiegman writes that there is a desire "to organize the many intellectual genealogies about bodies, identities, sex, gender and both racial and economic genealogies that have come to exist uncomfortably and without identitarian coherency within the institutional domain first named in Women's Studies" (37). Recasting the image of the feminist movement from the 1970s may have to recast itself or be part of the dilemma of confronting the category of woman in the academy, but erasing history may not be that easy.

Exclusion and its determinant of inclusion denote a naming process that institutes a particular gender criticism in which the politics and ideology of self-conscious struggles and choices underwrite a national history of the women's movement.[2] Similarly, the Chicana feminist movement's emphasis on the struggle for recognition, with its own renaming, or transvaluation, as a political discourse, provides a new set of conditions for examining the national and nationalist discourse on Chicana women (del Castillo 1989). Numerous conferences, anthologies, and courses began, by the late 1980s, to move away from the idea of a single course in the Chicano studies curriculum, "La Chicana," to argue for inclusion in all disciplines or curricula.

My emphasis here on the national serves as an indication of the refusal to categorize Chicana women as a seamless appendage of larger history, whether in the Chicana/o movement or in the more generalized women's movement. Assertions of exclusion, while necessary to a foundational logic of Chicana feminism initially, have claimed the limited opportunities that postcolonial, transnational, and Third World women's movements have seized. The naming process is important, but it is not as significant as the elaboration of new technologies that intensify conditions of labor. Examples of the new technologies emerged as Chicanas and other Latinas began addressing discriminatory practices in, for example, reproductive health, beginning with involuntary sterilization programs.[3]

The academic discourse on the Chicano movement provides sobering examples of how women and gender issues continue to overlook marginalized women's voices. With the exception of a handful of recent studies, there are few serious attempts to assess women's participation and contributions to the Chicano movement (Espinoza and Oropeza 2006). The collective failure to address gender has adverse consequences for scholars' representation of the political nature of identity. Additionally, this neglect contributes to theories of political action and consciousness that cannot account for differences in perspective or the distinctiveness of Chicanas' activism. Cynthia Orozco explains:

> Mexican-origin women have participated in community
> organizations in distinct ways. Women's organizational styles

illuminate the fact that machismo did not keep women out of politics. Women did not merely participate as family members or because of a family ideology. Nor . . . to "just help their men." They have expressed a feminist heritage in mixed-gender organizations, women-only, and separatist feminist groups. Lesbians also have their own distinctive organizational heritage. (1995, 24–25)

What, then, accounts for the paucity of scholarship on Mexicana-Chicana activism and politics? The answer lies, according to Orozco, in scholars' assumptions about women's consciousness and actions and the sexual, gendered, and racial ideologies on which these assumptions are based. Looking at the trajectory that directly links Chicana feminist analysis from its earliest conception to today, this complex system derives from the argumentation of exclusion. Refusal to adopt identifications with Anglo-American feminism and the early Chicano movement forms a critique of nationalism and signals the originating basis of postnationalism emerging specifically from a feminist position. Linkages with grassroots work, intellectual production, and social politics provide a basis for postnationalism as political consciousness critical of nationalistic forms of representation and instead formative of national organizations dedicated to an ongoing critique of patriarchy and exclusion. Of the national forms I examine here, the Comisión Femenil of MALCS, Women of Color, U.S. Third World feminist organizations, and specific Chicana lesbian groups have provided a heterogeneous basis for Chicana feminism's emergence as a postnationalist feminist discourse.

The work of Chicana activists who came of age during the late 1960s and the 1970s collectively write into history the important contributions of Mexican-American women in the social movements of the U.S. civil rights era. While differing in historical and organizational focus, each study identifies the tension between cultural nationalists and Marxist nationalists or with Anglo-American feminism. The common tendency is to characterize the 1960s activist generation as radical and therefore markedly different from previous generations. It sets forth a challenge to left-leaning men, Marxists, and Chicano men in particular that radical activism meant transformed inclusion. The problem with the term "radical" is that it was thought of in terms of class analysis and social and economic structural change and did not figure into the assumption that men and women, while sharing goals of racial and ethnic experience, held different views on sexuality. In other words, "radical sexualities," as a concept about gender and sex, did not emerge until the late 1970s. Such disparate discourses were cultivated in the late 1970s, throughout the 1980s, and into the 1990s as a collective method of spontaneous action in developing a unique and familiar understanding of the feminist project, an undertaking dialectically separate from its origins in the U.S. civil rights movements (Hurtada 2003). Chicana feminism's departure from the Chicano movement led to a discourse on gender and sexuality and came under the additional pressures exerted by an advancing global expansion transforming gender and sexuality structures (Chabram-Dernersesian 1992).

Early critiques against nationalism and originating from a perspective of the women's movement explained that radical men were not open and willing to address the concerns of women. The most obvious and well-cited criticism of this was the problem of inclusion in a movement that purportedly was intended to liberate both men and women from the constraints of the dominant culture. Arguably, such discontent was not so much about the lack of inclusion as about the need for Chicanas to find self-expression. At stake in many of the confrontations with "revolutionary claims" of self-determination, whether feminist or Chicana/o, hinged the material claims that women made on their own behalf.[4]

It bears noting again that for Chicana feminists the various Chicana/o and Latina/o movements across the United States derived their character from a combination of solidarity movements across Latin America, including religious and reformist practice (Lamas 1991, Mendoza 2002). The tenor of such revolutionary movements in Latin America resisted the totalizing pressure of U.S. economic and political imperialism, what María Josefina Saldaña-Portillo refers to as an oppositional movement against the "developmentalist" era in the history of the United States (2003). At the same time, however, we must recognize that such movements too often deflected any discussion of gender or sexuality in the name of homogeneity or nationalism. Chicana feminism thus emerged as a series of discourses talking through emancipatory actions (organizations) and consciousness-raising methods (ideas and decision making) that developed from state, organic, and institutional models of thinking, namely civil rights, liberal economics, the countercultural movement, anti–Vietnam War sentiments, and Anglo-American feminism.

Despite the tendency of specific identity formations to propel a history largely influenced by organic intellectualism and revolutionary paradigms, what prevailed in, and perhaps even limited, the Chicana/o cultural revolutionary stance over time was its primacy of patrimony as a legitimate form of speaking and navigating the public space. Matthew C. Gutmann,

in *Changing Men and Masculinities in Latin America* (2003), calls this phenomenon "hegemonic masculinity." Citing a lack of focus on or knowledge
about men and masculinity produces its own privileging of masculinity;
the assumption that masculinity occurs without epistemological mediation
in the Latin American context further attests to the unassuming evidence
that epistemic biologism remains intact in the colonial context. Likewise in
the Anglo-American feminist movement, as Wiegman posits (2002), there
is a relationship between the countercultural movements and the development of a foundationalist feminism that maintains what Chela Sandoval
has termed "hegemonic" feminism (2002). All of these attempts to characterize a dimension of feminism, whether foundationalist or hegemonic, lay
claim to the nationalist imperatives that Anglo-American feminism constructed in its wake.

Under the rubric of civil rights, the collective voicing of the Chicana/o
movement has relied on naming this primacy of masculinity and resisted
it as the legitimate voice. The militarism inherent in colonialism marks the
masculine as the subject or agent of violence in history, as the masculine
animates the representational and cultural means of communication, all
indicating a need to sustain masculinity at whatever price and in all institutions, religious, political, and economic. And despite the revolutionary
imperative to elicit political change, this postcolonial pattern developed
into a cultural fissure in later conceptualizations of postnationalist communities. The fissure was taken up by the unfinished business of Chicana
feminist theorizations. Viewed from another angle, the private and public
spaces designate a spatial dynamic that privileged the structural formation of male discourses: public speaking and written language. Inserting
the male discourses into the racial language of the nation also feminized
indigenous heritages, and similarly, women's languages were racialized into
submission. Examples include the use of the masculine pronouns to denote
all persons.

Any rebuilding of a functional community must therefore assume a
postnationalist reference and explore the delineations of gender production that give primacy to masculinity and gave capital valuation to women
only through the retention of women as objects of the private space, something that contributed further to the rigid gender coding that has sustained
revolutions across Latin America (Vigota 2003). Thus even within a nationalist movement such as the Chicana/o movement, there was room for the
growth of Chicana feminism.

American feminism, or Anglo-American feminism, thrived in the 1960s
and 1970s. The American feminist movement prompted all sorts of per-

spectives from radical to leftist to liberal viewpoints. Groups formed in Chicago, New York City, Boston, Seattle, San Francisco, and Washington, D.C., as well as in small towns and in communes; they engaged in continuous conversation and action within a materialist feminist framework that had its origins in the late 1960s, when synthesizing feminist politics with Marxist analyses was common and necessary. Materialist feminism held that working conditions for women served as the basis for understanding all inequalities. That key theoretical formulation allowed many feminists to examine other material realities, including single parenting, divorce, poverty, unequal wages, job discrimination, and so on.

Early work on a projected alliance between Marxism and feminism directed itself to the problem of bringing feminist questions of gender and sexuality into some form of strategic dialogue with class analysis (García 1990). In keeping with subsequent developments within the women's movement, the materialist feminist problematic has extended to questions of race, nationality, ethnicity, lesbianism and sexuality, and cultural identity, including religion. In other words, it moved from class-based analysis toward race/color, ethnicity, and sexuality, growing more complicated in its understanding of why or how women were oppressed.

The desire for inclusion in equal rights curiously revolves around a notion of self-representation; and while exclusions could be determined, witnessed, or claimed, Chicana feminist organizations especially recognized self-representation as a desired goal. Chicana feminism arose from either small groups meeting for the first time (Encuentro Femenil) or caucuses following other formed organizations—National Organization for Women (NOW), NWSA, NACCS—in which feelings of isolation and disconnection from their own movement or from an identity frame congealed. This process for group development extended across major southwestern cities and towns and in some rural areas. Most Chicana feminist organizations developed primarily from Chicano-based movements or other community action organizations within a localized base. As I will explain later in more detail, cultural nationalism became less of an option among the growing number of Chicana feminist movements. Chicana feminist intellectuals and scholars made key choices that would ensure a heterogeneous orientation, but not without debate. The major turn facilitating the heterogeneous framing of Chicana feminism as a postnational critique hinged on the belief that cultural nationalism as it played out in the *movimiento* represented male-centered ideologies. What seemed like a casual commentary on the part of many women organizers and early feminists became evident: the *movimiento* did not liberate them from the kitchen or other menial duties associated with liberation-style politics. It did initiate the development of awareness about political action, which in turn foregrounded liberation.

Numerous organizations and representations in books and art developed in this period, and the foundation for Chicana feminism followed. In considering the many ways feminism challenges nationalist masculinity by emphasizing and putting into action a feminist method of desired outcomes, we see that Chicanas challenged foundationalist feminism by citing its cultural legacy of exclusion of other than "white, middle-class" women, as it had long been assumed that the Chicano movement's ideas developed from a foundational intellectual framework created in the late 1960s.

By the late 1970s, however, as the end of the Vietnam conflict signaled a return to some degree of cultural normalcy, one result was more aesthetic than tangible. In the course of an eighteen-year period in the Chicana/o movement's various constituencies, a consciousness and style emerged that set apart this movement from others. Chicanas set the pace for looking at the concept of women of color by creating a discourse on sexuality that became distinctive. While many facets of an idealized notion of a community remained in the articulations of Chicana feminists, a new feminist discourse did in fact develop to meet the goal of political, cultural, and economic inclusion (Chabram-Dernersesian 1992). As such, this newfound language, political direction, and focus culminated with the publication of essay collections and political projects that ushered in the "women of color paradigm" during the late 1970s and the 1980s. Chicanas were instrumental and central to that development.

SOCIAL JUSTICE ORIGINS OF CHICANA FEMINISM

Ideals of social justice consistently found expression in varied forms to advance the concerns of Chicanas beyond the immediate local and community interests. By cultivating a response that directly affected Chicanas in their communities, Chicana feminists asserted claims of injustice in a first critical analysis, which emerged from grassroots and activist organization across the United States.[5] Some feminist publications, they argued, dated back to the early twentieth century in regions of the borderlands. Chicana feminist collectives of the later periods cited both silence and exclusion in participation within the Chicana/o movement and especially from U.S. feminist movements.

Espinoza and Blackwell quote Marta Cotera and others in recent studies of the origins of Chicana feminist movements. In her 1971 essay "Hijas de Cuauhtemoc," Anna Nieto Gómez called for a critical view of sexism, citing its presence in Chicano families, in communities, and within the male-dominated Chicano movement. The internal politics within the Chicana/o movement also pitted Chicanas against other emerging groups. In the following passage from her famous essay, Nieto Gómez emphasizes the need to create a Chicana feminism that resists silencing strategies. She suggests that the struggle to find a Chicana feminist voice was also a struggle to define oneself outside the male Chicano patriarchy and outside Anglo feminism.

> Being compared with Anglo women has been the greatest injustice and the strongest device used to keep Chicanas quiet. Nobody liked to be called a traitor in a cause she feels she would die for. In addition, no Chicana who has worked in the movement deserves to be compared to any Anglo woman or Gay liberation. These comparisons are divisive and threatening to the strength of the movement. (7)

Nieto Gómez explores how distortions in Chicana feminism created havoc in the struggle to define a place in the different movements of the era—women's movements and/or gay movements. Such efforts were often met with criticisms. Not unlike the *traidora* (traitor) complex about which Norma Alarcón writes in "Traductora, Traidora" (1989), an essay detailing what Alarcón describes about La Chicana as intellectual, Chicana feminists of the 1960s and 1970s were caught in a historical bind because of the meaning of the translator/traitor; the term refers to La Malinche, who served as translator for the Aztecs and the Spanish conquerors (Alarcón 1981). Her intellectual skills in diplomacy and translation set her up as the presumed betrayer of culture after the Spanish conquest of the Aztec empire (see also Candelaria 1980). Even in early-twentieth-century Anglo-American liberal culture, the sedimentation of this perceived betrayal motif subtly cautions the Chicana in intellectual realms as well as in U.S. letters: from a branding of the scarlet letter "A" to an "M" for traitor in a state of abjection, the untrustworthy, adulterous, or traitoress is a figure used to control women and make them fearful.

Early Chicana feminist predecessors wove similar threads in provocative philosophical pieces that were intended for and read by those in the emerging movement. Like several other feminists in the movement, Bernice Rincón in her work in the newsletter *Regeneración* declared that Chicanas, as women, could no longer be relegated to marginal status within the home and culture since the domestic space was constructed to deny Chicanas a place in the public space of the Chicana/o movement. This sentiment, echoed by many Chicanas, expresses a concern that the "revolution" for social change did not make its way into the private space of the home; this was the "woman question" so artfully articulated in the cult classic film *Salt of the Earth*. Other Chicana feminists echoed Rincón's sentiments. For example, Enriqueta Longeaux y Vásquez, founder of the publication *El Grito del Norte*, wrote numerous articles on the status of Chicanas and cited sexism within Chicano communities while affirming that these communities also were dominated by a pervading system of racism in the larger society. These feminists encountered issues that a liberal nation-state directly articulated in civil rights legislation, in the War on Poverty, and across other programs. The issues continued well into the next few decades with little change or improvement for "minority" women, the term that began being used in the government (García 1997).

The most vivid example of the transformation of grassroots feminism and university research came in the formation of publication arms or houses that published women of color, notably Third Woman Press and others nationally, including Kitchen Table Press and Spinsters/Aunt Lute. According to the founder of Third Woman Press, Norma Alarcón, the idea for a publishing organization developed from a conversation among Chicanas and Latinas living in the U.S. Midwest. They aspired to form a journal that dedicated its publications to writings by women of color living on the margins of society. It took several years and university support to build Third Woman Press. In its first ten years, the house existed primarily as a journal titled *Third Woman*.

First published in 1979, *Third Woman*'s founders included Alarcón, Ana Castillo, and Sandra Cisneros, who organized the first editions of the journal. By the mid-1980s the women behind *Third Woman* had transformed the journal format into Third Woman Press, a publishing house producing critical anthologies by women of color. Today, Third Woman Press no longer exists. For more than twenty-five years, the press provided a forum for the written and visual expressions of women of color and sustained their support in intellectual activism by publishing the works of feminist writers. It was one of few presses dedicated to such work by women of color.[6]

A correlation thus exists between the activist grassroots publications in Chicana feminist thought and the rise of Chicana studies as an academic field of inquiry. The scholarship witnessed an interconnectedness of race, class, and gender assumptions and, later, sexuality and broadened into ethnic studies and women's studies with a cross-disciplinary approach that linked class to gender and racial inequity. As a model of study, Chicana-authored scholarship still was most apparent as feminist study but, with some notable exceptions, not necessarily considered within the attention of feminist studies.

Recent trends in U.S. feminist critical studies suggest a shift in subject matter—from a strictly U.S.-based race, class, gender divide to a more complex set of renderings—occurring partly because of the advancement of global and transnational capitalism. As the transformative aspects of global capital continue to define the living conditions for many Third World women, Chicanas and Latinas in the university setting are investigating the reorganization of the working-class labor sector within Third World communities and nations. While it has yet to be seen how the transformation from a U.S. cultural national movement to a global and transnational frame will affect the field of inquiry known as Chicana studies, clearly we have already witnessed major changes in the scholarship.[7]

Border studies, critical race theories, and transnational and global studies, as well as gender, sexuality, transgender, and queer studies, have emerged in recent years in response to the need to expand the terminology of an identity and methodology—Chicana studies—that took its prominence in the 1980s and 1990s. However, the commitment to social change and to questions of justice has remained a consistent part of Chicana feminist practice whether in the university or beyond it. As Chicana feminism gains visibility around the globe, the nature of its analysis, for example, its influence in contemporary leftist theory, is also changing.

COMISIÓN FEMENIL

The early 1970s firmly stand as a vital and active period in the growth of Chicana feminist grassroots organizations. Comisión Femenil, dedicated to the political organization of Mexican-American women, was founded out of a resolution drafted by thirty women attending a women's issues workshop at the National Issues Conference in Sacramento, California, in 1970. The resolution reflected concerns that the women considered priorities.[8] By 1971, with the formation of Comisión Femenil's first chapter at California State University at Los Angeles, the organization of Chicanas and some Anglos met regularly and in connection with other community-allied organizations such as Chicana Service Action Center. Comisión Femenil's goals to train and organize Chicanas to assume positions of leadership developed from organic ideals that a community should grow its own leaders from the bottom to the top, which the Comisión did by grooming members for leadership. It hosted workshops, seminars, and public speaking engagements. Comisión Femenil held the first of its annual conferences in Goleta, California, in June 1972. By November 1972, Comisión Femenil members testified on Chicana issues before the California State Commission on the Status of Women. What differentiates Comisión Femenil from other Chicana grassroots organizations is the members' commitment to grow leaders from within their ranks to serve in the public and political arenas: "If Latina concerns were to be addressed in the public decision-making arena, Latinas themselves would have to participate as decision-makers and policy-makers," they argued.[9]

As the Comisión Femenil grew, a philosophy developed to represent the ideals of the group. One document details the philosophy of the organization and some of the desired outcomes for the group:

- Enhance the image of the Chicana and develop awareness
- Educate members so as to be more effective in the advocacy of Chicana Rights
- Provide leadership training so that members could assume positions of power in the political, socioeconomic status
- Promote welfare of the Chicano community
- Provide a female-dominated organization for women to function [work] without the constraints that had been experienced in male-dominated community organizations

Comisión Femenil archives at UCLA contain documents reflecting the organization's second-wave approach to feminism. The group intended to formalize a political action committee for Chicanas. The issues and community problems that brought Comisión Femenil into existence became a directed, organized effort oriented toward building community, political infrastructure, and a representative leadership base. Of the social issues that mattered most to members, job training, poverty, education, child care, abortion, and forced sterilization were just some of the many issues the women of Comisión Femenil addressed in efforts to promote social change. The group celebrated its thirty-year anniversary as an organization in 2004 on the campus of UC Santa Barbara; participants brought and donated Comisión Femenil materials to the Center for Ethnic and Multicultural Archives (CEMA). This archive suggests the significance of one organization in the matter of how and why Chicanas began to organize for their own interests, whether within or outside Chicano nationalism. In some respects,

Comisión Femenil unintentionally paved a path toward a postnational understanding of Chicana issues.

MUJERES ACTIVAS EN LETRAS
Y CAMBIOS SOCIALES

By the early 1980s, the work of Chicana academics, which other social movements and men in the academy had barely acknowledged, became a vehicle for the founding of MALCS (Women of Letters Advocating for Social Change). In 1982 a group of Chicana and Latina academic women gathered at UC Davis to discuss their concerns as Chicanas in the academy and to share their academic work. Already having experienced a loss of voice and isolation within the echelons of higher education, these women were eager to communicate their knowledge and collaborate with other women; they desired to change society's perceptions that led to mistreatment, invisibility, and erasure. MALCS was established at this meeting, which followed previous gatherings of the same graduate students and faculty, as an academic organization that articulated Chicana and Latina feminist perspectives. The MALCS declaration, written one year later on the Berkeley campus, formally established the organization and affirmed the membership's dedication to the unification of the members' academic lives with their community activism. The MALCS *declaración* (1983), a plan of action, states the reason for the organization's founding:

> We are the daughters of Chicano working class families
> involved in higher education. We were raised in labor camps
> and barrios, where sharing our resources was the basis of
> survival. Our values, our strength derive from where we came.
> Our history is the story of the working-class people—their
> struggles, commitments, strengths, and the Chicano/Mexi-
> cano experience in the United States. We are particularly
> concerned with the conditions women face at work, in and out
> of the home. We continue our mothers' struggle for economic
> and social justice. The scarcity of Chicanas in institutions of
> higher education requires that we join to identify our com-
> mon problems, to support each other and to define collective
> solutions. Our purpose is to fight the race, class, and gender
> oppression we have experienced in the universities. Further, we
> reject the separation of academic scholarship and community

involvement. Our research strives to bridge the gap between intellectual work and active commitment to our communities. We draw upon a tradition of political struggle. We see ourselves developing strategies for social change—a change emanating from our communities. We declare the commitment to seek social, economic, and political change throughout our work and collective action. We welcome Chicanas who share these goals and invite them to join us.[10]

MALCS hosts a summer research institute (established in 1985) and publishes a newsletter. MALCS members helped establish a permanent research center at UC Davis in March 1991 to develop knowledge by, for, and about Chicanas and Latinas as scholars. MALCS published Trabajos Monográficos, a working-paper series that changed its name in 1991 to the Series in Chicana Studies. In its second volume, the series morphed into the *Journal of Chicana/Latina Studies*, which MALCS published into the 1990s. In 2004 MALCS officers and members agreed to a new journal title, *Chicana/ Latina Studies*, and the journal entered a new phase as it left its earlier home and moved to Loyola Marymount University.

The founding of MALCS was valuable to the formation of Chicana feminist critical analysis in the 1980s and 1990s. As an organization that has flourished because it offers controversial and, at times, dramatic presentations at the different sites and venues of its conferences, MALCS is the first group of its kind to link feminist issues with the specific issues of Chicanas in the academy.[11]

The concerns that MALCS has addressed from its inception are captured in the MALCS logo, an Aztec woman kneeling and working in front of an older IBM XT computer. The image captures the historical space and imagery of mixed-race and indigenous women with technology. Filling in the divide, the artist, Yolanda López, met with the group of Chicana scholars at UC Berkeley in 1982 and proposed *La Monita* for the MALCS logo. The women intended *La Monita* to represent MALCS in its mission vis-à-vis labor practices (boycotts, strikes, unionizing activity), discrimination, and racism as well as indigeneity. The formation of Chicana feminism has continued ever forward with its development as an academic discourse and practice. The two have not been mutually exclusive—the political organizing "out there" and the academic "within" type of writing.

In the 1970s small groups of Chicanas on and off campuses for the first time broke away from the mythology of subservience that had fossilized into a folkloric idea, not true cultural practice. The organizers of political groups and, later, academic ones defied historical memory, for example, that maintained that Mexican-origin women and mantilla-clad, Catholic-worshiping figures were tradition-bound. Chicanas who entered the academy fit neither this mold nor this image. The imaginary spaces proved critical to the first writings that Chicanas produced, in the works of Marta Cotera (1973) and Adelaida R. del Castillo (1989), to name just two. But among the most pressing concerns of a generation of first-time academics was the need to express issues that were particular to Chicanas as women of color (beginning with Third World liberation struggles). As the movement traveled from grassroots outside of universities to a research analysis supported by funding inside the agency that "produced" knowledge, the conceptual reframing of Chicana feminism grew and was magnified.

Most of this research developed from discussions at myriad feminist conferences or meetings; the majority took place at colleges and universities as well as in community centers in efforts to bridge the divide between town and gown communities. While many concur that the most important aspect of Chicana feminist critical analysis is the ever-present need for social change, the 1982 birth of Mujeres Activas en Letras y Cambio Social as still the only Chicana/Native academic organization has made it possible to organize critical perspectives in other ways. The institutionalization of MALCS stands as an example of the critical nexus between a commitment to social change and academic interests. In the publication of major Chicana critical texts over the past quarter-century, most of which have been written to "cross borders" or engage a critical vanguard by showing the need to alter the course of study, a MALCS goal is met: to voice, publish, and add to the knowledge about Chicanas everywhere (Alarcón et al. 1993). The organization's critical texts were published intermittently until recently, when funding was secured for the journal in which some of this material was first published.

The image of the 2006 MALCS annual summer institute tells a history. The Aztec "Mona" is replaced in the poster or flyer by an athletic, full-figured, young mestiza, flexing a tattooed arm on one side and holding a small laptop in the other. Her vest decorated with stars and the daisies in the background recall several important symbols, from the shawl of the Virgen de Guadalupe, Mexico's patron saint, to the Day of the Dead ritual. What died might well be the Aztec moniker so that the Chicana modern "take-charge" icon replaces her despite deploying such traditional symbols of mexicanidad as daisies.

The published material focuses on the internal contradictions within Chicana studies, whether viewed by its practitioners as group identity, as a culture, or as academic integrity. These self-reflective modes of analysis include queer, gender, and sexuality studies within the broader field of Chicana/o studies, along with the intersectional concerns of psychology, spirituality, transnationalism, and border studies. Some presenters premiere their work at MALCS and then refine it at larger gatherings; others only present certain work at MALCS for insider feedback. The intense struggle within the organization around sexuality and gender in particular engaged a relatively young academic community. Chicana/o studies was a growing discipline in the 1980s, and most departments of Chicana/o studies dated to 1969 and later. Foregrounding in its publications and at annual gatherings some of the most important political theories and practices, such as feminism, radical lesbian separatism, gender identity, and the discipline of Chicana/o studies, MALCS was a leader in presenting new or innovative methods and research. One result, then, was an interesting arrangement of critical inquiry that oriented the "stereotypically" Chicano "nationalist" position of identity formation from without to a critical Chicana analysis from within. At its most basic level, the Chicana position presupposes interesting facets of community building, but it also translates the goal from a setting "out there" toward a setting "within," because MALCS' annual meetings take place at colleges and universities throughout the United States.

The first time I attended a MALCS conference, in Los Angeles in 1990, was memorable because it brought to the forefront lesbian representation and was creative in organizing a visible manifestation of standpoint epistemology. Briefly, standpoint epistemology asks participants to investigate their viewpoints in relation to contradictory evidence. In older feminist practices, it was termed "calling out," that is, asking someone where she stood (Spellman 1988). Participants in the 1990 MALCS conference deliberated on two major concerns: the lack of inclusion of lesbians as presenters and the paucity of lesbian subject matter in conference sessions. In addition, a separate challenge arose about the inclusion of "white" women as presenters because one white woman sought to present her research in a panel or workshop. The difference between these two terms was critical. Both issues brought about intense debate. For one, MALCS cofounders recalled that workshops and panels were spaces for Chicanas to introduce research without the interference of censorship caused by a mainstream presence. Workshops instead allowed the presenters to inhabit a physical space normally not accorded Chicana feminist research: freed of a colonizing gaze. Not all MALCS members agreed in this interpretation of MALCS' bylaws.[12]

Conference sites, their institutional tensions, and the production of knowledge, all symbolized or embodied and emboldened by MALCS, allow a politics of the self to be created outside of traditional forms of knowledge production. In its theoretical presentation, Chicana cultural and academic production applies to history, social values, aesthetics, politics, and economics, along with other organized structures that determine the political subject's cultural frame. Immanent critique constitutes within MALCS, for example, a subtle mechanism of change that occurs from within a movement or organized social structure.

To account for a radical transformation of language or cultural, social, or semiotic structures, the resistance that determines such subtle changes is not always built or determined by economics, but it often does play a role in the power dynamics of social and intellectual formation. Sexuality and sexual politics clearly played a decisive role in MALCS' 1990 annual conference. Such a change has followed the establishment and growth of the organization MALCS, particularly in its discussions about leadership, identity practices, and creating a space where serious criticism, self-reflection, and spiritual renewal can all coexist. The coexistence was or has not been smooth in the matter of lesbian political practice, but Chicana lesbians have led MALCS into the future by serving as coordinators, chairs, and program committee organizers. Although accepted as a marginal discourse that traverses the boundaries of sexuality and culture, today's Chicana feminism offers a critique of nation, family, and community as well as of ideology and heterosexual hegemony in postcolonial and transnational studies.[13]

CHICANA LESBIANS

The invisibility of Chicana lesbian feminism changed with the publication of *This Bridge Called My Back* (1981). Other major books published in the 1980s stand as models of a feminist project that uses a radical format to illustrate its departure from conventional notions of class radicalism. The lesbian feminists Gloria Anzaldúa and Cherríe Moraga developed a feminism that arises from a Marxist socialist critique and derives its cross-interdisciplinary framing of critical analysis from activist, academic, and sociopolitical practices.

Among the many dispositions of *This Bridge* and similar books is a general response to systemic exclusion, silence, and divisive institutional politics. Central to such theorization has been the formation of lesbian feminism as a core element that challenges notions of nationhood in the sense of an intervention against liberalism or for equality (Alarcón 1995, 187).[14] Each time lesbians took a stand against exclusion, they were suggesting that they were still not full-fledged participants in the conference, on the committee, or at the festival (Bauer and Wald 2000).

In elaborating the field of feminist study, with a list of major publications and changes in pedagogical practices, Chicana feminist critical analysis has, however, been widely recognized in other venues, such as contemporary leftist theory, cultural studies, feminist studies, sexuality studies, and queer studies. One amazing result has been attention given to lesbian writers and theorists whose work had been largely overshadowed by Chicano publications that subscribed to other forms of radicalism. Only in recent years has Chicana feminist analysis found a new direction that advances a fresh set of political goals, but this originated in the most "radical" of sectors, with Chicana lesbian writers, both academic and nonacademic (Rueda 2006).

Lesbian critical analysis is thus the knowledge production by women of Mexican-American descent whose work has altered the structural and particular oppressive conditions that the colonial history of Mexico and the colonization process of the U.S. Southwest created. In the twenty-first century, identity frameworks reorient academic and political spaces to recover and designate a place and space for Chicana lesbian writing, what Emma Pérez encapsulated and theorized as *sitio y lengua* (1991). Such critical analysis by Chicana lesbians has been powerful in the transformation of cultural nationalism, but its reexamination of the nationalist heritage the past few decades has been largely overlooked in feminist and queer circles. The trajectory of Chicana feminist critical analysis incorporates theoretical and social political practices as well as a race and gender analysis in its main concerns. The goals of such critical analysis in feminism have been to interpret and dismantle historical and structural conditions that oppress women, to demystify the truisms within culture that hold Chicanas to a subordinate role in society, whether conscious or unconscious, and finally, to recast dimensions of power in all facets of life. Chicana feminist critical analysis thus assumes many forms, including such artistic projects as *La Ofrenda* by Ester Hernández.[15]

The image of the Virgen de Guadalupe, worshipped on the back of Hernández' lesbian lover with flowers offered to either the saintly image or the lover, meld a lesbian praxis, artistic and political. Only those "in the know" would understand the subtext of this popular painting, reproduced into posters and hanging in virtually every Latina lesbian household in the Southwest and beyond (Griswold del Castillo, McKenna, and Yarbro-Bejarano 1991). Numerous approaches of inscribing Chicana lesbian aesthetics have developed across new areas—including social justice venues; transnational, postnational, and global studies; and gender and queer theories and methodologies—and each emerges as part of the intellectual matrix of a new Chicana movement. The problem, however, is that within heterosexist representations rearticulated through the cultural domination of Chicanas, depictions pervade of self-sacrificing women as followers behind their men in battle or serving as nurturers and healers. The "cultural deficiency model," as social scientists term it, is sustained. This time, rather than poverty as a cultural determinant or poor role models in the case of discussing gang membership, the viewpoint is differently sexed. Women are weak or subsumed by men.

Within any revolutionary construct of the type witnessed in Latin America in the late 1970s and the 1980s, such imagery fails to challenge patriarchal domination, reinventing alternative representations of Chicanas but still mediated through the service of male authority and privilege. For example, in her powerful condemnation of what she termed "the Adelita Complex" (1997), Norma Cantú argues that despite their proponents' revolutionary claims, these images are nonetheless stifling for Chicanas because they fail to view women as potential leaders, as political thinkers, or as military strategists. Instead, women are seen merely as appendages to male-defined and male-led struggle. As Cantú notes, these representations were further commodified through Mexican films on the Mexican Revolution, which often showed Mexico's leading man, the actor Pedro Armendariz, riding into the next battle followed on foot by his equally popular leading lady, Dolores del Río. Hollywood helped perpetuate the notion of subservience or of a helpmate to the detriment of strong leading role models for Chicanas.

Within the Chicano movement, patriarchal heterosexist constructions of *la familia* were articulated in cultural politics and practices. With family becoming a metaphor for nation both as a site of birth and life, the term became discursively fixed, leaving unequal relations within the family undiscussed. These narrow conceptions of community rely on unexamined notions of home, family, and nation and severely limited Chicanas' struggles by extending a hierarchical and dependent aspect of family relationships into the political arena, which manifested intolerance for alternative negotiations and preconceptions.[16] Moreover, the structures of familial experience (such as authority, language, and participatory opportunities) construct different expectations and capacities for various family members, structures that, in turn, have profound and detrimental consequences for emancipatory struggles (Zinn 1975b). The ideology of *la familia* encoded gender roles for Chicanas that were often defined by ideas about nurturance and subordination. Their function was to maintain male power and authority. What was "authentic" was frequently defined by fundamentally unequal ideas about sexuality and patterns of interaction between men and women.[17]

Chicana feminist efforts to expose the Chicano male heterosexist monopoly on the construction of Chicana/o identity effectively exploded the notion of an essential Chicano/a subject and initiated a bitter struggle for the space in which to record an alternative perspective. Chicanas have been determined in their efforts to expose the practice of "selective memory" that conveniently repositions women in subservient roles in the name of cultural authenticity. Cherríe Moraga explains:

> In reaction against Anglo-America's emasculation of Chicano men, the male-dominated Chicano Movement embraced the most patriarchal aspects of its Mexican heritage. For a generation, nationalist leaders used a kind of "selective memory," drawing exclusively from those aspects of Mexican and Native cultures that served the interests of male heterosexuals. At times, they took the worst of Mexican machismo and Aztec warrior bravado, combined it with some of the most oppressive male-conceived idealizations of "traditional" Mexican womanhood and called that cultural integrity. (1993, 156–157)

Gloria Anzaldúa joins Moraga's stinging indictment, suggesting that in the process of reclaiming an Indian past, Chicanos privileged the more militaristic, patriarchal Aztecs and undermined the principle of balanced opposition between the sexes that had previously existed. "The Aztec people considered themselves in charge in regulating all earthly matters. Their instrument: controlled or regulated war to gain and exercise power" (1997, 26). This power extended into the spiritual arena in an effort to undermine female authority:

> The male dominated Azteca-Mexica culture drove the powerful female deities underground by giving them monstrous attributes and substituting male deities in their place, thus splitting the female self and the female deities. (81)

Reactionary political representations of "selective" indigenous images not only reinforce male interests and power but have the unintended consequence of undermining the potential solidarity between the sexes. The privileging of only the Aztecs (and not the Mayans, the Pueblos, or myriad others) as a role model for a new nationalist patriarchal Chicano community serves as a clear example of the tendency of nationalist movements to reclaim, reinvent, and legitimize traditions that disempower women in the name of cultural authenticity. However, once the implications of gender were introduced, it becomes possible to see how the debates over Chicano identity have been conducted within categories that bear the imprint of hierarchically defined sexual differences. Employing a theoretical framework sensitive to gender implicates the possibilities of understanding how power, knowledge, and resistance are tied to gender representations and produced and reproduced in historically contingent, and culturally variable, symbolic practices.

Viewing Chicana feminism against a traditional nationalistic backdrop is an important rejoinder to the slippery essentialist binds and limiting identity framework that so defined feminism in past decades. Chicana feminist critical analysis countered the idealization of culture and nation by citing its future-perfect grammars, possessing little or no investment in either the idealization of Chicano nationalism or Anglo-American feminism. It was located in art projects, academic collectives, literary expression, and publications. Newer views developed because of the failures of the earlier movements to account seriously for Chicana presence and Chicana agency. The idealism that informs Chicana feminism occurs because the practice of political difference incites new paradigms.

However, in an age of suspicion over essentialist identity conformity and antiliberal campaigns in the academy, one of the impulses that ought to be resisted is the summary rejection of any type of idealism as a community and social practice. Rather, we should not necessarily conflate as cause and effect the essentialism and universality of institutions and nation-states and the abuses of male-dominated epistemologies with the insurrection of different ideas and self-determinations of minority women. If we fear positive ideas about ourselves in order to appease the theoretical ordination of academic knowledge, which can be faulty and after all is intended to be a critique of dominant male culture, we miss a valuable point about such progressive movements as Chicana feminism and its aim to transform knowledge and history. The anti-intellectual claims allow easy conclusions and idealizations of cultural movements for civil rights. If anything, anti-essentialism and anti-intellectualism have thwarted efforts to promote some types of affirmative actions by reducing women of color to an oversimplified identitarian body count. Affirmative action programs, it has been shown, have at least initially benefited white women more than any other single group (Mixon and Uri 1991).

In addition, Chicana feminism's claims of exclusion from Chicana/o nationalism as well as from Anglo-American feminist movements necessitate a different historical understanding of Chicana as subject/agent in the academy and in the field; any idealized feminist future must reside in an understanding of the specificity of a Chicana past and in historically situated contexts several centuries old. To render Chicana agency as a recent phenomenon would be equally erroneous for Chicana/o studies and for feminist studies.

A summary review of Chicana feminist critical analysis reconvenes the area in which the Chicana/o movement has fulfilled some of its promises and holds the greatest meaning for a postnational future. Chicana feminism's internal dialogues have shaped critical discourses by responding to current issues: Has affirmative action helped or hindered the movement of Chicanas/os into academe? Where do Chicana academics belong in the discourse on globalism? What is the nature of Chicana feminist critical inquiry? These questions were not necessarily planned in advance of a quest for data or for publishing position statements and policy papers because there was limited funding. The renderings of its own history as a field or area of study make the outcomes of Chicana criticism, of Chicana feminist studies, less predictable than one might anticipate for other groups. With others, policy impacts or a shift in the direction of new research might be outcomes, but with Chicana-based criticism, an immediate or lasting value has yet to be determined.[18]

Embedded as a critical strategy of what I have labeled elsewhere "the future-perfect tense" lies Chicana feminism's impossible recourse to exceptionality that becomes subsumed under utopian positioning; the strategy of criticism, like that of resistance, simply cannot exist in isolation if it is to have a life beyond the urgent call for change. It should include maneuverings beyond the standpoint politics. In other words, an exploration and thorough review of *el movimiento* has value but not if left without a context about where resistance ended—losing steam while many sought to gain social, political, or class improvement, with uneven successes. Chicana feminism's critical analysis serves as a primary critique of hegemony and of hegemonic cultural determinism; the institutional dynamics of globalization, for example, possess their own set of silences and exclusionary methods that continue to marginalize Chicanas under a new set of terms—new world ordering or post-9/11 paranoia. In these global settings, due to massive immigration of Mexicans in particular, the quantitative data reflect a cycle of nonimprovement, economically speaking. The new immigrants, more than half of them female, tend to reinforce a dependent status built on low wages, hard working conditions, and few opportunities for advancement.

Attempts to universalize La Chicana—as an emblem of colonialism, liberal salvation, or moniker of labor, that is, always the maid—do not serve to improve class mobility but are important because they consciously linked intellectual and activist models in emancipatory and liberating terms. Liberatory strategies that materially and theoretically ameliorate the conditions within feminist practices in general and especially for Chicanas in the academy have not merely surfaced but have been deployed to move the scholarship and knowledge of the scholarship toward a recognition of what Chicanas need materially and academically to move out of poverty.

Symbolic currency fosters true leadership, which in turn transforms all critique into action or results. In a few instances when leadership might have been registered, it was viewed with nostalgia and not always as a transformative or powerful strategy; some exceptions among leaders in politics and education have been previously noted. Certainly leadership within Chicana feminist circles, whether in the society at large or in academe, is not individually rewarding because it entails sacrifice and little actual recognition; the reward comes collectively and usually without merit promotions or compensation of the type given to leaders of other movements—in unions, political action committees, educational initiatives, and so on. A glance toward the future where Chicanas might "arrive" is still necessary to Chicana feminism as a method of inquiry largely because it is self-fashioned out of the internal contradictions of history and recently in the publishing and organizational domains, within institutional practices of knowledge. The contradictions and the publications serve as the basis for all future development in feminist critical analysis. Drawing from the arguments advanced recently, it is apparent that Chicana feminism locates itself primarily within conventional academic domains while at the same time traversing the boundaries a bit warily between competing disciplines and interdisciplinary studies. The focus on labor and workers that dominated Chicana/o academic subjects in the 1980s, along with literature that also focused on Chicana "conditions," has recently moved into or toward theory, cultural studies, and women's studies, fields that did not originally accept Chicana writing as "sophisticated" or contributory in that way.[19]

Chicana feminism has in key areas achieved or exceeded many of its ideals. The ideal of collectively organizing and promoting a critical vanguard has become a major driving force in the academy. In literary production alone, Chicana feminist writers have dominated knowledge production within Chicana/o discourse, art, and literary representation; yet the recognition of this production is not accepted outside the closed quarters of small conferences and classrooms, where such gains profit little else than mere mention or exploitive recognition. The next step lies in carrying these efforts into political and business arenas.

That Chicana studies participates in the creation of something loosely organized in method and strategic practice under the umbrella term "critical studies" is important. Most critical schools of thought, such as the Frankfurt School, the Birmingham School, and the U.S. civil rights and feminist movements, developed in a post–World War II culture. Emblems of race and ethnicity until the 1970s gave primacy to differences determined by masculine, not feminine, biologics. However, the U.S. civil rights movements and feminist and queer liberation movements offer social and cultural critiques that challenge dominant ideologies and foreground the roles of women. This facet of the American formation of race and ethnic difference has often determined a lineage for culture by males. Even within current Chicana/o cultural studies, the earliest critical studies relevant to Chicana feminist studies have been Marxist critiques of class and gender (Chow 1993). The positions of Mexican or Chicana women in U.S. culture, in the nation's economies, and in popular culture, including forms of public sexuality, each based its discussion on class. The popularity of Selena or of Jennifer Lopez, cultural icons within Chicana/o and Latina/o communities, were based as well on poor girls making it "to the top." Although Marxist criticism has been used to discuss marginalization, oppression in the Marxist sense exists outside of the physical body or is of the kind of female subjectivity visited on such cultural figures as J Lo.[20] Thus, the struggle against the manufactured images is simultaneously considered a class-driven resistance to an external authoritative power and a question of agency. In the 1980s Chicana critical studies created its own dynamic style of feminism by founding feminist research organizations such as MALCS or smaller study groups sponsoring conferences.[21]

A feminist trajectory fueled a critical vanguard. The idealization of having a Chicana feminist critical model widely acknowledged and broadly applied has not come to pass in a manner that would not seem random or fatally flawed by chance. Rather, the production of knowledge by Chicanas over the years has advanced to the point that different patterns and contradictory views of feminist practice can now be named and recognized. Another example is the work of NACCS Lesbian Caucus, founded in 1992, which has engaged in a discussion for a few years about whether to change its name to include LGBTQI (Lesbian, Gay, Bisexual, Transgender, Queer, and Intersexual) Caucus participants. The male equivalent, the Joto Caucus, continues to function as a space for gay male attendees of the annual conference. For now, the possible name change sustains a discussion of queer identities with Chicana feminists at its lead, while the men retain greater autonomy or separatism.

Many similar advances have registered in the types of research, subject matter, focus of analysis, and concepts of gender and sexuality under way in a direction consistent with current feminist critical analysis globally. Questions about identity practices—about a group's purpose—reflect the questions arising worldwide. Twentieth-century Chicana feminism did not originate with a single issue of liberation, although the effects of colonization could hardly lend themselves to a cogent narrative to determine a logical sequence in undoing them. Despite the major historical turns that have shaped the outer layers of Chicana feminism, at this juncture, the millennium signaled a time for an overarching reassessment. Next, I outline some of the key themes that comprise Chicana feminist critical analysis—when it arose and where it might be headed.

IDENTITY AS POLITICS

Recently, it became fashionable to reject identity formation as a source of knowledge production. Chicana feminism's multifaceted and distinct political diversity offers a critical style that provides ideas in a new millennium for recasting the politics of identity. Since the late 1990s, social activism, cultural studies, and lesbian and queer studies, as well as colonial mestizaje and transnational studies, have illuminated Chicana feminist projects in ways that could not have been imagined in the 1980s. All have formed within them varied and multiple languages and discourses. Like migrants among the stiff disciplinary directions, Chicana cultural studies characterize these new academic projects that push Chicana criticism on to another level of engagement with the broader academy. More books published, more Chicana elected officials, more Chicanas moving into the business world attest to the practical side of a new identity practice. Rather, the distinctive tone, symbols, and tools used to fashion a Chicana praxis and analysis bridge the interconnections between knowledge production and diverse experiences.

In appeal and celebration, Chicana critical analysis promotes identity as a politics, and this identity also can be seen in resistance to the clever political ideology of the conservative agenda. Chicana politicians, for example, know that no conservative right-winger can outdo Chicanas/os on the question of the significance of family. For one, older identity practices scorned Chicanas/os as "familistic," a category that sounded like a disease. My concern is not to define what constitutes Chicana feminism as an exact science or practice; rather, the critique from within its own debates about men, or Chicano *movimiento* politics, about sexuality, as we have seen, accounts for its transformations. Therefore I do not explain here "who did or said what" individually but rather have focused on the "what" and "how" that question acts as the thematic and critical aspect that Chicana feminist analysis is fashioning. A projection of Chicana feminism's development needs to examine its path but also the implication of its questions for all of society. The future of Chicana feminist critical analysis appears to hinge on the development of multiple emerging discourses, some of which have been responsive to the social changes of a global culture (wages and transnational labor migrations, for example) and the redefinition of national identity. Given the structural poverty that serves as Chicana feminism's home, we might all well wonder how it is possible that such an analysis can lead the way or even contribute to other types of analytical movements that are viewed through the lens of "proper" credentialing of Third World women of color from the upper classes with access to policy institutes, large governmental grants, and other types of funding.

While critical ideas represent some interesting hopes and visions for the future, some scholars argue that Chicana feminism promotes an identity politics because of its focus, which shadows a largely inaccessible private view of participation only by Chicanas, Latinas, and women of color (Sotello and Turner 2002). Chicana feminism, as documented in the previous pages, actually promotes identity as its critical process, pushing the boundaries of knowledge and conditions that will benefit Chicanas for the long term. Ironic as it may seem, this measure to secure parity in the public expression of ideas has been seen as limiting access or excluding the participation of those interested in the study of Chicanas because Chicanas have regularly called attention to all colonizing gazes—masculinist, racist, or recently, heterosexist. Working on pure academic merit, those interested in such an exchange may not have any personal investments in the lived experience of Chicanas. A need to be included by those insisting that Chicana feminism is exclusionary (toward them) subordinates the place of Chicanas. Under this ruse, Chicanas become merely a study group, subjects or objects, formed by, but not subverting of, the process of creating a knowledge base on Chicanas.

The conclusion, therefore, is that Chicanas become the object property of academic knowledge, and the presenters, students, and professors become "maids of methodology" serving the repressed hierarchies of a global machine (Spivak 1993). The example is not fictional, as it has occurred at several critical junctures in the academy and extends beyond the campus to the awarding of fellowships and grants to non-Chicanas who are seeking to reap the rewards of "filling gaps," no matter how well intentioned (Rosaldo 1993). In the absence of a critical mass of any type, Chicana feminist or otherwise, those who award these fellowships or grants need to ask: What does the source of the perception of exclusion really address? What role do outsiders traditionally play?

The study of "identity politics"—a term applied to these seeming hordes of scholars of color who were really just cultural critics and have mastered legitimate fields of study having to do with race and racism—has reached into the lexicon of critical analysis. Its meaning should be carefully examined. The *Stanford Encyclopedia of Philosophy* gives this assessment:

> The laden phrase "identity politics" has come to signify a wide range of political activity and theorizing founded in the shared experiences of injustice of members of certain social groups. Rather than organizing solely around ideology or party affiliation, identity politics typically concerns the liberation of a specific constituency marginalized within its larger context. Members of that constituency assert or reclaim ways of understanding their distinctiveness that challenge dominant oppressive characterizations, with the goal of greater self-determination.[22]

Chicana feminist logics, and especially Chicana lesbian feminist logic, require working through the ideas in workshops and academic projects intended to develop intellectual exchange within a space free from the power struggles typical of American group dynamics. In mainstream circles, "speaking" is considered a constitutional right, but even more it is a cultural exercise of a constitutional right to power. In actuality, MALCS workshops and NACCS caucuses, to cite two Chicana spaces, do not set the terms for identity-based thinking but, rather, encourage actions by individuals who promote intellectual exchanges and develop new scholarly ideas. Plenary and roundtable dialogues help move Chicana feminism forward and disrupt a competitive pattern that dominates national academic organizations such as the Modern Language Association (MLA) and even the American

Studies Association (ASA), whose interests lie in "outsourcing" knowledge. That is, Chicana studies is presented to occupy a *sitio y lengua* of authority, to not give up the academic terrain to outsiders while informing them of the critical analysis being formulated.

Instead of adding to the hierarchies of power that so often pervade academic discourse, the logics of identity formation within Chicana organizations have distinctive features: Chicana critical analysis is expressive of a flexible identity process and is present in Chicana/o discourse. No matter how strong, loud, persistent, and dogmatic the presentation of the nationalist or revolutionary rhetoric in the earlier organizational period, whether at MALCS or at NACCS, the instability of language and the insistent mobility of feminist culture precluded any identity-based formation to flourish. MALCS was a precursor to NACCS' turmoil around feminist issues; from 1990 forward, NACCS had to respond to a combined Chicana lesbian feminist voice, organized as a Lesbian Caucus, and before that, in the 1980s, as a Chicana Caucus. Both caucuses continue today, although bylaws have been proposed that would require a "minimum" membership for each caucus to continue. Whether official or not, however, the caucuses advance cultural critique within the national organization from different perspectives and are vital to the organization's continuation.

Such identity formations can be understood as a temporal facet of nationalism or group enterprise intended to mobilize action as it resists the alienating effects of organized capitalism and the ensuing conditioning for ethnic female representation. The identity politics addressed here draw from the historical context in which "identity as politics" emerged, following intense debate that led to substantive changes in a cultural logic of Chicana feminist identity and its politics. Identity politics emerged in the 1980s (not the 1970s) with what was then perceived as the organization of culturally ethnic, feminist, and queer oppositional groups. The political context for identity politics was embedded deeply in the Reagan-Bush administration's cultural approach to changing the course of social dynamics and its intended goal of destabilizing liberal social politics and economics that had been constructed during the 1960s and 1970s. Whether the dramas emanating from the National Education Association (NEA) debacles of the 1980s or Lynne Cheney's conservative, micromanaging leadership on educational "standardization," the period induced a Chicana critique meant to revamp the traditional mainstream perspective on education. "Tenured radicals" was a common phrase cast first toward 1960s and 1970s Euro-American faculty on the political left, but it came to apply also to those few faculty of color who were pioneers in the academy. Chicana academic feminists took their place in the lineup and received few rewards for their organizing and theorizing (Thomas and Hollenshead 2001).

The pervasive sense of "dis-ease" that Deena González described (1998) is one of the reasons new approaches, textual practices, and thematic subject matter have taken on greater meaning over the past few years. In looking at the ways we are discomforted by one another's presence, even as a textual problem, we become better able to bridge the social and methodological issues presented by identity politics or a politics of identity. By the late 1990s concerns with identity politics became the source of a new knowledge paradigm in Chicana feminist critical studies, and several major books on the subject address continuously the reason as well.

CRITICAL MESTIZAJE

The project of a critical area of study that proclaims a basis in an interdisciplinary vanguard represents a "knowledge plan" as it interrogates oppressive power and the erasure of Chicanas across different areas of feminist studies. Emma Pérez' *Decolonial Imaginary* (1999) challenged the linearity of colonial historiography. Pérez, a historian by training, understands that by the narrowing histories women tell, through the use of narrative devices, colonized women are excluded from historiography. To overcome the problems with such colonizing discourses, according to Pérez, new ways of writing stories must replace the dominant discourse. Pérez arrives at a "decolonial imaginary" to create a new cultural logic for the colonized. She divides the decolonial imaginary into three segments: Part 1 provides a remapping of Chicano/a history and sets the foundation for the study; Part 2 uses new-historicism methodologies to analyze the genealogies of twentieth-century Chicana social practices; and Part 3 incorporates Freudian theory and Michel Foucault's method of genealogy to focus on a description of the "colonial imaginary" in framing patriarchal Chicano nationalism.

Pérez critiques both the Chicano studies canon and gender analysis in history. She clearly places herself in the next wave, part of a generation of scholars who will lead the way to postcolonial histories and Chicana/o histories that construct Chicanas/os as subjects, as well as creating new ways of knowing. Pérez' illumination of an "Oedipal Conquest Complex" argues for new ways of writing, teaching, and knowing outside of the colonial imaginary and has poignancy for the twenty-first century. As Prasenjit Duara explains in *Rescuing History from the Nation* (1995), a decolonial imaginary will require scholars to reconsider the very process of writing history. As yet another generation of historians comes of age; time will tell if we construct fresh ways of knowing.

Work produced in the same area has afforded Chicana feminist criticism additional understandings. In *Methodology of the Oppressed* (2000), Chela Sandoval structures a new approach to feminist thought by centralizing women of color in the postmodern frame of reference. In a work with far-reaching implications, Sandoval does no less than revise the genealogy of theory over the past thirty years, inserting what she terms "U.S. Third World feminism" into the liberal narrative of liberation and revolution.[23] What Sandoval has identified is a language, a rhetoric of resistance to postmodern cultural conditions. U.S. liberation movements of the post–World War II era generated specific modes of oppositional consciousness. Out of these emerged a new activity of consciousness and language that Sandoval calls the "methodology of the oppressed." This methodology—born of the strains of postmodern cultural identity struggles that currently mark global exchange—holds out for the possibility of a newfound historical moment, a new citizen-subject, and a fresh form of alliance consciousness and politics. Utilizing semiotics and U.S. Third World feminist criticism, Sandoval demonstrates in this women-of-color methodology how people can mobilize "love" as a category of critical analysis.

Methodology of the Oppressed offers an alternative mode of criticism, opening new perspectives on a theoretical, literary, aesthetic, and social movement or psychic and psychological expression. The authors who have introduced a Chicana cultural studies format in these books stand as examples of Chicana feminist knowledge production at a millennial turn. Their cutting-edge cultural (critical) studies approach blends the intersectional concerns of race and gender with a deep feminist social critique that could be virtually flattened, or recolonized, by "horizontal" Foucaultian logic in the academy. Edén E. Torres, in *Chicana Without Apology* (2003), renders an epistle of intellectual mestizaje brought to life within First World modernity—even postmodernity—that is, it is part feminist missive, part healing practice, and part existential philosophy guided by a healthy dose of Latin American socialism. This work returns Chicana feminist logics to an earlier time when liberation movements in Latin America also helped shape the discourse.

Torres' first chapter, "Anguished Past/Troubled Present: The Savagery and Promise of Traumatic Memory," a pointed retelling of her father's internalized colonization, makes this point: "For most of my childhood, my father was a ghost. I loved and feared him for many reasons, and never knew when he would appear or disappear. Nor could I predict whether his brief presence would be kind or cruel. I have come to believe that he has always hated the Mexican in him" (11). Torres' point, without stating the obvious, is that objectivity, scientific search for evidence, claims for truth, and socio-logical cause and effect cannot begin to measure the entrenched aspects of racialized, gendered, or economic trauma. Like many other works, *Chicana Without Apology* presents education as liberating for some, but the reality remains that most Chicanas, along with many women of color, serve as objects of study and not as subjects of their own analysis. Without a viable class critique and a middle-class base willing to strive for equality in educa-tion, politics, and the economy, it will continue to be difficult to translate the promise of success into visible social change. Without it, as Torres and Pérez have argued, our future remains wrought with psychic pain. Torres leaves the book with a reminder of what this social change means:

> The ability to make connections is often difficult, but we must behave as if we know it is absolutely possible and necessary. We have to do it despite the hardship and real dangers involved. Such a commitment increases our capacity to perpetually incorporate new voices, to critically think about and acknowl-edge questions as they arise, and to refocus on a larger vision. (186)

Chicana Without Apology offers a discursive practice that is true to its orientation in standpoint feminism and cultural studies. Within Chicana feminism, the interdisciplinary format spans the literary, including its social politics, the poetics of identity. These perspectives, methods, or standpoints (epistemologies or logics) orient us to that familiar place we call home—or better yet, that is nestled deep within the contours of the scariest place of all, the political unconscious. In the following chapters, I will explore other instances in which postnational Chicana/o discourse has facilitated entry into transnational culture, for better or worse.

Three

CULTURAL BORDERLANDS

The Limits of National Citizenship

> *The myths that once grounded our identity become bank-*
> *rupt. Sixties-era pan-Latinamericanism,* la mexicanidad
> *(unique, monumental, undying), and Chicanismo (with*
> *thorns and a capital C) have been eclipsed by the process of*
> *borderization and social fragmentation. Like it or not we*
> *are now denationalized, de-mexicanized, transtechnized,*
> *and pseudo-internationalized. And worse, in fear of falling*
> *into a new century we refuse to assume this new identity*
> *roaming around in the Bermuda Triangle. We live in*
> *economic uncertainty, terrorized by the Holocaust of AIDS,*
> *divided (better yet, trapped) by mass cultures and new tech-*
> *nologies that appeal to our most mediocre desires for instant*
> *transformation and psychological expansion.*
> GUILLERMO GÓMEZ-PEÑA, THE NEW WORLD BORDER,
> 1996

The New World Border, Guillermo Gómez-Peña's apocalyptic vision of the U.S.-Mexico borderlands, follows a nihilistic thread of global culture. The uncertainty and gloom that characterize *The New World Border*'s provoca-tive angle of cultural citizenship proclaim that the lost identities have now been replaced by a world of "borderization." The textual montage of bor-der representation composed of photography and spoken word, arranged in endless and unnerving chaotic narrative sequences, forebodes and at the same time beckons the instability of the Mexican and Chicana/o identity within globalization. Taking aim at static culture's failures, represented in the political styles of Chicana/o nationalism and Mexican folklore, Gómez-Peña portends that the revolutionary postmodern of border "Chicanidad" takes place across a circuitry of networks and subterfuge. While the founda-tion of Gómez-Peña's terminology arises from the inevitable dissolution of nationalism, he decries the unfathomable—that the future offers national citizenship and its attendant identities.

The postnationalism of Gómez-Peña's work suggests that a critique of nationalism on both sides of the U.S.-Mexico border is necessary to challenge inherent limitations of citizenship conveyed across the media and other technological networks. While Gómez-Peña fails to locate a plausible scenario for this conversion into the transnational border spaces, the question that looms far and above is the nature of citizenship. The edgy performance-art style that is quintessentially Gómez-Peña intentionally simulates panic and revolutionary fervor in a Gramscian sense.[1] Globalization has made a nationalistic claim obsolete. No group of people can claim exclusive rights to mass-scale, multinational work. As the world gets smaller, the American dream of self-improvement no longer belongs exclusively to American citizens.

In this chapter I focus primarily on the postnationalism of the U.S.-Mexico border culture that occasions one set of interpretive conditions for the emergence of transnational culture that Chicanas/os are able to access. Because national literatures, representations, and politics use an enlightened subject for their citizen-subject model, notions of an enlightened subjectivity do not apply to border residents. In most instances, body figurations, or embodiments, arise as the site of border encounters. This aimless body assumes the metaphor of border culture; while seemingly preoccupied with citizenship in U.S. public discourses, in actuality, the body forms citizen-subject relations through crisis, abjection, and confrontation. The politics of such an identity framework depend on the body, whether as laborer, immigrant, trader—and female as cultural purveyor—or as globalized human being.

In *Mexican Encounters* (2003), Rosa Linda Fregoso examines the disappearance of Mexican women along the El Paso border. In it she describes how "the politics of gender extermination in this region took the form of the apparently random yet seemingly systematic appearance of brutally murdered women's bodies and the equally horrific disappearance of many more" (3). The processing of bodies by the formerly named U.S. Immigration and Naturalization Service (INS), the recovery of corpses along the waters of the Rio Grande, and the subjects of violence override the desire to classify humanity into a semiotics of enlightenment, which is already wrought with complications. Along the border, because there are two systems of recognizing the cultural citizen, one has to confront the different value systems of humanness and humanities. Fregoso correlates the disappearance of women in Juárez with the state's unwillingness to recognize women as its own citizen-subjects. She notes that "one would expect the modern state to intervene on behalf of its citizens and limit extreme expressions of gender violence such as that unfolding in Ciudad Juárez, but the Mexican Government has failed dismally. It has justified its failure through a rhetorical strategy of deflection that has taken on two narrative forms: negation and desegregation" (ibid.). Fregoso disputes the easy conclusion that the murder of these women has anything to do with globalism. In her critique, Fregoso challenges a theory that rampant globalization of the maquila murders furthers American leftists' continuous and desired construct of victimhood. Both Gómez-Peña's and Fregoso's interpretations of the complexity of global culture focus directly on the darker side of the globalized border, but neither purports to emancipate it.

If the identity concerns raised here also signal the end of the interpretative logic of an enlightened subject's location, freedom, and entitlements, one might ask what sort of culture is being created from border culture's never-ending quandary to produce ever more problematic meanings with its deteriorations of humanity (Calderón and Saldívar 1991, 1). The transnationality of U.S.-Mexico border culture conveys a semiotic system in distress, one confounded by the limits of its own national representation. The in-between spacing of national and transnational does not occur overnight, and historically, the transition into a global transnational mode did not take place so effectively. Postnationalism, as I have illustrated, does not necessarily suggest to us an antinational claim, that is, against a certain representational embodiment of the nation. Rather, the postnational refers to the discursive scene where the loss of nationhood can at the same time be both politically disadvantageous and aesthetically stimulating. A primary disconnection between aesthetics and political economics has been an ongoing dilemma for border representations. This dynamic has been especially relevant for Chicanas/os and Mexicanas/os who rely heavily on the metaphors of migration or movement as cultural transgressions yet seem caught in a political struggle between two countries without an organized transnational movement linking Chicanas/os with Mexicanas/os or Latin Americans. Alliances could counter some of the state-perpetrated violence or neglect of citizens.

HISTORIOGRAPHY

Our earliest and most memorable account of the U.S.–Mexico borderlands originates from frontier narratives, storytelling devices that often depict an antagonistic relationship between European settlers and the amorphous threats of the frontier. From Mary Rowlandson's captivity narrative to Natty Bumppo's lonesome treks through Indian territory and even to Herman Melville's holy war against the great whale, such encounters with the frontier always pushed forth the border of U.S. expansion.[2] Historically, at least, the border has shifted greatly in the past two hundred years, but this history seldom frames American culture as an uninvited transgressor. For border historiography, the problematic issues lie in remaking the concept of nation. Shaping the great American historiographical struggle with the wilderness becomes the first encounter with the transformation of the notion of nation in the United States. Nowhere is this pattern more evident than in Frederick Jackson Turner's classic essay "The Significance of the Frontier in American History."[3] Turner's model presents the view of the advancement of Anglo-American culture as the inevitable progression of both democratic principles and the exercise of rugged individualism. Turner describes the basic tenet of this resolve: "But the most important effect of the frontier has been the promotion of democracy here and in Europe. As has been indicated, the frontier is productive of individualism" (1947, 51). Not only does this view enlist U.S.–Mexico border policy, but it also may have set into motion the cultural antagonisms in citizen conflicts along the U.S.–Mexico border that continue with us today. In looking further at the dimensions of postnationalism, I will review the formation of borderlands as a model for transnational discovery. Because the creation of the U.S. borderlands has been in the making since the mid-nineteenth century, an actual formalization of border consciousness occurs specifically during the 1980s in U.S. cultural studies' views of nation.

Early canonical representations of American narratives lead to some fantastic, often romanticized narrative of citizenship in which the predominant themes of piety, heroism, and manifest destiny served as ethical precepts of western expansion. Most important, however, these early American narratives obviate the need to dramatize a narrative of citizenship in order to shape an American literary canon that lacked a sense of place. Because the U.S.-Mexico border is viewed as one of the last vestiges of this American frontier, such a refusal to allocate citizenship is necessary, if only to establish a basis of ideological power in the region.

This characterization of the border deforms citizenship and enacts dislocations from national representations. These dislocations are the disruptions within a border space that cannot be sufficiently contained within the nation: the economic interdependence, cultural borrowing, and history of the exchange among its inhabitants. The disruptions, however, belie the interdependence of one nation with the other as a community.

I use the cultural production of citizenship to draw attention to the way border subjects disrupt the transparency of citizenship. While "cultural production" seems like a huge term with dimensions beyond the service of any project, a useful reminder of the way citizenship works in culture occurs through Pierre Bourdieu's analysis of culture productions. Bourdieu theorizes (1991) that the cultural practices of a given society inherently use the role of culture to generate power and social differentiations in the attitudes, tastes, and practices of that society. His is a position suggesting that the most proficient way of administering citizenship is through cultural attitudes conveyed in music, art, fashion, and such sensibilities. In working out some of the connections between citizen relations between the United States and Mexico, I use the concept of cultural productions here to discuss how popular narratives, films, music, and political issues about U.S.-Mexico relations undermine the symbolic value of U.S. citizen culture. Border subjectivity deforms the cogent narrative of citizenship by disrupting its reproductive potential. Cultural productions of the border work against the assumptions that nations share a separate system of representation. Because citizenship is socially constructed, any discussion of exactly what citizenship is will vary according to the circumstances of its origins or relations. However, attitudes about citizenship herein refer to the ways culture works to produce and reproduce social differentiations among citizen groups. Chicana/o subjectivity presents a problem of legible citizenship. While state and federal laws advocate for legible citizenship, one determined by documentation, as the only means of situating citizenship, Chicana/o cultural productions attend also to oversights and invisibility by design of federal and state processes to recognize or reject certain individuals as citizens. The rules of citizenship within transnational and global culture will be increasingly determined on cultural means of organizing and rendering visible individuals.[4]

Legal and juridical discourses construct a phantasmal alien body through two social currents: criminality and immigration. As a result, visual spectacle—and visual sexual transgression—of the transnational become evident. The border is a geopolitical space that elicits translation of experience into narration through a questionable body; that is, the body belongs to others, in the case of the undocumented worker. *Lone Star*, a 1996 film by John Sayles, makes this point. The film begins with the narrative trope of the law but results in a critique of the racial and cultural interactions between Anglos and Mexicans. In the end, interethnic relations are doomed or circumscribed by a color-coded world, by history, and by race where race mixing is an illusion. Sadly, protagonist Pilar's final line, " . . . forget the Alamo," might as well have been "Remember it, but remember it differently."

Defining moments across frontier and expansion have brought about the fervor to create a national consciousness.[5] It is fitting to associate the terse ground we see in border cultures with the border's effect on the production of national citizenship. Most people who read the national aesthetics of the culture of the U.S.-Mexico border view it as a vertical split, delineated as a boundary between two nations. Since the nineteenth century, this split has become emblematic of the spatialization of "the border" as an antagonistic space, a wanton ground that needs and invites police and hegemonic surveillance. Obviously, the compulsion to set limits on the border is not new. What is more fascinating is the desire to extend control of the national borders vis-à-vis the sexual, that is, through gender.

The management of the border through agents of the U.S. Customs and Border Protection (CBP) and Drug Enforcement Administration (DEA) thus becomes subjective and, as such, an unconscious impulse—a drive. In this, border subjects become inscribed as illicit and, within the hyperregulatory space, as "questionable bodies." The readership of such bodies points to the regulatory and scopophilic tendency that accompanies the liminal spaces of a nation. The border, with all of its unintended crossings, conscious or unconscious, relates analogously to the boundaries of gender and sexuality. Theorizations of "the border," formed in the unconscious discourses of national citizenship and as a space of questionable persons or embodiments, also make salient other phenomenological issues. The cultural panic associated with the border warrants examination, as it is part of an ever-growing array of cultural fears: of road rage, of transgender identities, homophobia, and panic leading to institutional aggression and many varied forms of societal despondency. Anxieties have often been a basis for a state's formation, as the state constitutes its authority over its citizens in order to discipline them. The intention to discipline a body renders intelligible (readable) representations that fall outside a conventional logic—a view may seem true that the world is no longer negotiable in the old Fordist sense or in the pre– and post–World War II eras.

Scholars have shown and policy makers confirm that before any social or economic policy makes its way into the legislature or boardroom and before any textual analysis makes its way into an academic screening, there are determinations, regulatory in nature, that are being waged a priori with the intention of determining exactly what and who constitutes the "alien," "the illicit," and "the transgressive"—the border subject. Regulatory compulsion emanates from our gendered, sexual, and racial identities because the originating structures of national consciousness originate with the familiar tropes in shaping our conscious reality through the birthright of gender and citizenship (Alarcón 1994b). The epistemological hazard that might be perceived in a border subject's apparent disassembled disposition (whether sexual, gendered, national, or aesthetic) leads to the emergence of a questionable body: such persons have few rights.

Border frameworks in Chicana/o critical studies offer a rethinking stage in Chicana cultural national subjectivity (the Chicana/o movement). Border studies have achieved status in Chicana/o critical studies in recent years because in the 1980s the social organization under the "protest movement" had been exhausted by the malaise created under a conservative cultural agenda (Bruhn 2006). A significant proportion of Chicana/o border studies was based on the need to rethink the political and aesthetic questions progressive scholars faced during the 1980s. From Anzaldúa's reconfiguration of the borderlands as a zone for such rethinking, resexed, gendered, and sexualized, to postcolonial studies examining the porous nature of the border, writers and thinkers have turned national attention to a neglected geographic area. Carl Gutiérrez-Jones has argued (1995) that "rethinking" the totalizing narrative of national culture becomes necessary as the terms of hegemony co-opt the terms of identity. If borders engender a geographic tendency to refuse or accept a citizen's teleology "of a people," a national, utopian model (most visible as 1960s counterculture and youth movements) makes sense. Is it therefore the case that the transgressive nature of border cultures and people creates another instance through which to understand gender and sexual relations in the material sense? The resurrection of "national citizenship" has been at the center of producing a readable body for the purpose of nationalizing aesthetics in the unconscious analogues of gender, sexuality, and race.

Transnational and global conditions have oriented our course for understanding political, economic, and social terms. "Border subjects" enter into conversation with a national discourse as a problematic concept, especially when the terms of citizenship affirm rather than question the national culture as an intelligible and transparent body. The same holds true for an embodied notion of borderlands as Anzaldúa imagined them (1987, 29). I will try to emulate the aesthetics questions that a border effect creates by delineating a horizontal mapping of space to get a better feel for the way "the border" works to inform our traditional academic sensibilities. On this

I pivot the central concept of "the national citizen" across disciplinary corridors and among illicit textual practices.

A gendered interactive space is what the cultural critic José David Saldívar establishes in *Border Matters: Remapping American Cultural Studies* (1997). Saldívar traces "a genealogy" of the border as discursive and a hybrid extension of Chicana/o subjectivity. Saldívar makes an interesting observation when he views the U.S.-Mexico border as a "new temporalized-spatial logic of the simulacra [that] has an ethno-racialized underside" (34). From the outset, Saldívar resists ascribing the "postmodern" in the "borderlands" as a glib antifoundationalist scheme. Saldívar concludes that the postmodern is "a major consequence that follows from Gómez-Peña's . . . riffs on postmodern Tijuana. . . . [The fact] is that we can no longer conceptualize the U.S.-Mexico border self as 'alienated' in the sense that Marx defines it, because to be alienated in the classic sense presupposes a coherent self rather than a scrambled, 'illegally alienated self'" (158). Obvious in Saldívar's intended global claim of reading the border is his pointing to the possibility that Marx' "alienated" subject does not negotiate the materiality of consciousness in the same way that a border subject might navigate the paths of hegemonic relations. By adjudicating ethnicity, race, and sexuality within a repressed set of boundaries in a national discourse, Saldívar suggests different material relations for the "undocumented" and "alien" within the terms of "nationality." Are we then led to conclude that the border subject might convince us of another effect in reading capitalist labor production? As such, can we say with a straight face that Marx' alienated subject of labor could not appeal to some of the wilder urges experienced when the marriage of postmodernism and postnational Chicanismo have materialized into what appears to be a cultural transgendered experience?[6] If the workers are not just male and they are also not only workers, not simply pawns of border industry, then their place and belonging must be expanded to include the complexity of their identities.

If one is able to comprehend the semiotics of the border as a transgendered experience, readings of both gender and sexualities provide a transnational geography. The body's metaphors apply to the traffic and intersections of a given national boundary as well. Saldívar's remarks reveal this point with respect to Gómez-Peña's border visual work as "a vast textual machine, a hybrid cyborg that can also map out social and bodily realities" (Saldívar 1997, 154). This "hybrid cyborg" is reminiscent of the technological medical opportunities that have figured into the transgendered body. But what is actually being figured and resignified in the body of the borderlands subject? And how are we to align this multiple configuration of the (post)national body when it is seen as a last recourse to some missing progressive search for justice? If the border as the subject of illegality and as the subterfuge of body is by calculation not intended to be seen or recognized as a legitimate subject that slides through the registers of nationality altogether, what should be the constitutional basis of the subject whose only previous qualification was to elude hegemonic recognition? What basis of cultural citizenry do we assign a temporalized noncitizen who resides outside of capitalist production? Moreover, as Saldívar suggests, in the course of remapping the border subject as the central, if not critical, axis from which to understand U.S. hegemonic relations with respect to Mexico, we might, as a result, recognize the imagined high-tech world of an alienated "illegal" subjectivity beyond the national compulsion to reduce gender and race to their lowest common denominators.[7]

Saldívar's cultural studies work arrives at much more elaborate readings of the border than one of an economically determined, historically constituted subject located primarily in Marxist terms (Raat 1996). "Alienation," Saldívar reminds us, appears as "coherent" self-expression in capitalist terms. Saldívar points to the borderlands as a place where we might reconfigure our notions of a national literary subjectivity, and it questions the role of national identification in its intended claim of promising a clear sense of identity. When we think of border crossings or borderland spaces, we immediately review the excessive or transgressive processes that mark the border as naturally prone to prohibition and regulation (Gutiérrez 1996). Some would even welcome the transgression of the borderlands as an entry point into new intellectual currents. This inclination may be true for some, but the issues point to a different set of concerns. One must therefore perceive that this interactive relationship between nations has given pause toward actively questioning some of the unconscious impulses that national identification in literary and cultural representations provide. The preoccupation with gender roles and assignments, with the resurgence of traditional ideologies within the seamless narrative of the political economy of exchange, and with the difficulty in establishing fair immigration and citizenship policies are examples of the impulses. One must not be fooled by an apparent liberating quality of the border because, if anything, the U.S.-Mexico divide is one of the most regulated zones in the United States.[8]

Another immediate problem is that the inherent lack of a discernable center makes it useful to reflect on how national bodies are being interpellated and reformed by a hegemonic production through populist modes of administering citizenship.[9] It has been convenient for some to think of the border as an endless site of possibility, but such hype only masks the potential of another form of reading socially determining effects. We could say that by constituting a mode for cultural production we can better see the interactive relation that appears to seize or demonstrate an "authentic experience" in a border framework. Cultural production reveals the overlap between two conscious modes of constructing reality, one belonging to the previous century and the other in today's, as depicted in the following table.[10]

Mode of Representation	Materialist Method, Nineteenth Century	Postnational Border Method, Late Twentieth Century
Experience	authentic	cultural production
Economics	territorialization	free trade
Aesthetic reflection	sentimentalism	performance art
Location	original	displaced
The real	organic	commodity
Emotions	stoic	humorous
Violence	physical	psychic
The people	folkloric	popular culture
Desire	romantic	fantasy

A system of representation is caught, as it were, between these two overlapping historical views—the nationalist past, represented by the nineteenth-century model of conflicted historiography, and the unruly cipher of the contemporary border, with all its transgressions—both of which struggle for some recognition in late capitalism's terminology.[11] The moment is an irreconcilable history because neither the nineteenth-century model, dominated by nationalistic uprisings, nor the more recent post-national current, marked by a Foucaultian institutionalization of the body, can effectively speak to the aesthetic and political questions that current critical study demands. "The border," like "the postmodern," may have some resonance with the spatial division in materialist readings of the national subject. But unlike the postmodern, the border is possessed by a national configuration of two tensions. What appears to buckle under the disposition of the border framing, however, are those excesses and transgressions that might create a third space—an irreconcilable, if necessary, historical posture. Using a simple framing and a conscious mode of border culture, several possibilities of the semiotics of border subjects played out in a social discourse of the body. A questionable body arises from the effects of the globalization and transnationalism taking place in these border zones. With it, regulatory practices based on "documents," "proof," and other quantifiable evidence takes effect to mask an unconscious hermeneutic process, one that predominates as the political question (Cox 1997).

Female iconicity, the deployment of positive female images that is central to the liberating effect of postnationality, does not necessarily depend on a feminist ideological trajectory in the same way embodiments do in the case of transnationalism. Recent accounts of Chicana/o production capture the immanence of female iconicity in such films as *Selena* (1997, directed by Gregory Nava), based on the life of a young, rising Tejano music star. The story of Selena Quintanilla y Los Dinos tracks the Tejana singer's ascent in the reluctant, masculine Tejano music scene. The embodiment of mestiza consciousness, however, occurs subtly throughout the film, as the viewer witnesses the star's image sink into the quandary of sexuality and a traditional role established by the unconscious cultural domain of the family: father, mother, brother, sister, and boyfriend (Saldívar-Hull 1991). The film begs the question of how Selena maintains a figurative iconic status as a sexually autonomous woman if her brand of sexual agency is what ultimately allows Los Dinos to cross over into uncharted mythic terrain, a borderless Aztlán. She embodies English-speaking Mexico in Texas and limited-Spanish speech in Mexico. Her sexualized body, however, sustains a "borderless" language.

Selena's father is positioned to give us a diachronic view of national consciousness. Abraham Quintanilla facilitates Selena's "crossing over" from traditional Mexican to Tejano music. Selena's discontinuous presence as an autobiographical figure in the representation of Chicano and Tejano discourses serves as a pivotal construction of mestiza consciousness. The mixed racial identity is an uncertain narrative locked into an eschatological dream sequence because impending doom looms large over her sexed, overdone body. By contrast, Abraham's long-winded references to the "Mexican American's" existential conditions are plainly visible in a scene in which he drives Selena and her brother, Abbie Jr., to another gig. At this point, the father delivers a pedantic lecture to Selena and her brother on what it is like to be Mexican-American. Abraham explains, "Man, it's hard to be a Mexican-American . . . you have to know English and Spanish . . . you have to know Frank Sinatra and Pedro Infante."

The guile behind Abraham's remarks is ingrained early on in Selena and becomes visible in both the pitfalls and her potential to cross over as a singer, but the borders she is traversing are unclear. She was English-dominant and yet was viewed as the Tejano sensation who "made it" to the English-listening audience, as if she had crossed from Spanish to English. It is Selena's ability to access the transnational aspects of her "local" subject position as a popular Tejana singer into a sexual female icon who transcends the value of her work within the predominantly masculine music scene.

A promoter who attempts to underpay Selena notably remarks to Abraham, "C'mon man. . . . She's only a woman." Despite the obvious misogynist rhetoric implied in Selena's encounters in the local Tejano music scene, her ability to access the American cultural pop scene as well as the Mexican *norteño* scene proves to be the basis of her success. The height of her achievement occurs when she receives a Grammy award for Best Latina/o Artist, an accomplishment that placed Selena at yet another level of success as the first Tejana Chicana to cross over into American popular music. In this she followed in the footsteps of other women, including, as she says in her speech, "Paula Abdul, Janet Jackson, and Madonna."

Selena's dream ended, however; for as she completed her crossover album and anticipated the "crossover" tour, she met a sad fate. The rumors about her alleged lesbian relationship with Yolanda Saldívar, *a la lesbian continuum*, are not given voice in the film except for a few subtle glances Yolanda casts in the direction of the virginal Selena. The rumors were quickly dispelled by family members who proceeded to characterize Yolanda Saldívar as a disturbed woman whose fascination with Selena turned fatal. The good girl—the *buena hija*—depiction of Selena in the film compels yet another understanding of the Chicana female subject: even as Selena accesses the level of accomplishment in a transnational economy as a sexual icon, she is still confined by her traditional role to that of a virgin who can do no wrong, evoking a sentimentalism reserved for the Latina star.[12] Selena's mestiza consciousness achieves its representation through a series of dream sequences built into the film that add dimension to the material struggle of her success, even though the eschatological dream narrative later signals the singer's sudden fall.

Selena's ascension into iconic eminence is represented in the final scene of the film, in which her death is immortalized by her fans paying their final respects. It is reminiscent of the scene of the faithful paying homage to the Virgen de Guadalupe in Mexico City and transcends the image of the fallen star into an economic (if not religious) state of perpetual eminence. The conflated images of the *homenaje* (tribute) to Selena as popular icon and the image of the faithful praying to the Virgen de Guadalupe carry over by way of a synchronic cultural moment when the transnational female identity came into play in the popular imaginary. Selena's convergence as a popular icon and traditional deity through her ability to cross various borders, national as well as transnational, creates the vision of an ascent to consumer culture over the product of female identity. By challenging the precept of social desire and self-production, Selena's music speaks of a social and cultural desire that transcends the boundaries of romantic love in one of her songs, appropriately titled "Amor Prohibido" (forbidden love). Selena sings in Spanish of the social divisions, class and race, that divide her from her beloved:[13]

> *Forbidden love—They murmur*
> *on the streets*
> *because we are from different*
> *societies*
> *Forbidden love—Everyone*
> *tells us*
> *money doesn't matter*
> *to you nor to me*
> *nor to the heart*

The ethos of the song suggests a hegemonic crisis informing Selena's lamentations. The "forbidden love" is built in as a cultural prohibition where "the lovers" are formed. The figurative societal pressures to live in accordance with a class construct are implicated along racial and linguistic boundaries that code a new subject relation. Much of Selena's music forms similar tensions, such as this one, in which the dominant precepts are fashioned as a murmuring, a catty whispering that achieves a certain primacy as a hegemonic discourse. The love Selena claims in the lyrics is paradigmatic because it also is capable of leading her to an emotional banishment from family and culture. Risking everything for this love is not at all an innocent choice but a decision abundant with agency and consciousness that begins as a consequence of the forbidden. Is the class analysis implied in this song also a musing of the racial boundaries that create libidinal boundaries in class divisions, and if so, what exactly is being desired—the lover or the forbidden? Selena sings about social exile, couched as a subjective type of exile, as a love, that resides outside of the national geography of race.

What is even more fascinating about Selena's representation as a pop Tejano female icon is that her life appears to mirror the complexity of another female Latina. The film debut of *Selena* marked the rise of Jennifer Lopez' career as one of the most celebrated Latina pop icons in current American culture. There is the ascent of the "minority" female artist, usually charismatic figures such as Lopez and Quintanilla, whose accomplishments are noteworthy for their femaleness in talent and in beauty, no less. Whether it is the artist exemplar, the resilient personality, or the innately gifted character, the exaltation we experience from the rise of the female icon occurs as a daring defiance against social and cultural constraints as well as state and interpersonal antagonistic forces that form these psychic boundaries of difference. It is worth mentioning that a different counter-rhetoric of the "female exemplar" develops in concert with the narrative of survivorship, a category that gives special significance to the female figure in contemporary feminist thought. We notice in "survivorship narratives" that the subject position of the victim is reinvented into a proactive generative being who achieves a new sense of articulation and political agency. It is not even plausible at this point to consider a cultural nationalist intervention in such readings of the female Latina or Chicana icon, and it might even pose some troubling critical questions about the roles of culture and femaleness. The dubious and naive qualification of a cultural national project within the Chicana/o context may at this juncture seem more of an impulse than a serious critical investment of limited possibility. The use and abuses of this cultural national imperative within the particularities of the *movimiento* leave us with a different set of challenges (Alarcón 1994a).

We should, for the moment, suspend any conventional tracking of the border subject as a free-floating signifier. The agencies of the border are well inscribed in a long, well-documented historiography of conflict and its subsequent mandate of state regulation. In such a borderless world, the suspension of an individual's autonomy is the first existential qualification. How to deal with a being that is elusive, ambiguous, and questionable is one of the chief sources of debate. Much has already been said about the aesthetics of the border subject, but one must also return to its principle location in the cultural production of citizenship. The failure to actualize a given national citizenship in the border subject works through an understanding of the body. One can consider the relationship between historicity and the agencies of the border subject as an excessive embodiment of historicity that not only traverses the geographical location but that is capable of producing its own signifying elements free from the productive cycle in capitalism. In the case of Selena, she is also "just" her body, although in feminist theory we would say she is more than her body.[14]

In their present incarnation, U.S.-Mexico border relations can be thought of as a defense of American citizenship and a number of reform measures that modify citizen perceptions about noncitizens and/or racialized subjects, even popular cultural icons.[15] Discussion of immigration and educational policy, in addition to other social concerns, related and unrelated, can be viewed as an attempt to resurrect the production of a new citizen model in the United States to offset the effects of globalization and invigorate a new hegemony of citizenship (Spivak 1988, 1990). One need only review current policies on U.S.-Mexico relations as they manifest in California as part of a growing conversation on U.S.–Latin American mutual concerns over matters such as immigration and the swell of prison populations to understand the role state institutions play in creating these desired effects. Because the U.S.-Mexico border is often viewed as one of the last vestiges of the American frontier, the application of citizenship along border lines is seen as a necessary beginning to establishing a basis of power and social differentiation in an effort to create a disposition for a new citizen sensibility.[16] The cultural production of citizenship in this environment augments a desire for new citizen sensibilities—sexualized citizens who sing in English, for example—because of the ever-present need to secure the national border.[17] The desire for a new citizen sensibility of the border subjects as produced and manufactured through popular media lends an embodied example of the types of dialogues and tensions surrounding this region and knowledge about it. Who really knew Selena, after all, beyond the large physical space of the Texas-Mexico border, and how did they know her?

Border subjects disrupt citizenship. In literature, the tropes of citizenship, heroism, and triumph over evil all but encompass the American national canon. As we become more indifferent to citizenship as a powerful cultural trope during times of peace, it is the reliance on cultural citizenship that appears to spur national interests in forming new citizens who sing, dance, and play on the border. In recent years, the desire to invigorate the national spirit has turned our nation's attention toward domestic issues. These have included single motherhood, AIDS, salacious television programming, the affairs of heads of state, the Internet, and threats of foreign invasion; all have generated a preoccupation with the *behavior* of citizens rather than the inherent *rights* of citizens. Even Hollywood understands the value of the role of citizenship. This fascination with the trope is tied with "freedom" against the amorphous threats of the post-9/11 outside world.

Bourdieu's theory of cultural productions suggests to us that the most proficient way of administering a model of citizenship is through the cultural attitudes and sensibilities of a people. In Bourdieu's analysis of habitus, for example, he argues that the administration of cultural production takes effect through everyday practices (normal, discrete) exhibited primarily in the attitudes, tastes, and habits of the society. While the phrase "cultural production of citizenship" seems like a huge term with dimensions beyond the service of any project, Bourdieu's theory of cultural practice, in this case, accounts for changes in viewing U.S.-Mexico border relations. While these changes in policy can be regarded as an attempt to respond to the economic and social demands of globalization, "citizenship" refers to an element in Bourdieu's theorization. His habitus asserts that the cultural productions of a given society achieve legitimacy through the internalization of social habits, rendering matters of citizenship virtually transparent—a tautological construction.[18] The habitus of citizenship can be said to be the assumed privileges of national origin and the modification of this citizenship over time to suit the national interest—birthright, labor trends, territorial and commodity accumulation, and administration of immigration protections.[19] At the rhetorical level, citizenship should be looked at as tautological because it fails to provide a tangible description of the physical disposition of a citizen. Because of its composition, citizenship becomes a self-referential act that requires modification and reproduction over time. For this reason, among others, citizenship appears self-evident and transparent to those who possess it and is visible outside the realm in which it is produced (Alarcón 1994a).

In working out some of the connections in citizen relations, Bourdieu's theory of cultural productions anchors a discussion of the way citizenship produces a questionable body. Next I lay out the production of a questionable body across two paths. The first derives from a reading of excerpts from Debbie Nathan's essay "The Eyes of Texas Are Upon You" in her *Women and Other Aliens* (1991), followed by an examination of citizenship in John Sayles' 1996 movie *Lone Star*.

Culture plays a critical role in the reproduction of citizenship. Since citizenship is socially constructed and based on related national experiences, references I make here to citizenship will vary based on the circumstances and the participants in the narrative. Cultural dynamics reveal the way society secures the production and reproduction of citizenship by differentiating outside groups through phantasmal classifications. For example, "illegal alien" is phantasm. People, workers, are real, and they do cross the border. But they are not from other planets, and many argue that Mexico is still "theirs." I will foreground various moments when the discourse of citizenship is thus heightened. Finally, I suggest that the border undermines the role of citizenship by disrupting its iconicity, if we view citizenship through the idea of its fantasies.

THE IMMIGRANT EXPERIENCE

The immigrant body registers a disassociative experience in the visual production of the questionable body. In her 1991 collection of essays, *Women and Other Aliens*, Debbie Nathan captures the problem many Mexican immigrant women face and explores the complex relationship between the immigrant "alien" and the Border Patrol agent in the surveillance of immigrants.

The Border Patrol mediates between the state and the public citizen, and immigrants become the questionable bodies under surveillance (Alarcón 1994a). The use of surveillance in such "low-intensity conflict" (Dunn 1996) varies in form and application. Border Patrol agents wittingly and unwittingly, as a paramilitary police force, engage in a hermeneutics of a cultural citizen, a "body" that in turn leads to a social hermeneutics.[20] The obsession with the methods used to survey the border recall Foucault's theorization of power and knowledge, when he describes Jeremy Bentham's idealized apparatus of confinement in the "panopticon." Foucault's panopticon arises from the need to systematize the surveillance of prison populations (1995, 195–228). But the amorphous quality of the border makes it next to impossible to structure a clear-cut apparatus to survey and discipline a given body. In this case, the border must be understood as a free-floating signifier that escapes the compulsory rules of control. The methodology of control used to survey the border is administered through the visual gaze. With the rise of technological methods of surveying the border, including infrared and night-vision devices, a systematized form of reading the immigrant body is administered by Border Patrol agents in their attitudes and their perceptions of reading citizenship (Fernandez-Kelly 1983).

One of the critical devices used in this visual economy draws from a simple profile of the body to determine a certain "look" of illegality. The method of surveillance used in profiling renders categorical judgments about individuals through the clothes they wear, the cars they drive, or the color of their skin. Nathan cleverly documents accounts by women who try to cross into the United States without such papers as certified birth certificates, driving licenses, and passports (1991). Borrowing from one of Texas' most popular songs, Nathan titles one essay "The Eyes of Texas Are Upon You" to illustrate this low-intensity method of surveillance as a cultural hegemonic apparatus that instructs a visual economy assigned to "the look," a way of dressing in sneakers, gym shorts, or T-shirts and jeans that undocumented immigrants use to pass as U.S. citizens. It is an interesting social interaction based on reading the body, because the immigrant manipulates the way a citizen looks in order to cross into the United States without the border agent becoming suspicious of her or his actions. In turn, it is the Border Patrol agent's job to examine dress or styles to classify "illegal aliens" in contrast to "real" citizens.

Arbitrary surveillance appears to be the sole criterion with which to approach noncitizens. Appearance therefore becomes Foucault's panopticon via culture and is a visual exchange enlarged by citizen cultural productions. Since the structure of surveillance is decided by one body over another, for the Border Patrol agent and the undocumented immigrant, the application of the practice is arbitrary and tyrannical in its effect.[21]

Participants in this exchange, the Border Patrol agent and the undocumented immigrant, in their visual manipulations, trade off parodies of the way a so-called real citizen appears in both real and social imaginations.[22] In detailing a scene, Nathan refers to a woman named Reyna, a Mexican woman contemplating crossing over to the United States to visit her husband, who has found work in New Mexico. From the beginning, Reyna is frustrated by the lengthy and expensive process of crossing over via a *coyote* (smuggler). Because Reyna does not have enough money to cross using the more conventional, expensive, smuggler route, she chooses a different plan. Nathan describes her choice: "Reyna didn't have the money to pay another smuggler, so she begged and borrowed enough for an off season airline ticket to Albuquerque" (18). Reyna decides to take her chances at the airport, but first she has to shed her old look, "the Mexican look." Nathan goes into detail about Reyna's style: "She favors wobbly high-heeled sandals with tight plastic straps, shiny royal purple dresses with patent leather belts, magenta fingernail polish, peacock blue mascara, lumpy fire-engine red lipstick" (ibid.). By some U.S. standards of dress, Reyna's ensemble may be said to disqualify her on the grounds of shear garishness. The "Mexican look" Nathan describes is really one formed out of poverty and an attempt to appear feminine with all the colorful displays of feminine dress.

Here the economy of "passing" employed by Reyna suggests her strategic use of cultural monikers of U.S. citizenship such as fashion and health to successfully cross the border. Strategies of passing are often used by gays and lesbians and by blacks and Latinas/os in their attempt to escape social vilification. The hegemony of cultural compliance works similarly in this encounter with Reyna since she knows all too well that passing requires a presentation of self that can be manipulated. Since she has only one chance to cross, the whole process of "passing" for a U.S. citizen must be well thought out, that is, if she intends to pass the checkpoint without being noticed and stopped. Reyna enlists the help of her friend Lupita in an effort to transform herself into the citizen who can "pass without question." In one scene, Reyna and Lupita rummage through a used-clothing shop to get Reyna the right "look." Taking her chances at the airport meant that she had to begin the process of forming a new look as soon as possible.

> A college educated Trotskyist from Mexico City, Lupita was
> up on the border organizing for one of the Fourth Internation-
> als. She wore Italian leather sandals that looked nicer instead
> of crummier the older they got, wire rimmed glasses, and
> Wranglers. Unlike Reyna, Lupita was thin—but in a healthy
> way that in Mexico they call *protenizada*. Literally, that means
> you can afford to eat milk, cheese, fish, and meat regularly,
> maybe even for snacks. Figuratively, it means you've got the
> whole gestalt, the Look that would make you blend into any
> airport in the world. (Ibid.)

The acquisition of an appearance is more complicated than Reyna imagined. The differences between Reyna and Lupita appear written on the physical body. Health here is underwritten by good nourishment and a First World demeanor. This passage suggests that unlike Lupita, Reyna must have a high-carbohydrate diet that makes her look overweight and unhealthy. Even by Mexican standards, the well-nourished body can blend in at the airport, where the global citizen is recognizable for his or her supposed health (diet pills, gym membership, costlier food) as well as clothes. Reyna's inability to shed the colorful clothes further suggests that she was not able to locate the right to pass. "The Look" thus represents the "ideal" citizen.

> Reyna made it to the airport all right, but anyone could see she
> was one big faux pas. Purple jeans. Pumpkin colored jogging
> shoes. A peach polyester blouse with fluttery sleeves and a scal-
> loped Emmet Kelley collar with a big dip in the back where
> her horizontal bra strap stuck out like a T-square. A border
> patrol agent tapped her on the shoulder just as she reached the
> escalator. "Your Citizenship," he said. (19)

Reyna's immigrant experience is subject to examination as a questionable body. In this essay, Nathan draws attention to the way the immigrant experience is simultaneously rendered as visible but questionable. The immigration process eliminates certain individuals. Michel Foucault calls this process of elimination *asepsis*, the means of removing unwanted, "degenerate organisms" from a pure environment or culture.[23] Women like Reyna with less exposure to or sophistication in a dominant culture are logistically identified and targeted as "unwanted." With no access into the United States and no acceptable documentation, women in Reyna's situation share the experience of unwantedness. As a demonstration of concern about the national border, the surveillance of style and demeanor assumes conditions of power that determine who is acceptable and who is not (Arteaga 1994a). But this surveillance does not address some important questions: What exactly needs to be protected? What sort of threat does this person pose? Is bad fashion a threat to national iconicity? Is poor health a threat to national citizenship? The scenario characterizes many traditional and historical effects related to patterns of surveillance against immigrants in the United States (Calderón and Saldívar 1991). The underlying threat this method of patrolling poses to citizens is that perceptions of a body are arbitrary and can be altered to define undesirables at any moment.

BORDER CULTURE AND THE DISRUPTION OF CITIZENSHIP

Bodies are a basis of cultural production. Even dead bodies, if they have had enough of a life, appear to haunt the living. The movie *Lone Star* (1996) opens with the unearthing of a trace, a bone, attached to a circumstance, a past and a history, a narrative. The unearthing of the skull sets into motion a series of events that leads Sam Deeds to find the murderer of former sheriff Charlie Wade. But inside the skull lies another trace, Wade's badge. The unearthed "lone star" is an emblem of the phalloconic presence of law and order in an otherwise forsaken place. Wade's presence in the community was by design an unforgettable one. He made sure everyone understood his position and power. His heavy-handed exercise of the law extended to abusing anyone who dared to undermine his authority.

The film mimics the local expression of a border culture similar to that depicted in examples above of border subjects, legal apparatus, and cultural production of citizenship. Set in a composite border town, *Lone Star* represents a cultural breakdown of history and a cultural production of citizenship through its complicated drama about the lives of local townspeople. The story revolves around various sheriffs who all seem to have connections to the same murder mystery. The first, Buddy Deeds, overshadowed his son with his larger-than-life presence as a judicious and fair-minded agent of the law who is admired in the community even in death. His son, Sam, lives with the presence of his now-dead father. The story comes together when Sheriff Sam Deeds believes that his father may have killed Sheriff Charlie Wade nearly thirty years earlier.

The skull unearthed by a couple of military trainees on an excursion in the rough brush country along the Texas border unleashes Sam Deeds' confrontation with the past. In an effort to solve the mystery and dispel the superheroism that surrounds his father's legacy, Sam Deeds sets out to find the murderer of Charlie Wade, convinced that his father had something to do with it. He is entranced by the psychological implications of disclosing his father's past and therefore producing a symbolic death of the "father." These circumstances create a situation in which the loss of patrimony propels the law and its influence in relation to the cultural changes taking place in the small town.

We never really understand, however, if Sam Deeds is simply looking for the culprit in Wade's death or if he wants to end his own hostility toward his father's interference with his romantic affections for Pilar, a young Mexican-American he encounters in his youth. We learn, as part of his investigation, that Sam is disturbed by his father's legacy. The unearthing of the skull in many respects produces a desire to close a chapter by solving the death of Charlie Wade and by disclosing his father's secret corruption. This process leads Sam Deeds to believe that his father may have committed the murder to gain the powerful job of sheriff.

Mixed into the personal power dynamics of the masculine drama are various racial constructions. On one level, there is the rise of the Mexican middle class and its stake in gaining a balanced representation in local history. Pilar challenges the school's reading of Texas history by offering her own account of the Battle of the Alamo. The scene triggers a debate among the Anglo history teachers at the school, who believe that Texas history ought to be represented according to traditional readings that favor Anglos over Mexicans. Pilar counters this by declaring that history depends on the perspective in which the events took place, a perspective she says casts Mexicans at the Battle of the Alamo in a false light. As the figure of the Chicana intellectual, Pilar, now a single mother, is still attracted to Sam, an Anglo. Since their adolescent involvement was cut short by her mother's and his father's interference, it appears as if Pilar and Sam can now rekindle their sexual desires, except for her mother's meddling in her life. Miscegenation is implicated in this exchange, but it will prove to be a sexual transgression of a different order that propels Pilar's mother to intercede.

Pilar's mother, Mercedes Cruz, cast as the middle-class émigré, represents the traditional Mexican (neocolonialist) woman whose assimilation into U.S. border culture rings especially clear at moments when she reminds her restaurant employees that they must "speak English." In a bold annotation of local politics, the class constructions simply conceal the divisions of race that underlie the discussion on speaking English as proper citizen behavior. Mercedes Cruz represents the traditional Mexican female figure who has made a life for herself in Los Estados Unidos by literally capitalizing on the one business she knows best, cooking Mexican food. Pilar resents her mother's excessive presence in her life. Their relationship, like Sam's relationship to his father, draws a generational division between the cultures and histories they represent. In turn, Pilar is the resident Chicana, an organic intellectual who has a more provocative and dim outlook on the small town. Her tensions with her mother loom beyond the expected complications of mother-daughter relations; this stress is tied to Pilar's sexual liaisons as she grieves the loss of her husband.

On another level are the black characters, represented by the U.S. military as emblems of the federal law. The Army colonel is a stalwart patriot who is self-conscious about his achievements in the military. The colonel's attempts to discipline his soldiers demonstrate his precarious location as a black male who has succeeded through climbing the ranks of the military. The colonel's preoccupation with success is undermined by his lack of discipline at home. At times, he grapples with his son's rebellious and curious nature, as displayed at the local bar. The colonel tries to handle his family, especially his son, with the same qualities he uses in directing his enlisted recruits: commanding yet vulnerable. A searing reminder of the fragile composition of the family narrative along the border, the colonel's return as the leader of the military base is symbolic of the family dispute that has kept his family apart. He keeps the knowledge of his own father's history in the community a secret from his family to break ties with a part of his past.

One fascinating aspect of all this is not revealed directly. Implicated in *Lone Star* is the anticipation of a lost era. We sense impending changes in the educational system and in who guards the law. Sheriff Sam Deeds, when challenged by one of his deputies, will likely be defeated in the upcoming election. The fight over high school history curriculum signals as well the inevitable progression of the influences of the Mexican-American perspective. The presence of the military run by the first black officer at the post adds to the dimensions of a waning era of Anglo domination.

The film's message is held together by a commentary on the reproduction of culture. While subtle and secretive, the fact that Pilar and Sam are half-sister and half-brother offers an apparent incestuous message, masking how Pilar was conceived through a secret love affair between her mother and Buddy Deeds. The transgressive, incestuous narrative is therefore driven by the fears of miscegenation. Sam Deeds, unable to reproduce his father's legacy as the forebear of the next generation of Anglo culture, and Pilar, unable to have more children after a difficult pregnancy, are the sterile legacy. The sexual interactions between the various participants recall familial transgression that breaks down the cultural production of a citizen-subject's relations in the family narrative. If the culminating effect of *Lone Star* is to provoke controversy over sexuality and race, this frontier romance of the border disrupts the reproductive paths of the family and the succession of the traditions and legacies bound by it. The basis of the transgression is held together by a covert and, at times, overt commentary on interracial sex and fear of miscegenation.

The lone star in the film is but a worn emblem of individualism cut short by its own arrogance and inefficacy. The progression of the image of the law makes Sam forlorn and quiet. The death of the father, symbolized by Charlie Wade's murder and Buddy Deed's phalloconic order, are supplanted by living desires to forget and put to rest the ignominy of past relations in border cultures. In the end, Pilar tells Sam to "forget the Alamo." When Sam finds out that Wade was indeed killed by his own deputy, Earl, he lays to rest the myth of his father in order to comply with the repressed desire to sleep with his sister.

The model of the inherited cultural legacy of twisted Anglo-American culture is slowly undermined by imminent changes, by sexuality between the races, and by the inability to reproduce or heal the past. The cultural production of citizenship is like a haunting that is only put to rest by disruptions. It is not unlike director John Sayles to try to capture the local color of a given community, but in later work, such as *Men with Guns* (1998), Sayles utilizes polemical situations that arise within the global intervention into local communities. Communities like those in the border culture of *Lone Star* invite a different understanding of the influences of the larger discourses on subjectivity that have been routed through the simple or ordinary lives of their people.

These instances reveal how the border produces its own signifying elements. While the crisis of representation may be perceived as an effect and a byproduct of the decline of transparency, as some suggest, the border becomes critical as a zone in which the scholarship of Chicanas/os develops because it draws on the effects of globalization and a transnational economy. Ethical and moral questions arise from a removal of boundaries. Few seem prepared to read the agencies of the border outside of a political economy of those exchanges, whether composed of people, goods, or products. Such a political economy raises the question of whether a new hegemonic relation is developing from this situation. The concerns over the border have materialized as a certain cultural response to public policy debates. One goal of humanities research is to regard problems and sites of possibility that are already occurring in some of these spaces whether as popular culture in origin or in true, actual, daily interaction. Later, I will look at playfulness on the border to balance this layer of serious investment. Here, I have tried to emphasize examples of a visual process that goes into the cultural production of citizenship and its construction of questionable bodies, questionable within the frameworks of past and present and of racial and sexual boundaries.

Such analysis of the cultural production of the U.S.-Mexico border demonstrates how culture works to structure its own counterhistoriography. I have positioned the border subject as a "gestalt" of citizenship, to borrow from Nathan's reporting on an attempted border crossing, with discourses that trace genealogies through cultural production as their own "organic" historiography. This process occurs methodologically in literary, film, and other representations of the Chicana/o experience that are embedded in the twentieth century. Many seek to illuminate a marginal subject of the United States. If we consider the broader narrative of Chicanas/os in the United States, the narrative is marked by linguistic, racial, class, and sexual differences. Representations of the border offered as examples vary according to the location and different cultural interests that intersect with other narratives, including the border as a war zone, the border as an economic exchange space, and so on.

As a narrative condition, the border develops from a network of cultural productions that includes materialist concerns in a transnational context, but it is not simply that. For this reason, the cultural production of the border as a narrative condition also places these subjects within a state of contingency as individuals but also as legitimate constituents. A borderlands paradigm serves as a methodology for cultural production because it supersedes the authenticating cultural body found in Chicana/o nationalism. The body's self-referential claims to grievous historical errors are an effect of transvaluation. Discursive tracking occurs by the nature of the subject's relations to the authentic body; a process unfolds in yet another instance in which desire foregrounds the basis of this dissimulation, as disclosed in Pilar and Sam's *amor prohibido*.

Citizen-subjects' formation may have reached a saturation point in the nation. The border bears witness to this condition of the excesses of the nation and its limitations by spilling over onto the boundaries of the other culture. What will this mean for those whose sense of the nation is still in place? What will become of history without the signifying puissance of the nation to adjudicate such ideas? Gloria Anzaldúa anticipated this process and appeared to suggest that mestiza consciousness is exactly the condition by which radical changes can or will take place.

As an epistemological concern, the racial borderlands may advance specific cultural differences that exist within Chicana/o discourse. The fact that these borderlands function in Anzaldúa's work as a basis of limitation or barrier can been seen from the correlation that the myth of reconciliation plays in Chicana/o literature as a naive rendition of emergent forms. It is actually a complex intrusion of a self-conscious voice that serves to articulate critical self-renewal. As Emma Pérez configures the method in what she terms "the Oedipal reconquest triangulation" (1999), when examining Luis Valdez through his Delgadina figure, we might leave behind the worry about Pilar and Sam in their incestuous embrace and imagine what already occurs: a high percentage of "outmarriage," a strongly interracialized nation where color will no longer suffice to justify imprisonment of illegal border crossings as signifiers.

The questionable subject is the person whose sense of identity is neither registered within the legal discourse nor affirmed as legitimate in terms of citizenship. The narrative condition of the border presents an irreconcilable condition and emerges from a conflicted history. The attempts to decipher the cultural productions of the border popularly inscribe a historiography of the border plush with nineteenth-century racist ideologies of Mexican-Americans. Anzaldúa introduces another popular historiography by presenting the discourses of traditionally disenfranchised groups. The conviction espoused by Frederick Jackson Turner more than one hundred years ago is no less explicit in highlighting the need to "protect" the U.S. border from immigrants, drugs, and a long list of other presumed and real social pathologies. Mestiza consciousness, Anzaldúa suggests, creates an epistemological problem of difference; it is also an embodiment of a consciousness that offers a critique of western expansion as a unique narrative about the border. In terming the border narrative an irreconcilable history, I conclude that racial desires are the residual effect of a colonial legacy that is then written onto a narrative of, among other things, lesbian desire. Within a self-critical location, what becomes apparent in Anzaldúa's borderlands, because she writes from a position of a feminist woman of color, are practices that locate difference in a critique against traditionalist-conservative assumptions of westward U.S. expansion.

Chicana/o literary subject formation has taken a critical turn in rethinking the theoretical grounds by which Chicanas/os as subjects deliberate emergent concerns and consider the essentialist problems of minority discourses that claimed first a position of historical grievances. The critical turn from a Chicana/o discourse to that of the borderlands leads the discussion in literature to a self-critical location. The idea of a historiography of the border rooted in popular discourse is fraught with problems not discussed here because my analysis has been balanced with sources besides popular culture. Instead, here I have demonstrated how the westward expansion of the United States led to a grand narrative of Anglo-American dominance that supplanted local history through discourses on cultural differences; the narrative is disrupted in the image of Pilar and Sam reuniting a family "of the same." As a school or historiography that has come to represent Mexican-Americans' tenuous position within American history, the border inscribes the local history of the region. In the next chapter, I will refer to some of these historiographic characteristics in both factual and fictional accounts.

Four   CHICANA/O FASHION CODES
The Political Significance of Style

Chicana/o fashion trends throughout the twentieth century constitute a series of political encounters in American culture. The political use of clothes or fashion elicits a "stylization" of ethnicity and captures Chicanas/os' subject formation across the vast historical and intersectional political moments of identity play. From the rural to the cosmopolitan, youth cultures and even structural elements inhered in social gender and class relations influence dress codes. The provocative, emblematic stylizations offered by Chicana/o culture's fashion codes oppose dominant culture in creative ways (Parkins 2002).

While fashion predominates as a powerful consumer element particularly in a vibrant youth market, emblems of stylized dress codes produce cultural identity in a process that cuts across all segments of U.S. ethnic populations. In mainstream culture, however, fashion trends constitute an element of high culture, appearing as haute couture or ready-to-wear designer emblems. However, the subversive wearing of street fashion still occupies the outer register of political thought, because ethnic and minority populations lack participation in the production of high culture (Rubenstein 2001).

Within a hypercapitalistic U.S. economic context, fashion trends are not at all benign, whether they signify an artful expression of self-fashioning or a market condition of commodity organization. The political significance of clothes elicits unique political exchanges in virtually all instances that are taken seriously and as ethnic communities have achieved acceptance in the middle class. By the early 1990s, retail, catalog, and online clothing markets boasted $10 billion in sales annually in the United States and global market sales that reached as high as $36 billion annually (Allenby, Jen, and Leone 1996); the continuing upward trend suggests an intensive area of self-production at work. These figures also constitute the competitive nature of twenty-first-century economies and perhaps quantify the allure that fashion offers an individual in immediate self-value and instant valorization of a self-image. Clothing and accessories give the consumer the ability to easily manipulate his or her appearance. This ability to generate a self-image offers an agency of self-creation. As a political statement, however, fashion functions in an entirely different set of maneuverings. Read against the historical context of race and ethnic formation, fashion serves as a semiotic sign system that informs and disassembles normative race politics.

Fashion, especially the marketing of clothes, is a popular phenomenon garnering mass appeal while also embracing high culture's inventiveness. Nontraditional forms of analysis in cultural studies view fashion as a valuable social context from which to review ethnic body politics, which respond to the structural ploys of capitalism (Allenby, Jen, and Leone 1996). Clothes reflect a sense of personal identity and demonstrate a person's social demeanor, and fashion trends profoundly and blatantly reflect collective social desires. Fashion statements, especially within an ethnic community, are a salient rejoinder to a lack of political inclusion, especially as the distinctive elements of communities of color coordinate fashionable expression to resist normative constructions of racialized citizenship. By destabilizing the "normative" style, such consumer sensibilities prove to be more proficient at expressing personal and political discontent than any other type of consumer products.

Chicanas/os' relationship to fashion also reflects political and economic cultivation under hegemonic conditions. The mirroring of clothes as an oppositional stance destabilizes fashion's innate tendency to homogenize social character. Chain-store branding in companies like The Gap serves as a tangential attempt to create a metaphysical style, in a Habermasian sense, by stylizing conformity.[1] At the same time, the ability to create and maintain a given "style" suggests a creative outlet and agency within capitalism that, when properly deployed, can be a rewarding, politically charged experience. Wearing certain clothing—in itself or taken out of context—does not signal a defined liberatory practice. Rather, fashion codes address the network of ideas and circular interpretations that form stylistic sensibilities, disseminated in a semiotic interpretative field, while at the same time delineating identity and community in a way that informs new resistances and methodologies.

Chicana/o fashion codes, frequently marked by social alienation, delinquency, criminality, romantic hyperbole, historical pastiche, hypersexuality, and cosmopolitan chic, maintain the community's oppositional stance and retain a measure of political significance in the image production of the community. Conclusively, no singular code of dress represents all of

Chicana/o fashion sensibilities. Instead, Chicana/o fashion encompasses a spectrum of cultural and political differences that express geographical, class, and sexual distinctions. Recent examples of some of the codes reside in such prime-time television situation comedies as *Ugly Betty* and standup comedian George Lopez' former weekly show. From the mantilla-clad, pious women to strapping vaqueros during the period of colonization and expansion, these fashion elements tend to be the most loaded with prejudicial commentary. Later Chicanas/os, an ethnic category and group identity that forged its own path in the United States beginning in the 1960s, received wide circulation in popular magazines like *Harper's* and *Ladies Home Journal.*[2]

Shelly Streeby, in *American Sensations* (2002, 63), notes that journalistic representations of women found their way into U.S. popular culture through such means as illustrations of a fictive "heterosexual union" between a feminized Mexico and a masculinized United States. Fashion codes are meant to properly signify gender coding of women, especially those fashion codes that define gender and race. Notably, nineteenth-century fashion's social construction of the Anglo-American female in Victorian dress featured exaggerated hats and high, rigidly encased necklines that maintained a sensibility of controlled decency by forbidding any suggestion of sexuality to pass through the encased body.

Fashion, with its subtle caricatures and hidden motifs vying for the spectator's or viewer's attention, adorns the most enduring false images of Chicanas/os in the most innocuous places. The ordinary contexts in which many of these images occur ought to receive attention that is more critical. Unlike the popular representations of Mexican men in sombreros and ponchos and the unnerving but sublime passivity of conventional images of Mexican women, contemporary representations of Chicanas/os manifest themselves in magazine pages, restaurant logos, and tourist advertising. Even as clothes function to offer mostly provocative social encounters, fashion codes also express a dominant culture's figuration of ethnic prejudices by representing the oddly attired body in ways that seem useful but hardly realistic. The images of Speedy Gonzalez, Frito Bandido, and more recently the Taco Bell Chihuahua dog typecast Chicano masculinities by superimposing crude forms of representation in markedly racist impressions over the presumably benign commercialized object. However, the trail of such images takes on an even more deplorable dimension when gender and sexuality reveal a means of formulating racialized representations of Chicana/o and Mexican culture.

In these commercial caricatures, the exaggerated historical features and animalism assemble the oddity of race. The shrinking of the masculine form creates a diminutive characterization of the Mexican or Chicano male body and at the same time maintains its ethnic codes with the dog's large ears, which defy reality, hinting at the characteristic sombrero. The image of the mustachioed mouse Speedy Gonzales cheerfully poised to eat a taco with the Chihuahua in it goes so far as to suggest a form of cannibalism ascribed to Chicanas/os.

LA SEÑORITA

Like the fictive qualities of these name-brand commercial goods, the cartoon animal and its renegade style rely heavily on dress codes to outline the ethnic body. Similarly, representations of Chicana and Mexican women sustain an arrangement of the body historically with a perverted capitalism fictionalizing a subhuman stereotype and persona of the Mexican.

The *señorita* is assembled as part fact and part fiction. By all accounts, *la señorita* refers to an "unmarried" Mexican woman, including immigrant women and Chicanas living in the United States, who ascribe to the gender codes of traditional marriage. The marriage status of *la señorita*, i.e., her sexual identity made public, leaves a strong fictional aspect in American culture. Katy Jurado, for example, the most recognized Mexican film actor of the twentieth century, garnered much attention in the 1930s and 1940s with such films as *High Noon* and *Arrowhead*, often portraying the mistress of the heroic figure. Katy Jurado's characters draw heavily from the construction of *la señorita* as temptress—unmarried but sexually conscious and always provocative.

Less respectable renditions of *la señorita* facilitate this contradictory construction of the virginal yet hypersexual woman. Most of these representations impose—across an image landscape of American commercial advertising, street logos, and cinematic representations—an unmediated view of gender and race. While fashion codes predominate in the visual economy of the Mexican woman, her lack of political efficacy as a person repeatedly emphasizes a combination of visual effects: clothes, makeup, hairstyle, posture, and facial expression. The aesthetic codes of femininity, accentuated and exaggerated so as to never espouse sufficient agency in the public space but always remain available as a sexual object or as a symbolic passive element of male desire, became a desired feature of the Americanization of the Mexican woman. From the unreconstructed *charro* or rural rancher-cowboy depictions to the temptress, the hope lies in a fashionable reconfiguration.

La señorita, perhaps the most widely recognized image of Mexican women even in a random sampling of online restaurant advertising, evokes a contradictory set of elements. First, the sexualized naiveté of the Mexican woman implies both racialized and sexualized habits of mind. Generated by brightly colored and often flowered clothes and excessive makeup, the personification of the *señorita* organizes a framework for the romanticized pastiche of American culture's interpellation of the folkloric Mexican past, which foregrounds ethnographic Mexican women's "desire" in repressed postures. In representations artistically rendered, the Mexican female remains repressed in terms of her actual sexual desire or knowledge. In the economy of sexual desire, knowledge of a certain contract of sexuality produces the agencies of a woman's sexuality. Such images simultaneously adorn the female fiction of naiveté as it evokes sexual desire under capitalism. Although their facial expressions might register innocence, *las señoritas'* stereotypical postures and off-the-shoulder dresses convey coquetry as an innate characteristic of the racialized gender of the subjects.

By the turn of the twentieth century, the cultural boundaries of sexual prohibition ironically rendered the female in an "always available" posture textualized in fashion codes for the consumer audience. This pose opens the female subject to multiple opportunities for the gaze of capitalism to instantiate its desired goal: in this case, the hypersexualization of the Mexican woman and her social disempowerment produce doubly inscribed images to achieve both dominance and submission even in presumably benign advertising images.

The possibility that such representations or images have a disempowering quality and are contemporary as well as historical, particularly for women of color, is an idea that students resist in the classroom setting. In other words, it is common for students to contend that a greater interpretive agency exists to overcome image production of ethnic and sexually evocative representation. No one image has the power to create a socialized notion of women, such students will argue. However, the recurring image of *la señorita* and its place within capitalism suggest that the concurrent racialization and sexualization of the Mexican woman intend to fragment her politically and at the same time totalize her as an object of sexuality by drawing upon and sustaining this as an unassuming facet of American life. Under this interpretation, she is available.

Even in this moment of postmodern intention with unstable notions of differences, the ideological underpinnings of gender codes remain solidly in place in the name of a facile history called upon by consumption. Among the best-known critical projects on fashion, Roland Barthes' *The Fashion System* (1990) offers a study of fashion as a cultural system imbued with semiotic codes, in other words, one system of communication within another. In Barthes' fashion codes, the semblance of clothes disrupts the historical containment of subjectivity procured by the written word or narrative production. A wordless schema for the production of a subject applies to intersectional readings of the Mexicana/o and Chicana/o racialized continuum. *La señorita* does not remain static in her representation across contexts; despite the pervasiveness of the stereotypes and apparently racist undercurrents, an element of nostalgia for an earlier, simpler time returns with images; an element of pastiche cannot be forgotten. Although pastiche is commonly dismissed as an innocuous aspect of the sign, aspects of Chicana/Mexicana fashion do not measure up to scrutiny when read against the oppositional stance of the revolutionary climate of the 1960s or 1970s.

REVOLUTIONARY CHIC

The revolutionary images of Pancho Villa and Emiliano Zapata appear in other commercialized venues as caricatures of Mexico's past. During the 1960s a cult of revolutionary heroism began to take shape alongside the U.S. countercultural movement. Revolutionary chic from the 1960s draws its influence from the Mexican Revolution (1911–1917) and from later U.S.-based movements like the Black Panthers (Joseph 1986). The drama created by the social politics of the Brown Berets reimagined the revolutionary figure as harbinger of change, demanding political recognition in the public arena. Several popular representations feature the dramatic pictorial images of revolutionaries wearing their deliberately patterned uniforms, demonstrating political agency and cultural determination. More than any other facet, revolutionary figures in Chicana/o cultural aesthetics have been influenced by multiple sites of history. These figures offer elaborate readings for Saldaña-Portillo in *The Revolutionary Imagination in the Americas and the Age of Development* (2003): this revolutionary rendition depends upon military modalities. First, a progressive developmental narrative provides the motivation for a given national identity to emerge; second, the citizens desire to develop "within" themselves. Saldaña-Portillo describes the second modality in detail:

> The second modality of developmentalism is expressed in the idea that this movement in societies is contingent on the development of the members of these societies into free, mature, fully conscious, and self-determining individual subjects. While it is now evident that most, if not all, twentieth century revolutionary movements subscribed to a developmentalist model of history, the impact of the second modality on revolutionary politics over the last century has been less recognized. (36–37)

These two sites of emergence stand out. More than any other means of recognizing the revolutionary subject's placement, clothing occurs as a materialist and idealist basis in Marxist subjectivity. As such, Saldaña-Portillo's "revolutionary modality" applies to the formation of a subject that is self-fashioning of the protest movement and represents the political spectacle in cultural terms (Joseph 1986). Because clothes feature a dramatic, ritualized form of dissent that occurs in both the materialist and idealist states of emergence, its ability to transform the public space as well as identity production is incalculable.

The use of military garb by "the revolutionary" stages a confrontation in the public space as a counternarrative to varying nationalist agents. The uniforms intend to disrupt the visibility of naturalized "good citizenship" by instead inviting the viewer into the public domain of political stance. The poetics of the revolutionary generates image sensibility, creating visual political discontent, and emerges in the public discourse as a new historical process that lends voice, presence, and visibility in times of silence and marginalization via photogenic encounters. The concern with fashion and its deployment under political upheaval and social change offers a paradoxical context in which gender and fashion fuse effectively into the political codes of dress. The codifying styles of dress produce both the desired effects of public spectacle and revolutionary chic.

"Dressing down" was a signifier of moral, rebel fiber that was a valuable social asset. Contrasted by the preppy look popular in the 1980s, the dress-down aspect of the 1970s and 1980s commented on the homogeneity of class as well. U.S. writers on fashion have described dressing down as a means of downplaying material wealth; an example would be grunge attire that aspires to a revolutionary role through its scruffy and worn-out presentation, like that of the late Kurt Cobain. The politics of grunge may be unintentional because its cultural defiance falls apart with its disaffected and drugged-out offering as a style of defiance. The questions, even if unarticulated, were in operation by virtue of the stylization: beret, raised fist, long hair, and other accoutrements made up the politicized Chicana/o and distinguished her or him from an earlier zoot suiter or 1950s "sock hop" fashionista.

In the early-twentieth-century photograph *Soldadera mexicana*, a *soldadera* took time out from the Mexican Revolution to pose for the picture. She stands at attention, holding a rifle and wearing hat, pants, ammunition belts, and pistol while a few male bystanders look on. In this scene within a scene, two revolutionary moments captured in one frame draw attention to the female as revolutionary. The gender of the *revolutionaria* and the masculinity of a Mexican soldier captured in the moment create the effect of a spectacle. Obviously, her dress signals one aspect, as her clothes typify Mexican revolutionary garb. The determined expression on her face executes the uniform's political invectives to initiate change by force or "by any means necessary." From her demeanor emanates her devotion to "true change." The element of revolutionary chic derives from the uncompromising location of the *revolutionaria* and is accomplished primarily with her manner of dress.

Brown Berets capture the Chicana/o movement's culturally nationalistic style. The beret stands out as emblem of the revolutionary 1960s borrowed from the Black Panthers (Davis 1994). The beret, worn by both women and men, possesses gender-neutral intentions. The Brown Berets' clothes reveal the idealist narrative of the revolutionary figure (Ogbar 2004). While some photographs consciously emphasize female and male figures in a certain framing of gender, most were not necessarily intended to evoke sexuality. Rather, the sexuality emerges in the photography—specifically in full-length shots of Chicanas wearing then-fashionable miniskirts that seem to recall the female aspect of political assertiveness and sexual liberation in the Brown Berets. Still, no matter how one looks at the intent of the movement, the miniskirt, of its own semiotic accord, can only affirm sexuality, even in the name of political conflict. Much of this act of affirmation captures the camera's framing of the body and assurance that the entire body of each woman finds representation. The miniskirt functions as a gesture toward a media war rather than preparing the wearer for a real war, unlike that of the *soldadera*, whose rifle alongside her reveals the clear notion of physically fighting an enemy. The performance of war or suggestion of revolution through clothing fictionalizes and inscribes the gendered and sexualized elements of the miniskirt into a choreographed moment.

While the militarized, stoic glares of the Chicanas in such photographs proclaim their political urgency and suggest seriousness in the movement, their clothes, a reminder that outlines the provocative play of sexuality, could not be forgotten solely in the name of one type of liberation. Yesterday's revolution would become today's political drama, as Chicanas wrote about Brown Beret brothers who did not accept them as equal revolutionary comrades but instead as traditional cultural "vessels" (Espinoza 2001b).

SARTORIAL SPLENDOR AND THE COMMODITY

The creations of the revolutionary moment have departed into another set of spatial aesthetics. The postmodernist era in the 1980s resisted affiliations with the countercultural movements' zeal for political representation (Scranton 2001). A political desire remains supplanted by a consumer style supported by regional and distinctively marked attire. Although fashion trends represent a great element of postmodern consumerism and mass culture, trends feature styles that range from urbane to rural, suburban, slacker, funky, and downright cool. Dress codes and fashion sensibilities, postmodern cultural critic Dick Hebdige found (1979), define the historical moment as well as the identity frame of the wearer. In a manner of speaking, clothes of this more modern time frame, though less organized as a political aesthetic, mirror the capacity to both affirm and radicalize dominant ideologies with a seamless impression of social codes. In his study of post–World War II British subcultures, Hebdige found that "*postmodernity* is *modernity* without the hopes and dreams which made modernity bearable" (13). Hebdige's adroit lamentation of the modern "displaces" or disorients itself as the heir apparent to dominant culture. The role of Chicana/o fashion codes similarly assumes a new level of play with the intensification of capital, commodification in ethnic cultures, and entry of a few Chicanas/os into mainstream U.S. upper and middle classes.

One of the distinguishing features of hegemonic capitalism is its unstable commodity experience. Some of the more celebrated examples of the commodity experience include the fleeting exercises of consumer participation. The U.S. fashion industry, no less benign in its ability to market and promote a specific physical mien and cultural sensibility, finds itself with uniquely gendered and racial codes offered as marketing ploys (Ewen 1991). Taking advantage of the ethnic experience, the fashion system can override values taken as "normal" and "just" within dominant culture and in turn impose the new values on the rest of society.

True fashion is, above all, daring and propagates individuality and verve. Even trend-setting clothing lines such as The Gap, Eddie Bauer, and Abercrombie and Fitch have struggled to appeal to audiences outside of the Anglo-American identity. In the 1990s, executives of leading design house Ralph Lauren Inc. deliberately set unusually high prices for Lauren clothing to discourage people of color from buying it (Zukin 1996).[3] While fashion follows mass-marketing trends not specific to Chicana/o cultures, some fashion trendsetters view the Chicana/o market as lucrative. Designer Tommy Hilfiger and hip-hop design label Phat Farm intentionally appealed to urban Chicanas/os with polyester blends and oversized jeans lines, although rumors over the Internet in the late 1990s cast Hilfiger as exhibiting disdain for women of color.[4]

Other trends have followed in the path of the postmodernization of Chicana/o fashion. Boutique stores in Los Angeles use low-rider aesthetics to create their own urban chic via the Internet. Top-selling name-brand T-shirts feature such exclusive silkscreen logos as "Mamacita" and "Caliente" for the sexy "object A" on the go (de la Haye and Wilson 1999). Vato—among the cutting-edge brands of T-shirt apparel rooted in Los Angeles urban culture—sells to a more upscale clientele a line of clothing specific to the L.A. Chicana experience.

Oddly enough, the commodification of the Chicana/o experience transcends the typical meanings of *mamacita* (babe) and *caliente* (hot) to say that this is about the city of Los Angeles and not women's bodies. The selling of L.A. culture does not comment on or disrupt the sexist overtones and instead capitalizes on its edgy take on gender.

Religious subject matter also comes into play at the Rojas store on Melrose Avenue, where owner and designer Freddie Rojas sells a line of T-shirts that proclaim, "I [heart] Jesus." Implied in this T-shirt is the rejection of feminism. It replicates an aspect of clothes versus fashion. What distinguishes clothes from fashion, however, is the collective, interactive play of stylized dress in which the consumer and seller engage. Clothes express the mundane function of daily life, the utility of clothing, while fashion stands outside the frame of clothing. Chicana/o movement politics and Chicana/o nationalism were inside the civil rights struggle for autonomy; feminism seemed to some to stand "outside" that point of reference. Among those distinctive features of self-fashioning, here I consider the different historical patterns that mark ethnicity with, and from, sexuality.

HISTORICAL MEMORY
AND ITS CODING

Chicanas/os have not settled on a useful definition of the modern or postmodern. Saldaña-Portillo presents an economic explanation, but the aesthetics of the modern do not properly follow economic processes as easily. Across the short time that Chicanas have existed within modern American culture, they have exhibited an inventiveness of style, a sense of community, cultural defiance, and a definitive political standpoint against traditionalism and conventional attire. What commonly typifies the politics of dress among disempowered groups like Chicanas/os is the practice of reinscription—new ideologies whereby existing images from the prevailing order organized in innovative combinations resignify meaning. A maneuvering of style thus incorporates the practice of consumer economics, iconoclastic daring, and a desire to signify, all in one. An example of the practice resides in Chicanas' assembly of "looks," highlighted hair color to match particular clothing tones or sunglasses imitative of high fashion.

After all, fashion codes manifest themselves in varied stylizations—from the offbeat to suave sophistication. Typically, it is not what one wears but how one wears it that produces the desired effect. It is also interesting to note how the distinctiveness of the body renders certain looks plausible and other looks impossible. In all circumstances, fashion codes require some measure of aesthetic plausibility, as a different combination of items for the wearer leads to lingering impressions. In designing "a look," the workings of power operate on grids of meaning and intelligibility, such that a given look can "hail" others into the wearer's sphere or set a boundary to offset intrusion. High-swept hair fashion makes a statement to "Keep your distance," while "letting your hair down" connotes a friendlier position. Fashion systems codify the unconscious boundaries of inclusion and exclusion.

Stylized fashions in contemporary postmodern Chicana/o cultural expression have become more self-conscious in their design, no longer borrowing from existing codes of fashion from the past or from the lackluster surplus of clothes from malls and luxury outlets (Bryndon and Nissen 1998). The unique arrangement of Chicana/o stylization occupies the postmodern space of high culture, with its modernist impulses servicing the desire for novelty, public appeal, and visual recognition. From the hip-hop

Chicana/o urban hipster to Los Lonely Boys' Tejano-barrio look, fashion codes often reflect self-expression in youth cultures. In many situations, fashion codes offer commentary on the body and, more specifically, on the sexual freedoms implicit in areas of the body to which the wearer intentionally draws attention.

An obvious and enduring example of a look is the zoot suit as it personifies a specific burlesque of Chicana/o counterculture, with the oversized coat and pants departing from the constraints of the traditional fitted men's suit popularized in mid-twentieth-century Western cultures. The exaggerated design of the zoot suit announces its own sexuality by codifying its "sex" with excess. Color, size, and exuberance mark the zoot suit's transgression and underlying aggression. So much that has been written about the zoot suit documents the race wars of Los Angeles that it renders the zoot suit a privileged place in historical memory. Mauricio Mazón in *The Zoot Suit Riots* (1984) looks at the social symbolic processes of ethnic confrontations. Mazón, Eduardo Escobar in *Race, Police, and the Making of a Political Identity* (1999), and Luis Alberto Alvarez in "The Power of the Zoot" (2006) have all attested to the zoot suit's presence in shaping Chicano male political subjectivity.

Other styles of dress follow Chicanas/os' daring entry into dominant mainstream culture. Like that of the zoot suit, the sexual evocativeness of the cholo and chola styles finds a deeply embedded notion of the forbidden nature of sexuality. The Chicana/o "look," though by no means limited by the predominance of chola/o stylizations or the preeminence of pachucos, pachucas, and the zoot suit, offers still a sense of uniformity across the different cultural spaces within Chicana/o culture (Lipsitz 1986–1987). While cholo and chola stylizations capture the public's imagination and curiosity more than any other style of dress in Chicana/o culture, the lore that characterizes these urban legends appeals to the imagination, dominating the stereotypical matters of dress (Surace and Turner 1956).

Not all contemporary fashion trends share equal regard in the marketplace; some have no appeal for youth of color across ethnic lines. For example, clothes catering to Anglo-American youth have become racier and dubiously déclassé by emphasizing a dress-down style that is risqué even by today's hypersexualized conventions. The Abercrombie and Fitch line of clothes has virtually no appeal among Chicana/o youth. Abercrombie and Fitch, known for its tawdry and boring aperture for an oversexed or overdrugged look, appeals primarily to the suburban Anglo-American college student. Such dress-down tendencies have prevailed in some circles for decades, notably the hippie styles of the 1960s and the grunge look of the

1990s. By the late 1980s, the countercultural statement of nonconformity may have lost some of its allure and persuasiveness with the dress-down look. Instead, the dress-down look typified by singer Kurt Cobain resulted in a cultural defiance marked by alienation and depression.

Only later did hip-hop culture influence Chicana/o youth fashion codes through successful marketing to youths of color. In other respects, youths of color often disdain dressing down as a class statement, as "power" fantasies run rampant in hip-hop song lyrics and culture in general (hooks 1990). Rather the sense of power and difference are enacted repeatedly in hip-hop culture, with its proclivities toward gold jewelry and lavish excess, marked by a casual look and intense colorization in clothing.

Although some aspects of the dress-down look relate to socioeconomic trends, such as the rise of homelessness and the visible and adverse effects of AIDS on the physical body, these social factors have significantly altered the meaning of dressing down in communities of color whose members hold different attitudes about the body's representation. Excess is an acceptable form of embellishment in communities of color where exaggeration and surplus are signs of abundance that are a highly desired effect. Among the most visible is the baggy-pants phenomenon that spread in the 1990s. This is the look donned by youth of color, especially boys and young men. The trend originated in the music world but carried over into suburban and mainstream culture by the mid-1990s.

Observers offer varying theories on how the oversized-pants craze evolved. One version explains that the trend developed from prison inmates who were routinely assigned oversized pants to wear without the benefit of a belt (Smitherman 1997). Others in youth culture insist that the phenomenon originated from skateboarders and snowboarders who wore baggy jeans to facilitate movement in their sport. While the variations in theory of the oversized-jeans trend reveal the dialectics of racial difference in the interpretation of youth culture's fashion trends, there is no denying that the meaning assigned to clothes differs because communities have different sets of political investments (Rose 1991). The trend in jeans transformed the embellishments of the bell-bottom pants, and variations of baggy pants have diversified and grown into specific subtypes of baggy clothing. Hip-hoppers, ravers, club kids, skaters, and snowboarders all wear different styles of baggy pants. Ravers' pants are huge, usually covering the shoes or completely draping the ground. Skaters wear baggy shorts cut from long pants so that the cuffs will not interfere with skating. Baggy pants also draw attention to the underwear and buttocks "crack."

Another way to consider the oversized-jeans phenomenon is within the *rascuache* aesthetic. Within the context of hip-hop culture, the baggy-pants phenomenon would certainly apply to Tomás Ybarra-Frausto's notion of *rascuache* (1990)—"the down but not out" aspect noted in his cultural analysis of style and representation in art as well as in the visual presentation of clothes in the public space. *Rascuache* signifies the organic and common expression randomly put together and organized out of necessity rather than high culture's excess. In some respects, the chaotic ordering of *rascuache* pertains to the disassembled aspects of Chicana/o coloniality rearranged in randomness. *Rascuache* represents the removal of coloniality and the inability of such creative freedom within a populace to assume a new guise, a conscious ordering in Pierre Bourdieu's sensibility of culture, having no recourse to the folkloric past and materially disposed of a material consciousness necessary for high culture's expectations. In this case, the space of the postnational *rascuache* is truly outside history.

Fashion trends also codify the individual at his or her "best," although the down-but-not-out standpoint of the *rascuache* aesthetics may not prevail entirely in the fashion world. Fashion is an attempt to enhance the position of the wearer, even when the slumming tendencies of grunge, hippie, and hip-hop fashion privilege oversized pants and torn T-shirts. Chicanas/os, like African-Americans, follow a different historical thread and logic that insists on a self-conscious choice for a dress-down look to seem possible, one that admittedly fails within a consumer marketplace where production of body ideologies are always assumed to be Anglo. One of the problems with postmodern chic and Chicana representations of fashion is the entangling of politically subversive dress with historical subjugation. After all, one cannot cure historical colonization with an aesthetic compromise. Fashion carries a distinctive message for the postnational: on the one hand, it suggests art and creativity; on the other hand, it remains bound to both its creators and to the past because what "worked" in one era is soundly rejected in the next.

THE BODY POLITIC

Another facet of stylized dress returns to the notion of cultural capital and rebuilding community. Chicana/o communities, having shed the costumes of the homeland and figuratively removed the headdresses, perform ethnicity in the industrialized world by building upon cultural capital. Politics and cultural capital, two of the most proficient ways of assuring success, consort with hegemonic norms and domination;

they still function as a regulating force that incites conformity but also resistance. To adopt a style is to participate in a socioeconomic milieu. Let us consider the role of women in relation to fashion trends. In the 1970s, Chicanas adopted stylized dress codes that suited the time and their own rebellion with bell-bottom jeans and halter tops accentuating the "exotic" Latina. This choice, combining part feminism and part countercultural movement, made a fashion statement about the Catholic female body on a modernized path.

The sexually evocative nature of Chicanas as stereotypically portrayed, departing from early 1960s sensible dresses, inspired scenes like Abraham Quintanilla's outburst in the film *Selena* when he challenges "the bra," or rather Selena's bustier, a rupturing of the Oedipal confines of an innocent daughter. Whether bra or bustier, the interpretation is in the mind, and in that one small example of many that Chicanas can recount, fashion is, indeed, tied to the body.

Men's idle claims of the objectification of "the look" or "the gaze" find themselves cast as making celebrated and glorious attempts at transgression of gender boundaries, taken as a sign of liberation from sexual mores and constraints. A trend in youth culture toward exposing midriffs as well as buttocks reflects, within a Chicana context, what we might call *la lonja por donde sale* or *con todo para fuera*—let it all hang out. This trend of recent years, common across U.S. college campuses, radically transforms attitudes about the female body. Exposure of the waist apparently does not depend on body type, size, or proportion—only on gender. While "crack" exposure appears to cut across gender lines, the bare waist phenomenon appears to be exclusively an expression of the female body (Simon 2004).

Exposure of physical excess makes even more sense as we consider the reversal of sodomy laws and the proliferation of queer chic in film and television (Fuss 1992). Greater relaxation about queer culture suggests that a trend toward exposing the buttocks reveals a relaxation of sodomy laws per constitutional law. Here, however, the emphasis on the rear end advances a theory, and queer rights happen to coincide with it. When I polled my women's studies classes to consider the reasons for the midriff and butt crack exposure, I asked the students to consider why many women do not express self-consciousness about their shapes in readily revealing their midriffs to the masses. About 75 percent of the students responded that exposing the midriff regardless of its condition reveals a different attitude about the physical body. Others suggested that figures like Paris Hilton and Brittany Spears have influenced the trend, and some respondents even referred to such luminaries as "skanky" and "loose." Some attitudes seem

dauntingly familiar as I concluded the poll. Attitudes about body conformity have indeed changed, and certainly common attitudes about weight
have likewise changed. Exposure of the body pales in comparison to the
excesses of reality television, with its sensationalized scenes and atrophied
lifestyles. The success of reality television has made it possible to return to
a "normal" or more realistic conceptualization of the body, not because our
desire for realism reflects our lives, but more as a salacious desire for oddi-
ties and enigmatic surprises, including tattoos, unusual underwear, and the
like (Lewis 1997).

Against the background of these sentient propositions of the female
body, *On Fashion* (1994), edited by Shari Benstock and Suzanne Ferris,
brings home a final point. In it, Benstock and Ferris take aim at fashion
magazines' extensive disciplinary apparatus, which, the book's contributors
contend, promotes unrealistic beauty norms that produce widespread anxiety and alienation among women. The reinscription of physical codes, especially among marginalized populations, typically employs body evaluations
based on featuring the emaciated Anglo-European woman as an ideal.

With heiress-actor Paris Hilton in jail or not and magazines full of images of her at age eight or nine and a few years later, on beaches and in
skimpy bikinis, on or off diets, the "discipline" to remain youthful and
healthy at the same time is loaded with multiple meanings. Fundamentally,
women in general and women of color even more so have little control over
their bodies or what they wear. This makes adornment all the richer as a
statement about resistance, alienation, or circumventions.

Five

PERFORMATIVITY IN THE
CHICANA/O AUTOBIOGRAPHY

The publication of the autobiography *Hunger of Memory: The
Education of Richard Rodriguez* in 1982 changed our understanding of the
Chicana/o autobiographical tradition.[1] The text, which we might also see
as one of the first Chicana/o queer texts, reveals the problematic fissures of
identity formation in Chicana/o discourse. As much disdain as Rodriguez'
political views have brought to Chicana/o and Latina/o studies alike, *Hunger
of Memory* is still widely read, taught, and written about from various perspectives. Rodriguez did set into motion several polemical issues, making the
case for performativity and more specifically providing a counternarrative
to national culture. Numerous critical revisionary readings have become
available to us in recent decades that account for Rodriguez' apparent ho-
moerotics. These critical readings, however, either view Rodriguez' work in
idolization as a "queer" text or as an "ethnic" autobiography. Rarely are the
questions of Rodriguez' queer voice and the conditions of national identification taken as simultaneous effects. In the national scene, for example,
the American literary establishment initially heralded *Hunger of Memory*
as an American immigrant experience. On the other side of the equation,
Chicana/o scholars were quick to point out that Rodriguez' stances against
affirmative action and bilingual education were in themselves assimilationist propaganda. Part of the controversy stems from Rodriguez' attempt in
his autobiography to model a narrative of ethnic success, intending to distance himself from the cultural Mexican national aesthetics.

   In addition to his sexuality, which was revealed only subsequent to the
publication of *Hunger of Memory*, one of the central points of discussion
brings to the forefront the role of the ethnic minority "intellectual." In the
course of the autobiography, Rodriguez explains his struggles to overcome
language and cultural barriers as a child of Mexican immigrant parents
and characterizes the ambivalences that "excellence" brings to such an

"ethnic" intellectual. Moreover, his autobiography rejects cultural national pride in Chicana/o discourse in lieu of an individualist identity but also as a rhetorical decision that has transformed the reading of the Chicana/o autobiography. Readers of Rodriguez often criticize his rejection of Chicana/o discourse because of the way he has benefited from the American ethnic intellectual literary tradition. In this chapter, I thus focus on the enduring criticisms against Rodriguez by Chicana/o scholars who sense his rejection of minority discourse and, more specifically, identification with the term "Chicana/o."

Rodriguez' *Hunger of Memory* embodies the polemical double bind in Chicana/o race formation. The problems Rodriguez raises for Chicana/o scholarship are distinct from other Chicana/o narratives in that his preoccupation with culture becomes circumscribed in discussions of masculinity, sexuality, intellectual prowess, and performance (Decker 1993, Ortíz 1999). The autobiographical genre thus becomes the locus of performative function, of shame in racial discourse because of the way Rodriguez uses his academic triumphs to sanction criticisms against liberal models that deal with the problem of disenfranchisement among ethnic minorities in the United States; for him, policies like affirmative action were a vulgar biologism in culture (Oliver 1991). One of the sustaining criticisms against Rodriguez is that he unilaterally rejects minority discourse and identification with the term "Chicana/o" as an answer to the problem of disenfranchisement.

Rodriguez contends instead that Mexican-Americans should relinquish their attachments to Mexican culture if they are to succeed in the United States. He proceeds to set up a model of individualism that is voiced through a private/public dichotomy, a distinction he makes to distinguish himself from his parents' disempowered location as Mexican immigrants. His response to the politicization of these identities becomes more evident in the following sequence:

> When, for example, Mexican-American students began to proclaim themselves Chicano, they taught many persons in the barrios of southwestern America to imagine themselves in a new context, the Spanish word slangish, even affectionately vulgar, and, when spoken by a stranger insulting, because it glibly assumed familiarity. Many Americans were consequently shocked when they heard the student activist proclaim himself and his listeners Chicanos. What initially they did not understand was that the English word—which is literally the

> same thing (Mexican American)—was a public word, animated by pride and political purpose.
>
> . . . Let the reader beware at this point: I am not the best person to evaluate the Third World Student Movement. My relationship to many of the self-proclaimed Chicano students was not an easy one. I felt threatened by them. I was made nervous by their insistence that they were still allied to their parents' culture. Walking on campus one day with my mother and father, I relished the surprised look on their faces when they saw some Hispanic wearing serapes pass by. I needed to laugh at the clownish display. (1983, 158–159)

Rodriguez' commentary of the Third World student movement is marked by an uncanny visceral disregard for any display of ethnic pride. His rejection of the self-enunciating claims of the Chicano movement takes root in his understanding of himself as a public intellectual. While his obvious disdain for any conspicuous celebration of Mexican culture is to be noted in this excerpt, he is, nonetheless, cognizant of the limitations of his location as an intellectual when he says, "I am not the best person to evaluate the Third World Student Movement." In the same instance, his characterization of the students' use of traditional Mexican garb as a "clownish display" lacks a certain political irony, one he expects of his readers with regard to his own contradictory location as a minority intellectual. More readily, however, the real threat underlying his response is the ultimate realization of a political alignment between the students' and their parents' social conditions when he says, "I was made nervous by their insistence that they were allied to their parents' culture." The double voice of pathos and propagation of reactionary sympathy for Rodriguez' struggle leads the reader to respond both to his social position as a Chicano and to his political views. This double-pronged effect allows Rodriguez to locate himself as a Mexican-American, without compromising his carefully constructed, public identity as an individualist and intellectual.

His interior struggle, shaped by the discourse of hidden shame, a queer affect, signals more than personal inadequacy, but also an identity function that averts and transforms the process of identification. Because Rodriguez' views on race and language find themselves structured around a private/public dichotomy held by his success in the academy, no less, he positions himself between American individualism and ethnic cultural nationalism.[2] Not only is this dichotomy a false one that magnifies his (personal and) political disdain for social protest, but Rodriguez' recognition of the Berkeley students' ethnic attire and their alliance with their parents' social-political interests also becomes an intellectual ruse for his sexuality. This economy of identification leads Rodriguez to spurn the students' display of ethnic identification as a challenge to his sense of individualism, which would risk fragmentation at the mere thought of being "ethnic." Rodriguez' public/ private split serves to facilitate an understanding of his alienation as an ethnic-minority intellectual. Consequently, Rodriguez' ideological position, managed by his calculated sophistry, departs from any other Chicana/o autobiography at the time in the way he manipulates the process of identification altogether. In addition to this manipulation, his work raises critical assumptions for reading the ethnic body in literature because there is no longer a guarantee of spiritual transcendence or triumph over state power.

If one of the functions of autobiographical disclosure is to locate the subject position of the reader to the author's experiences as an invitation for identification, shame bears some significance in the way the dual action of sympathy and the desire for personal triumph elicits a problem for Chicanas/os' identification. It is not solely the grammatical and rhetorical assumption with which I am concerned here. Rather, the performative influences subject formation generally in the literary process and particularly in narration of racialized subjects. The implication is that the source of power relations in an emergent literary form such as the one under review necessarily encompasses how performativity is one instance in which, as Judith Butler notes, "discourse acts as power" (1990, 5). Working with the same current, the question relevant to this project is: How does a performative function in citizen or racial subject formation take hold? In this case, because of the way Chicana/o literature has developed out of a social interaction with larger discourses of power, namely citizen-subject relations, as well as from racial and cultural factors, shame performs a particular function in forming a literary subject position in the autobiography and its productive effects on citizens.

Such an odd dynamic in Rodriguez' autobiography, I believe, derives from a performative function in direct relationship to the discourse on racial citizenship. Because of the way the adjudication of private citizenship provides Rodriguez with a sense of identification vis-à-vis individualism, he responds virulently to antifederalist notions of identity when he opposes affirmative action and bilingual education, provisions established in the late 1970s as federal redress against minority disenfranchisement. This appears to be one of the fundamental problems behind the private/public distinction. One manifestation of this problem becomes noticeable during his years at Berkeley, when Rodriguez appears conflicted between the gains and attention he has received as a minority student in the English department and his feelings of guilt for having benefited from affirmative action. Despite being labeled a "minority" student, this form of identity formation appears to be a chief source of conflict. It is a problem that he later attributes to the failure of minority discourse to access citizenship and to his family, as Mexican immigrants, having to assimilate into a hostile environment. Strange as it may seem, the problem Rodriguez introduces is one present in California's discourse on race: the discussions about race place a great deal of importance on assimilation, a process that bears specific consequences to immigrant populations. Such a hostile assimilation process could be attributed to California's frontier history, which has shown little sympathy—and much ambivalence after the U.S. conquest—toward immigrant populations.[3]

Even with this hostility, Rodriguez rarely expresses any indignation toward the problem that underlies his failed citizenship; if he does, it is voiced with the approbation of a martyr bent on self-reformation. But the problem that Rodriguez introduces for Chicana/o discourse is one that, I believe, has deconstructive dimensions. These occur as Rodriguez attempts to denaturalize the Chicana/o experience from the quaint explorations of struggle so much a part of the immigrant or the coming-of-age narrative. Rodriguez introduces a persona who is tortured by the condition of his ethnicity at the level of consciousness. The entire autobiography is but a composite of memories that demonstrates how memories are the source of a great deal of anxiety.

The moment of deconstruction, moreover, is tied to the way Rodriguez cannot return to his family and to his feelings of disenchantment with his family's culture. The notion of a point of no return leads the narrative into another realm of signification where his wandering and yearnings belie his restlessness with himself. In addition to this, his achievements in higher education coupled with his obscured (never discussed) gay sensibilities have reached the point of no return, both ontologically and culturally. In the same way, deconstruction forecloses any possible return to an ontological presence; Rodriguez anticipates the complications of his ethnic intellectual consciousness in a similar fashion.

Rodriguez' location as an intellectual and as a closeted gay Chicano leads him into a crisis of signification that is tied to deconstruction, with some detrimental results. It is not the kind of deconstructive moment that leads to "free play" of identity formation. This deconstructive predicament, for Rodriguez, rejects his identity altogether. It makes sense that his aversion to identity formation is tied to many of his racial anxieties, since his return to either his family or his family's culture would precipitate a different narrative outcome. Rodriguez' inability to reproduce the same family constructs through the culture derives from a performative function of shame as an ethnic intellectual. On the one hand, he demonstrates that as an intellectual (of any type), his voice and writing ought to stand on their own, as a condition of his "rights" as an American citizen. On the other hand, his dark complexion, his struggle to achieve a "proper" Anglicized accent, and his immigrant parents stand as examples of what will never be read in the traditional, heroic, "up by their bootstraps" American narrative.

In keeping with the conventional Chicana/o autobiographical narrative, however, Rodriguez uses the educational narrative trope to convey his insider status in Chicana/o literature. The educational narrative is a common form of narration used in contemporary Chicana/o literature to track the internal progression of the subject. Modeled as an ethnic bildungsroman, Rodriguez' autobiography revolves around his educational experience as a first-generation Mexican-American who maneuvers through the institution with some degree of success. This perhaps sets Rodriguez' work apart from other Chicana/o autobiographies in that he appears to distress the process of identification as a social narrative. Rodriguez' autobiography thus stands in bold contrast to other early Chicana/o autobiographies in that his story does not directly question the prevailing forces that structure stereotypes of Chicanas/os or, for that matter, the violent threat that underlies such damaging stereotypes that Chicanas/os sought to remedy through renaming themselves as Chicanas/os and not as Mexicans or Mexican-Americans during the movement.

In lieu of a sustaining criticism against identity formation within the autobiography, Rodriguez expresses a profound sense of self-loathing as a means of dispelling any romantic notion of racial identification. Because of the way this existential crisis of identification affects his intellectual consciousness, Rodriguez compels the reader to another understanding of the ethnic intellectual through the choices he makes to distinguish himself from his family and the unhappy memories from which he draws in stating his position. As with so many autobiographers, however, Rodriguez undergoes a transformation of consciousness through the educational process as a means of reconciling the problem of his identification with his family and their social location in the United States as members of an ethnic minority.

Rodriguez unwittingly collapses the perception of his private and public worlds at various stages of his life. Tension between his public and private lives further complicates the autobiography in the way he details his family life, surprisingly enough, through memories about his racial and gender perceptions. This reveals a rudimentary problem about his so-called private life. His early years with his parents appear to cause great misapprehension about Mexican culture, but a savvy reader senses that these apprehensions are really coded concerns about his masculinity—and his sexuality. These tensions lead Rodriguez to withdraw into an intellectual life that magnifies his disassociation from his family. Rodriguez' public/private distinction also subjects him to particular racial and gender problems, which I will more closely examine in the following segments.

Rodriguez reveals parts of his sexual life that appear carefully encrypted in a discussion about race. He scatters references to his gay sensibilities through the pages of the autobiography in covert details and sweet allusions. The chapter titled "Complexion" is particularly loaded with references to his sexuality. This is an ironic choice of connotation for a discussion that surprisingly appears to be about race, not sexuality. In those few pages, he manages to discuss his teenage years with his family, a time when Rodriguez' sexual anxieties surfaced. The teenage years proved to be critical formative years in the development of his entire autobiography, since they appear as the only references to his perceptions about himself as a figure with basic desires. For example, he writes, "Fifteen, sixteen. I was a teenager. Never dated. Barely could talk to a girl without stammering. In high school I went to dances but never managed to ask a girl out to dance" (127). His shyness could very well make sense were it not for other remarks he makes about his intellectual interests: "Through my reading, however, I developed a fabulous and sophisticated sexual imagination. At seventeen, I may not have known how to engage girls in small talk, but I had read *Lady Chatterly's Lover*" (ibid.). His cognitive desires and sexual awakening converge in a discussion about his love of literature, a trope that shows homosexual promise.

These references to "reading" and "sexuality" link up to another facet of his fascination, for what he, or rather his father, calls "men's work." In the paragraph immediately after the one cited above, Rodriguez moves into a description of the way his father teased his son about never knowing what it means to really work. His father's emphasis on "real" work is reminiscent of the 1980s popular aphorism "Real men don't eat quiche." His father's statement seeks to emphasize that "real" men work at hard labor, while he (Richard) partakes of the soft labors of intellectual life. Rodriguez responds, "At such times I suspected that education was making me effeminate. The odd thing, however, was that I did not judge my classmates so harshly. Nor did I consider my male teachers in high school effeminate. It was only myself I judged against some shadowy, Mexican laborer—dark like me, yet very different" (127). This preoccupation with seeming effeminate develops in concert with his intellectual work. It is his dark, Mexican, male body that feels betrayed by his intellectual pursuits. Perhaps the most perplexing aspect of this problem stems from one recollection in which his fascination for the dark, Mexican, male body can be seen as an enlargement of his sexual fetish:

> I continued to see braceros, those men I resembled in one way, and in another way, didn't resemble at all. On the watery horizon of a Valley afternoon, I'd see them. Though I feared looking like them, it was with silent envy that I regarded them still. I envied their physical lives, their freedom to violate the taboo of the sun. Closer to home, I would notice the shirtless construction workers, the roofers, the sweating men tarring the street in front of the house. In addition, I would see the Mexican gardeners. I was unwilling to admit the attraction for their lives. I was unwilling to admit it by looking away. However, what was denied became strongly desired. (126)

It is not simply that he admires the "shirtless workers" for their toil in the "hot sun"; he also admires them for their physical presence, their physical beauty. He is clearly gazing and forming a sensuous representation of these men at work. Reminiscent of Wordsworth gazing down at the marsh in *The Prelude*, Rodriguez begins the paragraph with a "romantic" description of the Rio Grande Valley and the men as they work: "I envied their lives, their freedom to violate the taboo of the sun." Violating the taboo of the sun encompasses the sexuality of the complexion he is trying to access; he envies their freedom to expose their bodies without concern for the way it may affect their complexion. Rodriguez' "fear" of looking at the men unlike himself suggests a self-conscious homoerotic gaze that is transcended by his admiration of their work. Rodriguez' gaze is once again fixed on the problem of identifying (openly) with a Chicana/o body, a point of identification that is diffused into an intellectual discussion about the sexually symbolic virtues of dark men.

In the passage regarding "the shirtless construction workers" it becomes clear that he does not simply admire the men solely for their work. He is more aware of the sensual presence of the men around him in ways that he may not have thought of in describing the women or the girls from his youth or even the students protesting on the Berkeley campus. However, the last line in this paragraph sums up the whole question of his gay sensibility: "However, what was denied became strongly desired." At first glance, it does appear that he is playing with words by declaring his attraction for these men as part of an unrealized homoerotic experience. The deep source of his sexual inhibitions, however, returns to his early childhood experiences, much of which, I suspect, relate to his linguistic development during his early childhood development.

Another popular trope of cultural difference is the instance of language fluency in which Rodriguez strategically situates himself as a commentator on bilingual education. He accordingly recognizes the symbolic power that language possesses in determining his ethnic identity. For Rodriguez, the English language is about mastery over the public space. By relegating Spanish to the private sphere, he decidedly turns on his parents for their inability to speak the English language. During these critical moments in the autobiography, he wrestles with some of the other complications that arise from issues surrounding language and the public space. These are moments when Rodriguez draws from childhood experiences regarding language and appears to veer into a conversation about his masculinity. This occurs primarily through Rodriguez' tensions with his father. It is already obvious that Rodriguez' father is a central figure to his son's perceptions of language. What is of significance here, however, is Rodriguez' relationship with his parents and his perceptions of language during these early years. It is an unusual relationship with his parents because of the way English influences certain aspects of his life with his family. In "The Middle Class Pastoral," Rodriguez describes some of these tensions from his childhood:

> I was a listening child, careful to hear the very different sounds
> of Spanish and English. Wide-eyed with hearing, I'd listen
> to sounds more than words. First, there were English (*gringo*)
> sounds. So many words were still unknown that when the
> butcher or the woman at the drugstore said something to me,
> exotic polysyllabic sounds would bloom in the midst of their
> sentences. (13)

This moment draws our attention to his awareness of difference in language. He distinguishes English as a foreign and exotic language of *gringo* sounds. Spanish is the language of his family and the colonized. This distinction denotes the divide between the Anglo world and the Spanish-language world of his parents. His revelations about the English language suggest his eventual desire to be immersed in the dominant language and to belong to American culture. Rodriguez, once again, distinguishes between the public, English-speaking world of the educational system and the private, Spanish-speaking world of his parents. The contrast in the symbolic power of language becomes obvious. Here Rodriguez describes the world as it shapes his perceptions of his family:

> But despite all they achieved, perhaps because they had so much to achieve, any deep feeling of ease, the confidence of "belonging" in public was withheld from them both. They regarded the people at work, the faces in the crowd, as very distant from us. They were the others, *los gringos*. That term was interchangeable in their speech with one another, even more telling, *los americanos*. (12)

"The confidence of 'belonging'" is a sentiment he senses with respect to his parents. Rodriguez' discomfort with his parents as outsiders in the language paradigm is a feeling that would shape his relationship to language later on, during his academic years. In this figuration, he recognizes English as the national language of the Anglo culture that excludes his parents. Sensing that his parents do not quite fit the American mold because they do not speak English, he constructs a public/private dichotomy to reconcile the segregated worlds. However, it is his relationship with his father that cultivates his desire for an American identity. It is a concern that is strangely attached to his masculine identity. The deep yearning for belonging, as a code for his outsider status, resurfaces once again in the "Complexion" chapter when he describes his understanding of the role of language:

> Language was crucial. I know that I had violated the ideal world of the *macho* by becoming such a dedicated student of language and literature. *Machismo* was a word never exactly defined by the person who used it. (It was described in the proper behavior of men.) Women at home, nevertheless, world repeat the Mexican dictum that a man should be *Feo, fuerte y formal* [ugly, strong, and reserved]. "The three F's," my mother called them, smiling slyly. (128)

The popular Mexican folk adage *Feo, fuerte y formal* is one that complicates Rodriguez' self-perception with respect to language. Once again language and literature appear in the same conversation about his masculine behavior. How does he then violate the macho world by "becoming such a dedicated student of language and literature"? Rodriguez appears to make the connection between language as feminine and reserved silence as masculine. If language was crucial to him then, how does his behavior now as an intellectual interfere with his identity as a macho and as an adult? He describes the macho ethos according to the *Feo, fuerte y formal* dictum:

> However, a man was not talkative in a way a woman could be. It was permitted a woman to be gossipy and chatty. (When one heard many voices in a room, it was usually women who were talking.) Men spoke much less rapidly. In addition, often men spoke in monologues. (When one voice sounded in a crowded room men spoke in monologue.) More important than any of this was the fact that a man never verbally revealed his emotions . . . Men did not speak about their unease in moments of crisis or danger. It was the woman who worried aloud when her husband got laid off from work. At times of illness or death in the family, a man was usually quiet. Even silent. Women spoke up to voice prayers. In distress women always sounded quick ejaculations to God or the Virgin; women prayed in clearly audible voices at a wake held in a funeral parlor. In addition, on the subject of love, a woman was verbally expansive. She spoke of her yearning and delight. A married man, if he spoke publicly about love usually did so with playful mischievous irony. Younger, unmarried men more often were quiet. (The macho is a silent suitor. *Formal*) (128–129)

Rodriguez' reference to the "formal" aspects of machismo extends into his description of the cultural codes of conduct for masculinity as part of the performance of masculinity. However, he clearly states that he has indeed violated the code of masculinity by "becoming such a dedicated student of language and literature." This violation of the macho code indicates at least two possibilities. One is the working-class assumption that real men do not undertake literary study as serious work. The effeminization of the academic profession is another possibility, because it is the literary field that allows him to gain voice—language and expression of language are effeminate. It is also quite possible that Rodriguez may be alluding to his homosexuality again, an aspect of his personality that remains a suppressed part of the autobiography. Still, Rodriguez, on occasion, manages to divulge little suggestive remarks in order to reveal those suppressed parts of his life. Rodriguez' autobiography could then be seen as a treatise on "belonging," whether it is a sense of linguistic belonging or, as a macho, a belonging betrayed by his homosexual desires and as the intellectual who is an exile from his ethnic community.

Robert Folkenflik, in "The Self as Other" (1993), suggests that one of the reasons for writing an autobiography is to contrast the self in opposition: "The form that the opposition between the two selves takes is accompanied by imagery of sickness versus health, darkness versus light, bondage versus freedom, sleeping versus waking, birth versus death" (216). Folkenflik indicates further that the displacement of the traditional Augustinian autobiography is a "self that comes through as self-hatred rather than self-love" (ibid.), and this refers to the way confession transforms the spirit out of decay.

Rodriguez uses similar motivations by directing his narrative from silence to articulation, from invisibility to representation, and from negotiating the problems that arise from this racial location to his intellectual reawakening. While the self in opposition may seem to be a series of dichotomies that structure his reality, with the private/public split as the most obvious opposition of all, his perception of himself cannot maintain this distinction without some serious understanding of the role these distinctions play in his mind. The self in opposition for Rodriguez is also between the Anglo world and the Mexican world, between the chattering female space and the formal, silent masculine realm, between the working-class world and the middle-class intellectual persona, and, finally, between a world filled with dignity to one that is shamed. The double voice of shame and dignity captivates the reader simply by virtue of the illusion of the narrative of the ethnic intellectual, wherein Rodriguez uses the educated voice in the autobiography to formalize an authentic narrative. I am not simply stating that his narrative is part fiction or that authors fall into the trappings of any account that may be an amalgamation of certain memories. Rodriguez' subject position is adjudicated by his public identity and not by those that are historically generated from his family's experiences, that is, experiences that would endear his family to him as a source of identification.

The performative, in his case and in others, is a stated action that upon its enunciation creates the desired reality. Rodriguez' sequence of life experiences is of less concern; rather, his form of articulation suggests that he is inhabited by a larger problem in discourse. The autobiography can be said to be a part of speech act theory, if in this case Rodriguez' identity is shaped upon the enunciation of his subject location. This is the first condition necessary for the performative function to occur. The second condition of the performative elicits the illocutionary force expressed at the moment of transformation or conversion. A dual function of both the autobiographical narrative (as constative) action and the illocutionary force attributed to his race are formed by the social discourse on shame. It is not important that it is not of Rodriguez' own volition that this performative function takes place, nor is it a product of the self-aggrandizing function of the autobiographical genre. It is the force that generates an effect that results from social conditions, and those determine subjects in articulation. This we can recognize through the young Rodriguez' recognition of power differentials in the distinction of the Mexican world as a racialized other. A condition is expressed as a condition of Anglo discourse that deforms his understanding of citizen-subject formation in an idealized fiction. The shamed self thus is the one that is acted upon through the cultural codes of citizenship presented through linguistic and, later on, racial deformations.

We can say that Rodriguez' narrative is tacitly about a dispossessed identity, and the point of reference is that of the dominant discourse. He speaks as a marginal citizen who has internalized the dominant culture, but consequently, his own self-making cannot purge him of the hegemonic discourse. His past may be the occasion for the story, but his present outlines the ideological forces that determine and structure meaning. The basis of shame thus revolves around an autobiographical scheme in which the individual's subjective relationship to the structures of power is revealed in a hermeneutic that involves identification and disavowal as a simultaneous effect. The adjudication of citizenship through racialization, affirmative action, and bilingual education would mark him in such a way as to render him as a subject in relation to the power dimensions that he is consciously processing and is determined to overcome. The reader is left wondering: Will he succeed? And that affords him enormous sway among mainstream readers who will or can identify with his "predicament" but not for reasons, as he suggests, that are important.

Thus far I have tried to illustrate how the performative in Rodriguez' autobiography reconstitutes the racialized subject as one who has developed from an undesirable past. The integrity attributed to the "I" in the narrative is one that readers impulsively attribute to Rodriguez as the author. Through the confessional aspects of the story, the autobiography properly places Rodriguez as a reliable source of personal information free from nefarious intentions. Most striking and odd about Rodriguez' autobiography is the way he experiences the assimilation process. It seems that the process of assimilation for the Californian hinges considerably on subject formation based on language. The terms by which Rodriguez expresses his subject formation develop more clearly through his masculinity or in adulthood. It is a complication he relates over and over again about the way he has to develop himself despite the obvious attacks to his person.

The shame in his life creates unstable moments for Rodriguez in the autobiography because the manifestation of power consistently acts upon his body through an emotive realization of racial subject position. This realization occurs as an injurious act that he reverts against his family. Because his own physical body cannot process the epistemic trappings of any racialization, Rodriguez is caught between politicizing himself and assimilating. This internalization occurs at various moments in his life. In one, he recalls his response to the racial epithets directed at him:

> In public, I occasionally heard racial slurs. Complete strangers would yell out at me. A teenager drove past, shouting, "Hey Greaser! Hey Pancho!" Over his shoulder I saw the giggling face of his girlfriend. A boy pedaled by and announced matter of factly, "I pee on dirty Mexicans." Such remarks would be said so casually that I wouldn't quickly realize that they were addressed at me. When I did I would be paralyzed with embarrassment, unable to return the insult." (117)

The paralysis Rodriguez describes here represents the physiological consequences of the racial epithet. The performative function of shame here suggests the act of naming him "Greaser." The direction of the epithet is from a position of perceived social power that renders him speechless. The power to name him and to render him speechless in the delivery of the epithet acts to force the reality of his racial subject position. The epithet is realized through the signifying economy of power differentials that secures the Anglo boy's naming of Rodriguez as an act of social aggression, because what is implied in the boy's derogatory remark is the ability to secure his racial status in the situation, however lame it may seem. Rodriguez recognizes that he is unable to counter such aggression with a statement that carries equal weight. The obvious direction of the terms "Hey Greaser! Hey Pancho!" serves as a reminder of his social position, as his race is called into the process of the naming to constitute his subject position.

In order for the racist slur to take hold, it must be reinforced by a larger discourse on race. It is not the mere incidental derision of one teenager alone that creates the impact of the racial epithet. It is the sanctioning of racial dominance that is achieved. As such, the racist slur has the power to name without consent of the one who is being named, and its potential for assault is part of the racist culture that Rodriguez experiences in his life. To conclude that none of these actions may have contributed to his indignation in the autobiography would be an outstanding breach of humanness, since in the rest of his life he seems to be trying to overcome these events. The effects the epithets thrust on the psychic dimensions of individual cognition are not only as real and irrefutable as a physical attack but also are putative throughout his life.

> In all there could have been more than a dozen incidents
> in name-calling. That there were so few suggests that I was
> not a primary victim of racial abuse. But that, even today,
> I can clearly remember particular incidents is proof of their
> impact. Because of such incidents, I listened when my parents
> remarked that Mexicans were often mistreated in California
> border towns. (117)

Rodriguez' suggestion that these dozen or so incidents could appear as just a "few" boggles my mind. He at least recognizes that the slurs implicate others, since other Mexicans are treated badly in California border towns. The threat of violence is marked by a condition of racial otherness that persists in the collective experience of his family as his parents comment on the condition of other Mexicans. Although the words refer to his racialized identity, he associates these accounts with an empathetic familiarity. Rodriguez follows this segment with a commentary about racial injustice in the Southern civil rights movement but makes little connection between his own dark skin and racism. As he speaks in more detail about his experiences, he grieves over his dark complexion: "Dark skin was for my mother the most important symbol of a life of oppressive labor and poverty. But both my parents recognized other symbols as well" (119). This sentiment pervades his memories of his family. The complication of his race as an expression about dark skin is reported, oddly enough, as a condition of poverty that blacks experienced during the civil rights movement. Again, the point of injury seems to be largely cathexed by the family situation he would later criticize through language; the public space seems to be one that problematizes his relationship with his family, as is marked by his comments on dark skin.

> However, it was one thing for *me* to speak English with difficulty. It was more troubling for me to hear my parents speak

> in public: their high whining vowels and guttural consonants; ·
> their sentences got stuck with "eh" and "ah" sounds; the con-
> fused syntax; the hesitant rhythm of sounds so different from
> the way *gringos* spoke. I'd notice, moreover, that my parents'
> voices were softer than those *gringos* we'd meet. (15)

Not only is Rodriguez preoccupied by his own abilities with the English language, he ascribes fluency as the dominant voice/body that he is attempting to locate. Saying that his parents have "softer" voices suggests that
they possess less authority than "those *gringos*." In this sense, the situation
qualifies as a misfire, because once again he assigns cultural dominance to
Anglo culture; he essentially ascribes the dimensions of power that consolidate racial differences. He, as a child, cannot process the relationship between his parents' language abilities and the Anglo world, and he therefore
internalizes his parents' insecurities with the language as their subordinate
position in the English-speaking world, from childhood into adulthood.

Rodriguez then makes the observation that it is not only diction and
pronunciation that clue him in on the dynamics of the discourse. Rather, it
is a deeply conscious gesture of inferiority expressed by his parents' "softer"
voices, that is, softer than the *gringos*', that causes him consternation. If
at that early age Rodriguez can understand the effect the language differences mean in relation to his family, then what, if anything, prevents
him from expressing indignation instead of shame? The role of shame, in
this instance, procures the subject location of the speaker in relation to the
language. One cannot help but consider how language shapes Rodriguez'
consciousness in relation to the social powers that appear to influence his
perception and memories in such a way that he conjures them through a
trope on race. At other times, Rodriguez' ruminations about his complexion suggest the internalized racism that some Mexicans express by favoring
light over dark skin. One unique moment offers a glimpse into his perceptions about his complexion in his family. Once again color plays a role in
his understanding of himself sexually through his "dark" complexion.

> Complexion. My first conscious experience of sexual excite-
> ment concerns my complexion. One summer weekend, when
> I was around seven years old, I was at a public swimming pool
> with the whole family. I remember sitting on the damp pave-
> ment next to the swimming pool and seeing my mother, in
> the spectator bleachers, holding my younger sister on her lap.
> My mother, I noticed, was watching my father as he stood on

a diving board, waving to her. I watched her wave back. Then I saw her radiant, bashful, astonishing smile. In that second I sensed that my mother and father had a relationship I knew nothing about. A nervous excitement encircled my stomach as I saw my mother's eyes follow my father's figure curving into the water. A second or two later, he emerged. I heard him call out. Smiling, his voice sounded, buoyant, calling me to swim with him. But turning to see him, I caught my mother's eye. I heard her shout over to me. In Spanish, she called through the crowd "Put a towel over your shoulders." In public she did not want to say why. I knew.

That incident anticipates the shame and sexual inferiority I was to feel in later years because of my dark complexion. I was to grow up an ugly child. Or one who thought himself ugly. (*Feo*) (39)

This passage begins with the admission that his first "sexual excitement" involves a recollection of his skin color. What is clearly depicted as a primal scene between a son and his parents turns into a moment of internalized panic about his own complexion. The moment just before his mother asks him to put on a towel to cover his shoulders, Rodriguez anticipates going into the water at his father's initiation, but he is disconcerted by his mother's remark to cover his dark body.

The scene is posed as a moment filled with anticipation when he carefully watches his mother gaze over his father, who is delighting in the water. The point of sexual excitement does not seem to be fixed on the mother as love object; rather, he admires his mother, as they both look at his father in the water. He describes the moment as such, seeing "her radiant, bashful, astonishing smile." Even though he watches his mother admire his father, he in fact responds to the sensuality expressed by his mother in response to his father. The emphasis of the action is centered on the father as the object of their attention. The connection between his sexual inferiority is without question a remark on his sensibility as a gay man, not being able to survive the reality of both his conservative political beliefs and the reality of his racialized body.

This entire episode could be regarded as what Judith Butler refers to as "refusal of identification" (1997b). This moment elicits the refusal of identification based on Rodriguez' initial recognition of a sensual experience between his mother and father as she watches her husband swim. The sensual act is then transmitted back into Rodriguez as a self-consciousness gaze refracted from his mother's caveat to cover his dark body and ultimately interrupting the assimilation of his sexual excitement, that is, a sexual excitement conditioned on a self-valuative claim that turns to shame as part of a homosexual prohibition—"cover your shoulders."

Butler notes that part of the "prohibition on homosexuality preempts the process of grief and prompts a melancholic identification which effectively turns homosexual desire back upon itself" (142). This turning back upon itself is precisely the action of self-berating that he feels, which stems from his comments about concealing his dark skin. This refusal of identification accounts for the way Rodriguez uses his "complexion" to conceal and discuss his sexuality and to viscerally discharge points of identification. This turning back upon itself is then expressed through the prohibition of exposing the dark body in the public space. The performative act of shame occurs through a delicate, coded discussion of skin color.

Drawing from the preceding segment, Rodriguez' relationship with his father is curious. Through it, he establishes the primary understanding of power relations that leads him to refuse to identify with his father as a racial and masculine figure and, in the same discourse, to disqualify the family and community as part of the shared experience of relatedness. The relationship between father and son is one that blends with confused apprehension of the discursive—shame or embarrassment. One such episode at a gasoline station captures the essence of this situation once again when he listens to his father involved in a conversation with a gas station attendant:

> There were many times like the night at a brightly lit gas station (a blaring white memory) when I stood uneasily, hearing my father. He was talking to a teenaged attendant. I do not recall what they were saying, but I cannot forget the sounds my father made as he spoke. At one point his words slid together to form one word—sounds confused as the threads of blue and green oil in the puddle next to my shoes. His voice rushed through what he had left to say. And toward the end reached falsetto notes, appealing to his listener's understanding. I looked away to the lights of the passing automobiles, I tried not to hear anymore. But I heard only too well the calm easy tones in the attendant's reply. Shortly afterwards, walking toward home with my father, I shivered when he put his hand on my shoulder. The very first chance that I got, I evaded his grasp and ran on ahead into the dark, skipping with feigned boyish exuberance. (15)

The muddled representation of his father trying to speak English is brought forth in a memory "of blue and green oil in the puddle next to my shoes." This was not the only time he "stood uneasily hearing" his father. Rodriguez creates a stark image of the memory using genuineness of feeling to portray the moment as "blaring" and "white," which add to the severity of the recollection.

Rodriguez remains quiet as he listens to his father's agonized effort to communicate with the young attendant. It is here that Rodriguez' masculinity is threatened by the loss of his father's authority. The discourse of power is firmly grounded in the diction and clarity of English. Even as a child, he recognized the social position structured in the telling of this narrative. He establishes this by comparatively situating his father with the "teenaged attendant." Rodriguez compares the methods of articulation each actor expresses. He notes his father's sliding words and, most tellingly, the way his father's voice reaches an imploring "falsetto."

He essentially effeminizes his father's manner of communication in a final disidentifying slam. The gas station attendant, though not specifically marked by race, still manifests the image of a young, white, English-speaking male unable to communicate with the haltingly bilingual Mexican man. The teenager speaks in "calm easy tones." There is, however, something strange about this episode that Rodriguez has left virtually unexplained, perhaps an oversight or in the fictionalized liberties taken by autobiographical discourse. Even though the voices are framed in the blaring gaze of the white and bright gas station, father and child possess no car and simply walk home that evening.

The episode suggests that his father's broken English produces a salient impression of the power of language. Even class is transcendent in this moment, whereby speech (or the lack thereof) creates subject positions despite the structural claims to power offered by the gas station attendant. Rodriguez, at a young age, understands power differentials enough to elicit a visceral response from the disparaging effects of a subject's positioning at the level of the unconscious. In some respects, power is generated within a "deep structure" of meaning, in which the cultural codes of articulation are impressed at the grammatical level. The unquestionable legitimacy of English stands out as a "blaring white memory" that figuratively derogates Rodriguez' understanding of his father to one of a powerless actor. The effeminization of his father's tone slipping steadily into falsetto heightens the sense of shame that Rodriguez distinguishes for himself. It is with assertive guile that Rodriguez attempts to rework the memories of his past through a self-reflective moment. He says of himself, "I remind myself of my separation from my past, bring memory to silence. I turn to consider the boy I once was in order, finally, to describe the man I am now. I remember what was so grievously lost to define what was necessarily gained" (6). The melancholia in his tone in the opening chapter does appear to set the mood of the autobiography.

Rodriguez sets up a social paradigm that embodies the public/private split, a distinction that further alienates him from his culture as a private citizen. But even the public persona is constrained by the problems in his autobiography:

> Language has been the great subject of my life. In college and graduate school, I was registered as "English major." But well before then, from my first day of school, I was a student of language. Obsessed by the way it determined my public identity. The way it permits me here to describe myself, my writing. (7)

Ramón Saldívar argues in *Chicano Narrative: The Dialectics of Difference* that Rodriguez constructs a false binarism between the private and public in order to situate an ideological dilemma. The existing problems are the identity constructions of affirmative action and bilingual education as interpellations of racial identity, which mark Rodriguez so as to render him within a set of psychosocial determinations that he cannot control.

> In Rodriguez' story, this privileging of the private is significant because of what happens to the assumed binary relationship between the "private" and the "public" self. His vision reduces the interplay between these two constitutive human realms to the overpowering order of the private order of the *private* world. The social, political, historical world of bilingual education and affirmative action is illuminated only insofar as it relates to his private fate. The essence of that world in itself remains, therefore, peripheral to the central concern of his story." (1990a, 161)

The privileging of the private is correct if we consider that the narrative is contemplative of the reversal of his past, and the conversion occurs from a position of *aphanasis* (a silence represented by his inability to speak English) to that of a willful agent. Other modes of communication arise—the tone and quality of the voice emerge and communicate power, while "calm assured" tones signify a stable place of articulation. The public Richard Rodriguez emerges as a category interpellated by cultural and national identities that provide him a recognizable structure of articulation—all the joy and pleasures of identity.

Rodriguez also experiences drama and passion in his religious faith. Both the private and the public sphere were considerably cast into the depth of his religion. The dourness and solemnity of being Catholic and practicing Catholicism separated him from his education and his existential sense of direction as well. Though religion in a sense interpellated his moral boundaries, he nevertheless wrapped himself in the veil of piety as the good boy.

> I grew up a Catholic at home and at school, in private and in public. My mother and father were deeply pious *catolicos*; all my relatives were Catholics. At home, there were holy pictures on a wall of nearly every room, and a crucifix hung over my bed. My first twelve years as student were spent in Catholic schools where I could look up to the front of the room and see a crucifix hanging over the clock. (1983, 77)

Religion seems to embody both the public and private designation. Unlike the separate sphere created from his language and family life, Rodriguez does not seem to separate the religion into a public/private split. The constancy of religion indicates a reverence for faith and practice that appears beneficial to his public and private life. For him, religion is comfort and resolution that remains constant throughout his childhood and on through his adult life. Rodriguez portrays this reverence for religion but is symptomatically excited by the possibility of its transgression. The segment "Credo" elucidates his interpretation of religion as it determined the moral and ethical views that contribute to his scholastic achievements.

> The Church, in fact, excited more sexual wonderment than it repressed. I regarded with awe the "wedding ring" on a nun's finger, her black wedding veil—symbols of marriage to God. I would study pictures of martyrs—white robed virgins fallen in death and the young, almost smiling. (84)

The passion with which Rodriguez regards the Catholic faith supports his ability to sustain one element of his childhood that remains with him in later years. This regard for religion is one virtue he constructs himself in the classical sense.

Raymond Paredes, in "Autobiography and Ethnic Politics: Richard Rodriguez' *Hunger of Memory*" (1992), suggests that Rodriguez' autobiography follows a conventional conversion pattern that parodies the Christian model of renunciation (285). Within this Christian worldview, the model of conversion is achieved through Rodriguez' renunciation of his "racial consciousness," while at the same time Paredes notes that Rodriguez "cannot ignore it (racial consciousness)" (283). Paredes believes the conversion narrative in the evolution of the American autobiographical ethnic tradition is a naive rendering of romantic yearnings and is symptomatic of a condition of intense alienation in advanced capitalist societies. This situation leads to what Paredes suggests is a need to create "a romantic recollection of one's past" (ibid.). Citing another contradictory reference to "The Middle Class Pastoral," Paredes notes that Rodriguez appropriates the conventional aspects of the pastoral to accentuate his "affinity" for Anglo-American values and tastes while renouncing his Mexican identity. Paredes elaborates on Rodriguez' class disposition:

> Such a literary undertaking would be laudable particularly if it induced political action on behalf of the poor, but Rodriguez' work has the opposite effect. His assertions of sympathy for the poor are undermined by his own eager abandonment of his ethnic traditions and his failure to present any details of lower class culture that the reader may admire. (286)

Henry Staten argues in "Authenticity, Class, and Autobiography: The Case of *Hunger of Memory*" (1998) that Rodriguez' critics (Chicanas/os) miss the point in Rodriguez' denunciation of identitarian claims: "I believe, however, that Rodriguez' critics have not sufficiently noted the irony in his view of himself when he describes his remade mode of being" (104). The sense of irony could easily be understood as an attempt to distance himself as a marginal subject. It is helpful to recall that the Chicana/o movement itself was based largely on the performative function that Staten calls "identitive," and the Chicana/o movement, like the Black Power movement, was based on the linguistic principle of transvaluation and not entirely on performativity. The renaming of Chicanas/os is indeed based on a politically self-conscious act intended to offset the damaging effects of racism. The biggest failure in Staten's essay is that he uses buzz words of the 1980s drawn from the characterization of minorities as participants of, or in, identity politics; such phrases are meant to characterize simplistically or reductively a movement that took place thirty years ago, but they miss the mark in the choice of descriptors.

Staten fails to explain the performative element in Rodriguez' autobiography and simply relates the performative function as an identity-based, self-enunciatory act attributed to the Chicana/o movement. The performative is by all accounts an act of power that is possible solely within discourse, and the power to actualize the performative within discourse can be self-generated for any political ideology, liberal, radical, or conservative. Like Foucaultian notions of power, the performative function does not espouse one institution, group, or individual; rather, as it is understood here, the idea of the performative in the formation of the racialized intellectual is to look at the conditions that predicate the autobiography.

The "identitive" Staten loosely describes fails as a performative function based upon the smallest criteria outlined by J. L. Austin in *How to Do Things with Words* (1980) and fails even more seriously at the level Judith Butler regards in the assignment of constitutive identity function in *Gender Trouble* (1990). Either way one looks at the identitive, performativity is not primarily a self-enunciating practice—one can find more performativity in magical thinking than in the political realm. The lack of irony derives from the simplistic binaries Rodriguez conjures in the public/private dichotomy. Norma Alarcón in "Tropology of Hunger" (1998) notes that the public/private split strikes an imbalance in the use of certain terms that reveal the author's ethnic identification:

> Rodriguez' deployment of these political categories [private/public] in his work is part of a noncritical education that in effect leads him to the "unsustainable" refusal of ethnicity, except as a private phenomenon of ethnic exceptionalism that is then opposed to his construction of a public persona. Notwithstanding the historical naiveté of his political positions— which make him a popular public speaker in neoconservative spheres—it is the structural and rhetorical traffic experienced between culture and politics, which he cannot neatly sever into the private and public, that undermines the political persona to which, in his view, we should all aspire. (142)

Alarcón locates Rodriguez' argumentation as an attempt to resurrect the liberal bourgeois subject and cites this slippage where the cultural and the political seem to pose a dilemma in Rodriguez' articulation of his ethnic consciousness through the public and private split. The "trope of hunger," which Alarcón identifies as a specter that develops from the fictive citizen, attains fruition because of the racial terms within the nation that render the immigrant short of a discourse of identity formation. Thus, the hunger for an identity within a divisive social apparatus becomes a compulsive action that is repeated within Rodriguez' autobiography and conditions the basis of the narrative. In this sense, Rodriguez' voicing of citizenship places him at odds with his disavowal of racial identification by focusing on the authentic citizen-subject as a substitute for a racialized position:

> Yet Rodriguez' marking of his difference works not only in the direction of the (im)migrant worker but also in the direction of the authentic (i.e., Anglo American) nonalien, without much grasp of the production of an alien(n)ation insofar as the immigrant has no "ground" for a "public" persona. The autobiographical impulse moves toward dis-alien(n)ation through the desire not to be ethnized as "Chicano" and "Mexican-American" but rather one who is an "American," as Rodriguez claims in his essay, "An American Writer." (144)

Citing the double consciousness with which Rodriguez positions himself provokes a more dubious understanding of the performative. Alarcón registers one such effect when Rodriguez dislocates himself as the immigrant subject. The overarching claim that Rodriguez makes from the onset is that language, as a public discourse, is a source of immeasurable power in his life, in its ability both to stigmatize and to activate personal pleasure. Once Rodriguez procures mastery over the dominant language, he therefore is less subjected in the public sphere and carries the ability to procure mastery through masculinity. Having already experienced failed masculinity through his father's discourse, he can now procure the effects of masculinity through an articulated (calm easy tones of) recognition of his manhood in the public space. The public space appears to consolidate his perceptions of a stable world. While he denounces the secretive aspects of the domestic sphere within his family, in autobiographical writing Rodriguez declares himself a public being:

> Here is my most real life. My book is necessarily political, in the conventional sense, for public issues—editorials and ballot stubs, petitions and placards, faceless formulations of greater and lesser good by greater and lesser minds—have dissected my life and changed its course. And, in some broad sense, my writing is political because it concerns my movement away

from the company of family and into the city. This was my
coming of age: I became a man by becoming a public man. (7)

Rodriguez' characterization of his political writings leads to a discussion
of the various conditions of power that he confronts throughout his life.
In this instance, the educational institution becomes a nodal point where
power acts as discourse. His voice, perceptions, and identity are cleaved
within the educational institution, and in other respects, breaking away
from his family also marks his entry into the masculine public space. This
entry into the public space, while indicative of his "coming of age," also
marks his "becoming a public man." Rodriguez' desire to be "an American"
reflects a sense of coherence and legitimacy, which he encounters as a necessity of citizen-subject formation. The autobiography of Richard Rodriguez
thus corresponds to the withdrawal of the "I" that he associates with his
Mexican family and his private life and the designation of his public "I,"
which is capable of renouncing his past. The distinction between the public and private, moreover, indicates how the social stigmatization of shame
that he encounters within the public space structures the public man. Rodriguez manages his words well and at times offers intensive metaphorical
language to underscore his intellectual prowess and his success. Here one
finds the private Richard Rodriguez, often cast as the "young boy," an innocent observer, the son, who is haunted by his childhood fears of inferiority. But it is Richard Rodriguez the dark-skinned, indigenous-looking
Mexican who characterizes the discourse of shame and the marked category of powerlessness.

> In adulthood I am embarrassed by childhood fears. And in
> a way it didn't matter very much that my parents could not
> speak English with ease. Their linguistic difficulties had no
> serious consequences. My mother and father made themselves
> understood at the county hospital clinic and at government
> offices. And yet, in another way, it mattered very much—it
> was unsettling to hear them struggle with English. Hearing
> them I'd grow nervous, my clutching trust in their protection
> and power weakened. (Ibid.)

The source of such powerlessness in this excerpt reveals that Rodriguez
is dealing with childhood traumas throughout his autobiography. The ambivalence with which he treats his parents' language problems suggests

that he blamed his parents for his own developmental insecurities. Urged to overcome his childhood fears of the public space, Rodriguez chose assimilation in an attempt to overcome "the wall of silence" that created the public/private split between his family and himself. Educated by nuns in Catholic school at a young age, Rodriguez underwent a long process of renewal when his parents encouraged their children to learn English. Rodriguez eventually overcame his shyness and diffidence within public Anglo culture, but his obvious sense of humiliation was directed later at the affirmative action policies and bilingual education programs that he associated with the Mexican-American plight in the United States.

Ramón Saldívar identifies one of the problems with Rodriguez' autobiography as a "lack of true philosophical self-analysis" and argues that the repressed economy of the "private" voice fails to consider the "historical projections that constitute him as subject" (1990a, 161). Rodriguez, however, constantly constitutes himself through language and therefore reconstitutes himself in the present as he rewrites his past. Saldívar's focus on ideology provides another answer about the trappings of discourse itself:

> I would also suggest that Rodriguez' autobiography suffers as a poetic self expression. He offers his autobiography as a "pastoral," a kind of literature that draws a contrast between the innocence and serenity of the simple life and the corruption and chaos of urban life. But even in its most naive forms, the pastoral always recognizes that the desire for the innocent and serene past is unfortunately always nostalgic. (Ibid.)

As a student of "Renaissance" literature, Rodriguez' references to Caliban in *The Tempest* likewise gesture toward his familiarity with traditional canonical literature while at the same time situating himself within the discourse of otherness. Shakespeare's Caliban figure in *The Tempest* represents the colonial condition of having to master the dominant language; an ambivalent relationship to the dominant language constitutes Caliban's role and his relationships of power that converge on the act of speech as power. In this sense, Caliban experiences the shameful act of speaking the dominant language, but Rodriguez, like Caliban, masters the language of those who subjugate him. The private Richard Rodriguez loses the Spanish language of his home in order to establish fluency as a colonized being. Rodriguez does appear to allude to the ironic position of the colonized in relationship to the dominant language. The trope of the colonized evokes deeper problems that arise for him as an ethnic-minority intellectual precisely because he handles the "master's" language, English, so well.

Like Caliban, Rodriguez is driven by the invisible hand that constructs his public persona within a larger discursive framework of the colonial narrative. Doing so works to highlight Rodriguez' "dark skin" as he persistently points to himself. Though shaken by remarks about his minority status, he is resigned to elude the identification with such racial categorizations. Instead, he becomes the exotic other all over again, as a marked figure of otherness, if not outright scorned for his appearance. The discourse of race and color equally constitutes his behavior, his conceptions about himself, and ultimately his narration. In this dual action, the contradiction of identity formation assumes an equal force that produces a struggle for his identity. At issue here is the relationship between "the subject" and the contradictory racial disharmony within discourse itself.

Rodriguez raises a compelling matter with respect to his sense of colonization as a contemporary, racialized Caliban. In a much broader sense, there are obviously two competing problems here within the colonial subject: one is having to contend with the alienating condition of colonization, a facet that Rodriguez chooses; the other is the nationalist search for a homeland to counteract the condition of colonialism that but leads the subject further into subjection. Chicanas/os chose the latter.

CONCLUDING REMARKS

As I have illustrated, *Hunger of Memory: The Education of Richard Rodriguez* is structured around a performative display of shame because Rodriguez himself sets out to remake the "infelicities" that citizenship should promise but fails to deliver because of racist perceptions of him and his family. Rodriguez illustrates the profound injury caused by the racism that surrounds his life. The fact that his injury occurs at the level of language suggests that the discourse travels into his psyche and through the body as an injurious act of naming when he recognizes his noncitizen status.

All of these effects blend together into an ideological weave that cannot be read adequately through conventional Chicana/o critical scholarship because it has yet to reconcile multidimensional issues in the dialectical models of a subject's formation. Rodriguez' ideological twists and turns suggest the irreconcilability of his in/out status, in terms of race, color, and sexuality. Rather than citing the structural similarities with autobiographies of other Chicanas/os, from which there are plenty to draw to counter some of the choices that Rodriguez makes, the rhetorical function of transvaluation is helpful. Several Chicana/o autobiographies represent the transvaluation of Mexican identity to one that is refigured favorably as Chicana/o.[4] Their transvaluation grounds Chicana/o subject formation commensurate with cultural determination to reverse racist discourses.

Because Chicana/o discourse engenders various ideological formations that I will discuss next, the primary locus in the case of Rodriguez simply relates to the condition by which shame shapes and makes a strong impression on the body of an individual; shame generates a calculated musing and reworks latent, existential angst. The motivation to narrate the struggle is upturned by a subject formation that maneuvers through an ideological chasm marked by the double bind in race as well as gender and sexuality discourses. The formation of the Chicana/o subject is divided between the realities of Rodriguez reconciling his past with the promise of a new future. He uses the stability of the individual as a site of autobiographical voicing for the social group, and he becomes entangled within the intellectual demands of legitimation and sense of freedom afforded by this individual creative expression. It is as if the autobiographical is insufficient to his purpose. Without political identification, whether of the *movimiento* or the postnational, Rodriguez is mired in *pomo* space with its instability of meaning.

For Rodriguez, transvaluation also undertakes the same function to collapse the designation of the alien (other) and the inarticulate citizen outsider. This redesignation of the Chicana/o is itself a performative and similar function of changing demeaning aspects of racialization in discourse; the redesignation in renaming the Chicana/o from the Mexican demarcates a desirable effect in one's own self-identification. A dialectical model of self-identification would in effect state that there is an authentic Chicana/o experience that can be named or disclaimed. This model would foreclose any discursive possibilities inherent in the Chicana/o designation and would be overtaken by the specularity implicit in the designation of the Chicana/o subject as a transcendent cultural spirit. As Rodriguez fails to transvaluate within the Chicana/o experience, he rejects immanence over self-pronouncement, that is, a self-pronouncement that largely suggests that identities are crafted by the individual and can exceed racial categorization. The autobiography thus affords the obvious function of providing a rare glimpse into the individual in moments of crisis, flux, conversion, and, yes, great or wondrous literary accomplishment.[5]

The paradox between the reinscription of the Chicana/o voice in its singularity and as an identity within the social group stems in part from the renaming of the Chicana/o subject as a group formation. The dual function of relating the self/social model within Chicana/o discourse illustrates a set of assumptions about the individual and his or her representational utility. When the autobiography offers an ironic critique of marginalization by dramatizing and upturning the function of the individual experience, the dual action of reinscription and narration posits the Chicana/o literary subject as an agent who seeks legitimacy through social modes of reinscription in citizenship, transvaluating racist demarcations and revealing a sensual discourse of self-awareness.[6] While there are divergent theoretical paths to consider in thinking about the composition of the Chicana/o autobiography in this postdialectic, not-quite-postnationalist scenario, one case in particular can be made for the reconstitution of the self through a performative action.

It may be premature to regard this moment as one of identity crisis for Chicana/o discourse, as some may be too eager to claim it.[7] Instead, this moment simply signifies a rise out of political naiveté from a nascent cultural nationalistic tendency that narrates or reinscribes erasure and all the complications that arise from that subject location. One could even argue that this marvelous unleashing of expression in the Chicana/o autobiography is to be expected from an emergent literary voice; boldly, it tackles the contradictions of minority literature as a thematic dilemma within the narrative structure of the autobiography. It has been my intent in this chapter to elucidate aspects of the basis of Rodriguez' shame, or his claims to such, as an incipient problem in Chicana/o literary subject formation and to illustrate the concerns within discourse that undergird this problem.

As may be the case with most American ethnic-minority autobiographical experiences, the autobiographical narrative is fraught with all sorts of contradictory claims.[8] The concerns are relevant because Rodriguez' autobiography is a vivid reminder of the limitations of identity formation. It would be shortsighted to say that Rodriguez does not entertain a much larger concern, which is a calculated conceptualization of the state as a temporal structure that is limited by the ideological flows that underlie subjects in discourse at all times. At what point, then, does an ethnic discourse recognize the provisional status of the state in certifying the terms of equanimity? Rodriguez at his best anticipates this dilemma as he undertakes a reevaluation of his life, and through his examination he ultimately succumbs to assimilation as the short-term answer. He does so without regard for the social structures that create these imaginary divides. Could we say, then, that *Hunger of Memory* is a self-fulfilling prophecy that makes valid claims against the historical conceptualizations of race in California? Or is Rodriguez simply a product of his time—the liberal conditions of the state have achieved a clear message in the designation of difference as an emblem of adversity?

As we have seen in contemporary U.S. society, there is antipathy toward liberal American social projects such as bilingual education and affirmative action. Although Rodriguez' autobiography has long been admired by those in the media who appreciate his candor or marvel at how well an ethnic-minority intellectual can write, others loathe his ostensibly self-deprecating style. While a different argument can be made that the Chicana/o autobiography of the 1970s utilizes a process of transvaluation for rhetorical effect in the renaming of the Chicana/o subject, the basis of this type of narration draws attention to the possibilities associated with the renaming process, from Mexicans who become Chicanas/os to nationalists who recognize the meaning of the postnational.[9]

Six   # DENATIONALIZING CHICANA/O QUEER REPRESENTATIONS

> *[T]he national culture industry is also in the business of*
> *generating paramnesias, images that organize consciousness,*
> *not by way of explicit propaganda, but by replacing and*
> *simplifying memories people actually have with image traces*
> *of political experience about which people can have political*
> *feelings that link them to other citizens and to patriotism.*
> LAUREN BERLANT, "LIVE SEX ACTS," IN *THE QUEEN OF*
> *AMERICA GOES TO WASHINGTON CITY,* 1997

Chicana/o gay and lesbian identities have not emerged from a single movement or from larger historical dialectics, such as it has been defined in U.S.
gay and lesbian methodological and historical theorizations or even within
Chicana/o discourses in which discussions about homosexuality have
been explicitly rejected and ignored (D'Emilio 1983, Rich 1995). Ironically,
Chicana/o queer sexuality and its representations predominated in scholarly arenas throughout the 1980s and 1990s due to the influence of Chicana lesbian thought and the movements toward social change. Chicana/o
queer formation facilitated a critique of cultural nationalism and of U.S.
hegemonic queer formation and its historiography and, at the same time,
facilitated the entry of LGBTQIS into transnational culture.[1]

In their directive as a representational device, Chicana/o queer formations have dislocated and rendered problematic national semiotic sexual systems. In anglicized popular culture portrayed in the television show *Queer
Eye for the Straight Guy,* clean, fashionable gay men help reconstruct nearly
irrecoverable heterosexual slouches, usually because the "straight guy" in
each episode wants to please "his" woman. At the end, the heterosexual
man demonstrates that he had it in him all along, essentially reconciling
his heterosexual, if substandard, privileges with queer sensibility. In similar

format, Chicana/o queer perspectives and intellectual thought disclose hegemonic cultural reliance on gender surveillance and on the manipulation of desires.

Chicana/o queer thought also investigates conformity as pleasure and traditionalism in Mexicana/o and Chicana/o culture and ultimately destabilizes the sex/gender binary system as beneficial to the labor and economics of capitalism. "Denationalization" is a term that became popular in the 1980s as Latin American and Third World countries generally were forced into compliant forms of capitalism such as structural adjustment measures that were intended to privatize their economies in a matter of years. Structural adjustment included selling national utilities to private companies, portioning off oil fields to transnational corporations, and dismantling heath care as a universal system. During the early 1980s, drastic measures were taken to curb national expenditures, lessen the burden on the state to offer certain social benefits, and promote growth in the private sector. This period in Mexico's history is called *la crisis*, when anti-inflationary actions led to the devaluation of the peso and the restructuring of Seguro Social, the national social welfare safety net. This period marks the transformation of the Mexican economy from a socialist-based democratic culture to that of an emerging global and transnational economy. In large measure, the effort to denationalize Mexico's economy meant deregulation and opening borders to new market conditions. This social and economic development is important as we consider formations of queer Chicanas/os' identity as both an aesthetic principle of transnational culture and a political process. In the course of the past twenty years, Chicana/o queer representations have flourished under a burgeoning transnational culture. Denationalization suggests privatization, and it means deregulation of the social patterns and norms, which we can also take to mean less regulation of sexuality.

DISCOURSES ON QUEER MOVEMENT

It is impossible to declare queer representation as the sole enterprise of Chicana/o queer experience. Representation may not be enough to categorize the experiences of resistance put forth by queers of color in their attempt to mollify a U.S. national public discourse that is limited in, and by, its views of sexuality. The hegemony of sexual citizenship and a U.S. public discourse on gay rights has had an effect on queer ethnic organizations that resist mainstream gay and lesbian movements.[2] This resistance includes recent elaborations of transgender, bisexual, and queer concerns that have materialized as a result of successful campaigns to reverse gay civil rights. Depictions and discussion of gay marriage, reversal of sodomy laws (in *Bowers v. Hardwick*), and changing attitudes about public displays of queer culture can be found on network and cable television.[3] However, a public discourse on queer culture assumes a historical thread of analysis shaped by a different regard for the meaning of race, ethnicity, and color in the 1980s.

Lauren Berlant, in her important survey of the cultural crisis during the Reagan administration in *The Queen of America Goes to Washington City* (1997), offers a detailed theorization of the hegemonic links between the rise of social conservatism and a sudden preoccupation with sexual citizenship and homosexuality as a necessary public discourse about gender and homosexuality. A national discourse on "homosexuality" (a term sometimes used as a pejorative) began with a cultural campaign against gays and lesbians and in response to the AIDS pandemic.

The establishment of "reform" culture, initiated by cultural conservatives during the 1980s, coincided with efforts to join the U.S. economy to a global marketplace and to foment a culture of ostensibly traditional values as the nation's privileged discourse (Bork 1996, D'Souza 1991). During the 1980s in the United States, efforts to restructure moral and ethical citizenship paralleled an intense economic restructuring. During the Reagan administration (1981–1988), Lynne Cheney, then the head of National Endowment for the Arts, along with Bill Bennett, then Secretary of Education, introduced campaigns on "family values" that targeted racial and sexual minorities as culpable for an apparent decline of American culture (Vaid 1995). The breakdown of the family structure, according to Cheney and Bennett, was due to the rise of multiculturalism in higher education.

Later, Robert Bork, in his *Slouching Toward Gomorrah: Modern Liberalism and American Decline* (1996), determined that an open education is synonymous with a hedonistic decline of the United States as a world power. Noticeably, the title for the book offers a direct commentary on the role of culture in the nation's waning status in the world; Bork determines that the United States' standing as a superpower is being undermined by minorities and by gay and lesbian culture. Other conservatives, including Jesse Helms and Ralph Reed, likewise voiced highly charged public rhetoric to criticize all aspects of homosexuality, from gays in the military to the use of public funds for the arts.

As late as 2001 and in the days immediately after the 9/11 attack on the

World Trade Center, Jerry Falwell issued his own remarks about the reason for the terrorism. In his reactive style, Falwell determined early on certain Americans' culpability for the attack:

> I really believe that the pagans, and the abortionists, and the feminists, and the gays and the lesbians who are actively trying to make that an alternative lifestyle, the ACLU, People for the American Way, all of them who have tried to secularize America, I point the finger in their face and say, "You helped this happen." [4]

Falwell soon apologized in an effort to quell the outcry an outraged and saddened nation made against his statement.[5] These examples reflect a certain public preoccupation with homosexuality arising in the United States within the economic global shift that includes transnationalism; the preoccupation also attests to, and begins to shape effectively, American culture's changing understandings about gender and sexuality.

The development of border capitalism in the early 1980s incorporated women and other marginalized people, including immigrants from Central and South America, into the local border economies by creating a flexible approach to labor and citizenship.[6] The formation of flexible or nontraditional labor sets up vulnerable sectors within the Mexican population. Historically, the border regions along the U.S.-Mexico border have been fraught with neglect and unemployment. Thus, development of its economic base has been welcomed by Mexico's government as a way to ease the burden of poverty in this region.

As suggested earlier, citizenship—in the formation of Chicana/o identities—expresses embedded nationalistic tendencies that stem from living simultaneously in both nations' cultural frames along the U.S.-Mexico border. Immigrants often enter into the semiotic sign system by using fashion or other cultural tropes to mark their citizenship or their passing. This unstable system carries over into the semiotic sign system of the social and cultural networks of sexual identities as each nation offers its own options for identification. A benefit of this instability is that it actually but indirectly works to promote gay and lesbian production by recreating assimilation to ease blending into the culture as queer and therefore as U.S. citizen. Another way to think about it is to consider the performance aspects of citizenship and the different passing strategies that a drag or transgender experience presents. The possibilities of experience are endless in this arrangement of coding.[7]

Departing from the national structure means that the site of desire creates infinite possibilities for sexual identities and their practices. In the United States, this translates into the multiple identities already created by the identity potential such sexual experiences bring. Working in tandem with capitalism to invoke a sense of privileged desire, "queer identity formation" appears as a unique characteristic of U.S. rights and is emblematic of advanced capitalism. The same does not apply to Chicana/o and Mexicana/o cultures because a formal gay liberation movement has been difficult to elaborate in those cultures. A mapping of U.S. history in gay rights originates with the formation of such groups as the Gay Liberation Front, the Mattachine Society, and Daughters of Bilitis. Despite their socialist leanings, these early political organizations did not factor in race or ethnicity. Such groups did not consider race or ethnicity as necessary because the focus of acceptability and tolerance within a critique of U.S. capitalism took priority over all other matters. Historically, the U.S. feminist movement did not integrate concepts of race and ethnicity either, or at least not until the 1980s.[8]

Identity formations were working through their own sets of contradictions toward construction of a progressive society that relied on internal conflict to lay out a different foundation for a diverse queer body. Discourses on the emergence of a queer identity have relied upon social activist models to discuss the different homosexual-based identities that have emerged. John D'Emilio notes (1983) that the rise of a gay and lesbian identity became possible only as the material situation for men and women changed in the years after World War II. Annamarie Jargose, in *Queer Theory: An Introduction* (1996), sets up such a model that begins with the gay liberation movement of the 1950s and 1960s. The model includes the foundation of such organizations as the Mattachine Society in 1951 and, four years later, the Daughters of Bilitis. These scholars attribute the material rise of gay and lesbian identity constructions and political contributions to more advanced levels of capitalism, even as each is critical of the operations of advanced, postmodern capitalism.

Other studies do not demonstrate the same concern with the rise and formation of queer identities. Global technology sectors look more at the *advantages* of queer populations. A Brookings Institute study conducted by the Urban and Metropolitan Policy Institute concluded that gay and lesbian tolerance is fast becoming an index for advanced levels of capitalism in major metropolitan areas of the United States. The authors of the 2002 study, Richard Florida and Gary Gates, suggest that "tolerance" of gays and lesbians in the United States provides solid evidence of a nation's potential for economic growth because high levels of tolerance lead to intellectual and technological productivity. In fact, the authors conclude, "The leading indicator of a metropolitan area's high-technology success is a large gay population" (1).

A speculative reason that sexual minorities tend to prosper under capitalism is that sexuality, since the nineteenth century, has occupied the realm of the private space (Somerville 1994, Weeks 1981). The private space offers capitalism opportunities to excite desires under the auspices of an aesthetic principle that promotes progressive views of the body that might not otherwise be possible under a nationalist discourse, whether capitalist or socialist. National(ist) discourses draw their cultural logic from traditional values similar to those found in nineteenth-century notions of sexuality and become viewed in the twenty-first century as fundamentalist, as if they had "always existed." To think historically, to a certain extent, means rejecting the notion of things as "always being this way" (Moallem 1999).

The appeal of gender and sexual identities within transnational and global cultures exhibits a tendency to relax conventional rules of sexual mores because of the cultures' exploitative dimensions. In contrast to D'Emilio's important essay and the Brookings Institute's interesting set of findings, a more common practice in Third World countries is to enlist vulnerable populations into the workplace while procuring their transgressive ethnic and sexual qualities to promote cultural attributes imitative of those in the First World, presumably to encourage investment.

INSTITUTIONAL ISSUES

Encounters with "cultural citizenship," represented by the sense of belonging generated by a marginalized group within a larger hegemonic system, offers insights into the formation of Chicana/o queer representation. In cases where economic policy or social crisis prevails over the cultural order, the tendency to relax sexual proscriptions may in fact lead to more progressive notions about sexuality and allow an emergence of a queer identity. An unwitting assumption about the role of capitalism in a Protestant Christian-based, driven society such as in the United States is that the society depends on advanced social power relations to manage the sexuality of its citizens. The regulation of sexuality in general and the monitoring of sexual identities became more problematic in the United States as the formation of political identities and social categories began to emerge as social and political phenomena by the late 1980s. The United States is unique in the way gay, lesbian, transgender, intersexed, and a host of other identifications yet to be articulated in the continuum of sexualities under late capitalism have been able to formulate a sense of politics and of expression based upon an identity process (Phelan 2001).

A question often asked is: How has the gay and lesbian movement in the United States fostered or supported the goals and successes of Chicana/o gays and lesbians? Identities have been articulated and developed across and beyond personal interests. However, one of the noted exceptions to this broader development of identity is the way capitalism excites populations into consumerism or promotes an expansion of capitalism into other countries. The influences of capitalism form a facet of global demeanor and change the character of a country or culture, in this case in terms of the regard in other countries for gays and lesbians. The expansion of capitalism throughout the 1980s required countries including Nicaragua, Mexico, and some in the Caribbean to denationalize and alter their economies by adapting modifications required by the World Bank and the International Monetary Fund (IMF). The emergence of global discourses and the movement toward postnationalism take place at the same time as alterations in the culture and in communities, whether socialist in direction—as in the case of Nicaragua for a few short years—or as driven by the hands of the World Bank seeking to lend "stability" to situations created by an interfering United States attempting to "rescue" these countries from any socialist project.

These correlates of capitalist expansion ignited a different motivation to control bodies and their desires. Consistently, capitalism has developed more advanced power in social relations to manage the sexuality of its citizens (Kirsch 2000). Nationalism's failure to proscribe its citizens from an ideal state of self-reflection cannot be achieved without some intelligent examination of sexuality. "Induced" forms of capitalism tend to shock the culture. Without an effort within the humanities to develop a link between the two systems, one economic and the other cultural, the ill effects will continue across all levels of society, environmentally, socially, and politically. Completely overriding the nationalist labor structure of the workplace of men as the "breadwinners" has an impact on the sex-gender systems in Mexican and U.S. Chicana/o cultures. Meanwhile, the material links between the national effort and the gender system in Mexico have been translated to accommodate a transnational economy (Díaz-Cotto 2001).

Because a stable gendered identity is next to impossible to categorize, particularly in a transnational economy, the work of the nation is to produce, regulate, and impose upon its citizens a national discourse that can be assimilated and reproduced. Under capitalism, however, what are the conditions that permit homosexuality to thrive? Queerness can be seen as the cultural attribute of homosexual life in which a nexus between race and ethnicity can finally be considered. I focus here on the ability of queerness to denationalize representation. While earlier public confrontations in queer culture over race and ethnicity have been mild when compared to some in the 1980s and 1990s, the later efforts to extend rights and legal protections to gays and lesbians have been paramount, whether in debates about gays in the military or in the discussions about a "right" to marry. Next, I look at the denationalization of queer aesthetics to occasion the critical basis for a Chicana/o queer methodology and practice.

Having gained entry into current Chicana/o discourse, in part due to an extension of the progressive ideals of the larger body and mission of Chicana/o studies, lesbians and gays moved in the 1980s into the opened spaces quickly and with fierce pride. At the same time, activist practice provided opportunities to open other types of spaces to gays and lesbians. Within cultural nationalism, queerness did not exist; in fact, it was necessary to inhibit homosexuality as part of the desire to create a stable and unified front for Chicana/o cultural production (Kirsch 2000). Gender and queer sexuality have been central to the formation of Chicana/o discourse if for no other reason than that the all-important literary movement was crucial to the formation of queer representation. It occurred, however, a bit later than the *movimiento* and despite nationalism and suppression, if not outright homophobia.

The question as to why there is no corresponding social movement until the 1980s and 1990s is important for understanding how queer representation works. First, writing is a solitary act that affords the writer the privacy and anonymity necessary for exploring the inner workings of many topics, including sexual marginalization. Second, there is a period when queer writers emulated a version of the gay and lesbian movement. John Rechy, for example, emulated queer writers from the Beat generation. Moraga and Anzaldúa took feminist and black lesbian writers as a source of influence. Poet Francisco Alarcón looked at Federico García Lorca as a source of inspiration. Third, the antigay violence in Chicana/o and Latina/o communities still threatened coming out, so the effort to create a characteristic of openness similar to that found in the U.S. Anglo-American gay and lesbian movement in the 1980s and 1990s could not have been possible.

All of the material conditions were lacking. No, or few, middle-class expectations for equity and justice existed as they did in mainstream LGBTQI movements in the United States. LLEGO (Latino/a Lesbian and Gay Organization) was founded in 1985 by Latino community activists in California and Texas who united to advocate for HIV/AIDS prevention, education, and treatment in Latina/o communities. Eventually, it developed into the first national Latina/o LGBTQI organization. From its early focus on HIV/AIDS prevention and education and its evolution as a civil rights and health advocacy organization, LLEGO became a powerful force for social change. In comparison to other U.S. LGBTQI national organizations, however, it began late in the movement for gay rights.

As underscored earlier, formations of feminism were important to gender and social constructions of queer identity in Chicana/o culture. One could say that the lineages of queer confrontations are matriarchal (female) and not derivatives of a patriarchal (masculine) origin. While institutionalized notions of queerness might have been later co-opted by masculinized institutions and as discourses took form in their respective disciplining processes such as academic institutions, the loosely fitting networks of queer productions denationalized sexual identities.

In his essay "The National Longing for Form" (1990), Timothy Brennan states that nationalism is a trope anchored in two main nations: belonging and bordering. The patriarchal imagining of a nation is done when the subject who belongs defines himself in contrast to an other outside of the borders imposed upon territories or identities. The "other" in national discourse may refer to those groups outside of national borders and/or to those within its borders but outside of the hegemony controlling that nation's discursive practices. One facet of the efforts to transform these hegemonic and normative traces of nation building resides in the confrontations that create queer spaces.

Formations of gay and lesbian representation, like formation in transnational culture, do not develop evenly. The direction of Chicana/o gays and lesbians differs dramatically from U.S. gay and lesbian movements. In documented works by gays and lesbians, the most proficient examples of Chicana/o queer representation and political practice originated from feminist texts and from their interpretations in academic discourses. The acceptability and critical vanguard work of Cherríe Moraga and Gloria Anzaldúa framed the basis for queer representation in the 1980s and 1990s. Later years would prove to be explosive in the transformations of Chicana/o discourse as a departure from a cultural nationalistic aesthetics. Dialectical inquiry, so fundamental to Chicana/o *movimiento* thinking, thus facilitates a discussion of the denationalization possible in queer representation. While some have articulated that queer representations simply emerge from identity-based movements, its postnational undercurrent suggests that the subject of "queer," different from "lesbian" or even "feminist," decenters masculinity and heterosexuality in Chicana/o cultural nationalism. Queer spatialization, to paraphrase Judith Haberstam (1999), provides a theoretical location in a social practice aimed at either revealing identities or implementing political perspectives in arenas that many Chicana/o queers found unaccepting. The choice or decision was to make the spaces less hostile or to withdraw from them. Many scholar-activists as well as writers and artists chose instead to stay and fight.

ENACTMENTS:
THE QUEER POLITICS OF AZTLÁN

How do radical cultural nationalist movements based on 1960s revolutionary discourses influence criticism of gender and sexual production in the 1980s and 1990s? Perhaps it is not a simple question, or it defies easy answers. As a critical problem, however, this question lingered in my mind, and only later did it actually develop into a discussion of the role of cultural nationalism in Chicana/o discourse, queer theory, feminist thought, and the problem of locating a critique of historical differences. Nations have a particular way of conceiving history. The ways we have historicized gay and lesbian existence, for example, made possible certain theorizations. The matter of queerness in the twentieth century gained some social impetus, as did other several other liberation movements during the late 1960s and early 1970s. Most American queer historians mark the Stonewall riots as a turning point in the transformation from a "homosexual" to a gay rights movement (Hennesey 1994, Sedgwick 1990). Because the 1969 protest at the Stonewall Inn, a transgender bar in New York City's Greenwich Village, gained little attention in the national media, the telling of the queer riots transformed and initiated organization and coalition building within other groups. The event by itself did not initiate the change in the general public's perception of gays and lesbians, but by gaining the media's attention in defiance of standard New York City police raids on gay bars, Stonewall galvanized a movement so closeted gays and lesbians could come out. The ideological transformation from nonidentifying, unnamed sexuality to the adoption of the word play and concept embedded in "gay" thus galvanized the gay movement's history as an identity and social protest movement.

Gays and lesbians built alliances with feminists in an attempt to challenge notions of sexuality. The Stonewall episode provided gay and lesbian protestors national media prominence and an opportunity to emphasize the harassment provoked by New York police against homosexuals during the summer of 1969 (D'Emilio and Freedman 1988). The event marked a cultural and discursive transformation that changed the way people perceive queerness today (Cruikshank 1990, 9). Gays and lesbians, however, were already organized socially in underground enclaves that gathered at bars, bathhouses, and private homes and subsequently formed a subculture; members of these enclaves comprised what became known as "the closet generation" (Nestle 1992). Since then, political and social transformation dramatically revolutionized dominant sexual paradigms in American society as well as those in institutional practices. Ed Cohen regards the terms "identity" and "difference" within the gay and lesbian communities as a potential crisis:

> [While] the assumption that "we" constitute a "natural" community because we share a sexual identity might appear to offer a stable basis for group formations, my experience suggests that it can just as often interrupt the process of creating intellectual political projects . . . By predicating "our" affinity upon the assertion of a common "sexuality," we tacitly agree to leave unexplored any "internal" contradictions which undermine the coherence we desire from the imagined certainty of an unassailable commonality of incontestable sexuality. (1992, 72)

Media representations have achieved a new level of acceptability recently, but homosexuality long seemed an impervious location. Still, queer communities offer considerable deference to place and terms, a context, as well as theoretical possibilities that emphasize uniqueness. Cohen nevertheless represents the larger critique extending throughout gay and lesbian communities. It is especially vital for any community formation to incorporate a sense of identification through difference, but the effectiveness of distinction in the social realm has proven difficult. Both community formation and the desire for individuation run parallel as two prevailing popular philosophical attitudes at the beginning of the twenty-first century. The August 1993 cover of *Vanity Fair* magazine featured a scantily clad Cindy Crawford provocatively shaving k. d. lang as she sits lathered up on a barber's chair. Intending to provoke attention, this shot exemplifies the use of queer sexual play in order to break down homophobic barriers in the national magazine. The image deployed among queer theories a critical impetus for gay and lesbian study by extending the play sexuality in queer discourses within a heterosexual audience. Broadening this scope demonstrated by the *Vanity Fair* cover uses butch/femme roles in creating the spectacle of the sexual usually reserved for male audiences. In this example, the imagery makes it seem as if the society is ready to embrace all kinds of sexualities. Encounters such as this one run rampant across popular culture and produce an exceptional set of circumstances for critical analysis beyond the gay and lesbian movement call for inclusion and visibility.[9] When we imagine concepts such as "diversity" and "social unity" within the same objectives, the outcomes produce a set of circumstances that provoke certain kinds of encounters. The encounter between the proponents of social unity and the dispersal found in identification as difference exemplifies a radical or queer encounter (Maffesoli 1993).

A cultural discourse no longer bound to the images of traditional representation gives social unity its new form, memory, and outlook and serves as a critical methodology for a radically new subject position and subject of study. Gay or lesbian identity became an increasingly diverse cultural dynamic during the 1990s, so much so that the categories "gay" and "lesbian" did not provide an accurate outlook for all the subcommunities. Gay and lesbian studies, within the various conditions and theoretical situations that comprise a queer discourse in the latter stages of the twentieth century, took on community interests with the specificity of individual identification.

Although I am interested in the way communities create cultural discourse within a priori sets of conditions, plurality and diversity within local or specific contexts instruct modern social formation and must also be recognized. The results here are to problematize and theorize some practices within popular movements in conversation with community, historical, and academic production. I am therefore not attempting to engage directly the polemics characterized in "difference" according to the embodiments of race, class, gender, and sexuality within the traditional sociocultural claims. However, some aspects of the theoretical are part of the ongoing discussion of "difference." Material conditions rooted in "discourse" and "community" are rarely linked; rather, the reverse is more often the case. Another reason guiding this method is simply to use a theoretical approach fluent with the community and the institutional enterprise as opposed to the philosophical debate that others have already argued (Butler 1990, Fuss 1989).

Ontology or essence cannot be claimed within a modern cultural discourse without creating the appearance of anomaly (Lloyd 1993, 10). Claims of essential difference in the modern political context arise from the latent urge to form naturalized sites of social unity (Fuss 1989, 1–21). Although the sites have been constructed as a program to naturalize the subjugation of women and others, the discourse of "liberation" plays an important role in the queerification of these related identities (Phelan 1992). Identity politics thus represent the existing urge to qualify constructions of essence as a legitimizing discourse.[10]

The arguments sustained by identity politics should be examined separately from the traditional ontological view offered by some theorists, as several have noted (Fuss 1989, Phelan 2001). To them, identity politics are about the intersubjective conditions within a specific material discourse or recent historical event, such as liberation movements. A temporal conditioning of history corresponds to the way difference performs within a specific historical moment. Identity politics incorporate the recent historical rime as a narrative of reconstruction, rather than identifying begrudgingly within an a priori set of assumptions.[11] Recent history portrays this tendency to naturalize social unity as a byproduct of social anomalies, such as fascism, Balkanization, separatism, monolithic reproductions, and solipsism, but does not account for its radical progression throughout longer dialectical strains of events within modernity (Habermas 1992, Jardin 1985). For Chicanos and Chicanas, this would be signified in the way Mexicans emigrate and are locked into the "national" economy as laborers: the basis of Mexican and therefore Chicano/a unity would be located in their identity as workers but not as artists, professionals, or unemployed. Their work, essentially, is their identity, under the terms of this type of identity politics.

Therefore, identity politics carry certain limitations for academic study. Other theoretical practices, such as the social constructionist analysis offered by various projects, bring some relief to the limitations. With all of the attention given to the formation of bodies and desires, the matter of historical representation becomes a testimony of material exclusion and leads to the development of minoritization (Foucault 1972). Exclusion of queers from mainstream historiography has been a legitimate concern. Historians in particular have had to derive the creative methods of "mapping the complex discursive and textual operations at play in the historical emergence of subjects who come to be called lesbians and gay" (Terry 1991, 55). There are nevertheless events and conditions that have led us to this discursive bonanza. John Boswell identified this phenomenon as the rise of "minority history" (1980, 17); its development as a method for eliminating discrimination from the American paradigm of civil rights exposed the systematic construction of minorities in the United States. This practice takes inclusive strategies that differ sharply from the strategies found in mainstream historiography. In another instance, Jennifer Terry delineates the role of history as a methodology that focuses on the "conditions" of exclusion:

> I do not attempt to correct the historical record through locating great homosexuals in the past to reconstruct their effaced stories. Instead I look for the conditions that make possible, and those that constrain, the emergence and vitality of "lesbians" and "gay men" who populate the present. (1991, 55)

Among the projects of a different and critical historiography is the intention to theorize new practices and to trace what Terry calls "a deviant subject formation" (ibid.) Jennifer Terry and John Boswell both engage in an interventionist queer historiographic approach. Both scholars, however, concur that a sense of history for gays and lesbians has actually been a form of political activism. The practice of historiography as a method of intervention challenges the dominant paradigms using the historical narrative as the foundational text. Queer history thus gets caught in the proverbial critical bind. On the one hand, history entertains the social science aspect that functions in part to create a sense of solidarity or legitimation for a given, if masculine, group (Lyotard 1984, 47). On the other, historiography represents an attempt to intervene using interdisciplinary strategies that decenter the subject of history.

The method applied by Terry reconceptualizes the subject of history and emphasizes difference through the deviant subject formation. Terry's deviant historiography offers a potentially radical view in that history is presented as an analysis of a set of "conditions" rather than exceptional stories about important people and their formation. By decentering the "exemplary person" approach from the historical construction of a cultural reality, the past becomes an enabling critical field for the documentation of deviants or those who are constructed differently. By creating this space in the historical narrative, those who have been unable to personify the character of greatness must be traced back to the conditions and, in some cases, to the events that excluded them to begin with. For Terry, history is no longer about reconstruction or recapturing the moment; rather, it is a methodology that can trace exclusion into its present form.

The constructions of minority scholarship and curricula have strongly influenced the advancement of oppressed groups in higher education and society. Women, racial and ethnic minorities, and currently gays and lesbians have added to that influence by demanding specific study in institutions of higher education.[12] Furthermore, the demands roused from the liberation movements of the 1960s and 1970s carved a path in educational policy and social development. To a very large degree, the liberation movements inaugurated minority studies as means of transforming oppressive social circumstances or exclusion from academic institutions.[13] Minority groups also relied on specific social measures and events to gain access in the institutions of higher education: civil rights legislation, U.S. Supreme Court decisions, and protests galvanized social grievance toward an enactment of protection against discrimination and, in some instances, protection from violence (Cruikshank 1990).

Minority programs typically do not have the resources and stability of traditional disciplines or established departments. Most major institutions with limited support of the humanities have garnered security through the development of a graduate division of study in which research is the primary focus and funding opportunities arise (Collins 1992). Still, minority scholarship has been the subject of a much larger debate in cultural discourse in the national debate against multiculturalism because programs receive comparably more criticism for the way specific study of a group gains representation in the institution (Springer 2001).

These challenges assert that minority experiences are inconsequential and potentially detrimental to the development of a unified domestic educational research policy, such as a university's curriculum, or other "national" domestic interests, such as the family or military security. One of the most miscalculated of these assaults, *Illiberal Education: The Politics of Race and Sex* (1991) by Dinesh D'Souza, a book sponsored by the American Enterprise Institute, depicts the "studies" programs as the "tyranny of the minority" (241). D'Souza sees malignancy in such programming, and this concern for the programs' reach or spread accounts for the basic premise in his book. He states that "diversity" within higher education has contributed to "a monolithic ideological focus" (ibid.). This assertion derives from the narrow assumption that the development of a study program will only serve that particular group. Such critiques, however widespread, are clearly politically motivated and represent the position of religious conservatives and the political right. The popularity of *Illiberal Education* cannot be downplayed, considering the level of charges directed specifically at minority studies over the years and its small impact on the growth of gay and lesbian studies as a professional model (Yarbro-Bejarano 1995b).

The third consideration to emerge from a shift in scholarship of the past thirty years or so, depending on the historical vantage point, has marked the matter of "difference" in hermeneutical and theoretical practices.

Twentieth-century literatures depicting psychological depth, dialogical narration, fragmented subjectivity, contradiction, and ambivalence—fictional and nonfictional—disseminate and disassemble previously held notions of a unified subject and community (Hassan 1987). Post-structuralist methods reveal the unreliability of linear thought, giving license to heterogeneity and the free play of difference. One critique of post-structuralism claims that the endless language games, arbitrariness, and apparent infatuation with ontological conditions are indifferent to political experiences (Eagleton 1996, 28). Post-structuralist methods frequently lead to the dissemination of any unifying "truths," calling into question a community's solidarity in the process (ibid., 29).

Regardless of how one views himself or herself in the heterogeneous process, these changes have radically altered the way we represent communities by adding further claim to the instability of social groups and their constitution within a given tradition (Anderson 1983). The practices found in post-structuralism have contributed further to the level of complexity found in cultural discourse. In yet another developing critique of textual and cultural criticism, current scholarship is at odds with community formation. In his 1990 essay "The Ivory Closet," Jeffrey Escoffier identifies two distinct groups in the development of gay and lesbian scholarship. He describes the first "wave" of intellectuals as "a group of writers and scholars who experienced the euphoria of Stonewall and the women's movement" (46). The second wave of intellectuals is then described as "a younger group of scholars [who] are ambitious young teachers and bright graduate students trained at elite universities and occupying jobs at the more prestigious institutions" (ibid.).[14] Escoffier constructs the first-wave gay or lesbian intellectual as an individual who experienced the "exhilaration of Stonewall." The second construction situates the group as "those who did not," and he terms them the "post-Stonewall" generation. The "first generation" in Escoffier's paradigm connotes a sense of "origin." In his claim, Stonewall motivated gays and lesbians toward the liberation movement. Still, Escoffier's framework can be summarized as follows: "In contrast to their predecessors, they [the younger generation] emphasized sophisticated interpretation of texts rather than the social history or the sociology of gay life" (46).

For some, then, difference is marked according to the "generations" of scholarly practice as opposed to the dialectical transformations, the political, transnational economic developments, and legal arbitrations that have occurred since Stonewall. Eight years of a Reagan administration and four years of the elder Bush administration dramatically shifted policy and social sentiments against gays and lesbians. Escoffier's paradigm is significant only to the extent that he includes in it the contributions by women of color. In an effort to make his claim, he nevertheless excludes the academics and writers of color who engage in theoretical projects. This is perhaps Escoffier's most problematic statement throughout the essay.[15] Escoffier insists:

> Turning away from social history and anthropology to the textual concerns of literary and cultural criticism, the younger generation uses a language that, for all its literary brilliance, is quite difficult. Links between the institutional languages in the university render communities less visible; this new wave of lesbian and gay studies has not managed to incorporate women and people of color into its ranks and analysis. (46–47)

The sentiments Escoffier expresses carry another set of arguments. He cites a breach between the social contract of the gay movement and the development of certain queer academic practices. This breach separates intellectuals into these groups: Stonewall generation, post-Stonewall generation, lesbians of color groups, and academic leftovers like Teresa de Lauretis and John Boswell (46). There are several underlying ideas not stated by Escoffier about the practice of queer theory. A summation of his underlying claims includes the following:

1. The scholarly language and methods used by the more recent scholars are esoteric and elitist.
2. Such methods are abstracted from the material experiences and the political discourse of diversity.
3. Complexity and abstraction, usually associated with theoretical and textual practices, undermine and appropriate the marginal texts while disembodying the agency and removing it from the condition of oppression.
4. Post-structuralism and its games are preoccupied with Western metaphysics, maintaining, as Spivak would say (1988, 271), "the subject of the West or the West as subject."

The assumption Escoffier brings suggests that a natural coexistence resides between the gay and lesbian communities and sociohistorical methods, which may not be the case at all. Literary and cultural critiques such as Roland Barthes' *S/Z* (1974) and Foucault's *Madness and Civilization* (1970) erupted just when marginal groups claimed their sociohistorical exclusion within pivotal events of social formation. There is a strange understanding among nonpractitioners of criticism that a theoretical language is naturally incomprehensible because of the level of complexity present in the analysis. If anything, post-structualism, as a methodology, decentered the institutionalized texts and opened the space for previously marginalized thought and ideas.

Escoffier contends that contemporary theoretical language has failed to incorporate into the analysis "women and people of color." Theory and criticism have been used to attempt to expose the structures in the disciplines that designate difference for institutionalized practices. Such knowledge has its limitations, since it does not claim to transform social texts or to link an understanding of difference with progress. Using terms such as "agency," "subaltern," and "alterity," the subject of difference still would be an object of study under traditional sociocultural methodology.

Escoffier's paradigms underscore a more persistent problem for the future of gay and lesbian studies: the studies will need to encompass a sincere willingness for dramatic change in practice and in their approach to epistemology. The nature of deconstruction, as a methodology operating from within the textual philosophical structures of Western metaphysics, does not rely solely on the body of the text, nation, family, or even Milton's *Aeropagitica*, in other words, a work as central to philosophy and literature as to be lost without the referent.

By design, deconstruction has created the possibility of never again situating a static reading of anything, such as that marked by, and particular to, nineteenth-century colonialism and twentieth-century cultural imperialism. Without examining the complexity of the problem inherent in the formation of language and discourse, a significant challenge will not be achieved even by using some of the more elaborate work in sociohistorical fields. The matter of theoretical discourse is not about sophistication; it is, however, about complexity. A deconstructive analysis is hardly an exclusive practice of the left or a matter relevant only to "hip" minority scholars. As Escoffier mentions, such theoretical practices are exclusive, but they are exclusive only to the extent that intellectuals from all backgrounds recognize themselves in this moment of change and cultural production. Diversity does not quite dispel the notion that such practices lead directly toward a full-fledged heterogeneous practice or approach, particularly with class and institutional hierarchies still in place.

Education and its varied and various literacies still reside exclusively in the arms of a class or group eager to duplicate itself, for the most part, and only recently have scholars and academics, as well as organic intellectuals, risen to the challenge that "theory" is not theirs exclusively. Theoretical sophistication is not the province of the trained elite but rather has more often been seen in that light only. Today, with postnational, global movement from First to Third World and everything in between as goods and products and human beings traverse the earth, deconstruction allows a different intellectual exploration to move along with the migrants. It is not, then, the sole province of any one group or institution or area of study.

A decentering methodology such as deconstruction will not exercise itself out of a literary text with political taunts from journalists quoting the Modern Language Association panels at the annual conference (Berubé 1999). Deconstruction, however, can be effective to the extent that health care policies can be read and analyzed as texts, as can institutional objectives, pedagogy, community agendas, art, and even the covers of such elite magazines as *Vanity Fair*, all for their linguistic and symbolic content. All these are spaces without a unifying structure and without evidence of contradictions or hyperbole. Identity, as community, under this theorizing, takes on a similar role: to be able to imagine the practice of deconstruction within cultural discourse suggests a different reading for politics and policies, which are based on a quest or search for community and identity. Right-wing conservatives, for example, recast the concept of the family during the 1980s as the "natural site" of social unity. This tactic realigned community as an unnatural potential threat to the family and nation. By centering the family as the subject of a democratic plural society, this initiative slowly undermined the notion of "community" development or something that had been recast as the site of waste in government.

No construction of difference would be complete without an examination of the sexual and national boundaries of race and ethnicity. Tomás Almaguer, in "Chicano Men: A Cartography of Homosexual Identity and Behavior" (1991), seeks to delineate a U.S. Latino homosocial or sexual desire. Almaguer's premise centers on the existing influence the American gay and lesbian movement has had on Chicano and Latino sexual identity. His approach locates within the unexplored or overlooked categories presented by a traditional sociohistorical frame the constraints of representation within a gay and lesbian analysis. The racial and ethnic differences explained in Almaguer's essay cover several intersecting transnational cultural identities. Almaguer evaluates Chicano male homosexuality and the formation of identity within a sociohistorical apparatus: "Sexual behavior and sexual identity of Chicano male homosexuals are principally shaped by two distinct sexual systems, each of which attaches different significance and meaning to homosexuality. Both the European-American and Mexican/Latin American systems have their own unique ensemble of sexual meanings" (75). Almaguer then specifies how the two different systems mark sexual practices: "The rules that define and stigmatize homosexuality in Mexican culture operate under logic and a discursive practice different from those of the bourgeois sexual system that shaped the emergence of contemporary gay/lesbian identity in the U.S." (80).

Although the cultural claim to sexual difference is derived from the patterns within the social science categories, these illustrations suggest the identity is manifested solidly in categories that somehow developed from modern sociosexual practices in cross-cultural sexual identity. Almaguer also cites this progression of cultural national differences according to constructed racial disharmony in the United States:

> The ambivalence of Chicanos vis-à-vis gay sexual identity and their attendant uneasiness with white gay/lesbian culture do not necessarily reflect a denial of homosexuality. Rather, I would argue, the slow pace at which this identity formation has taken root among Chicanos is attributable to cultural and structural factors which differentiate experiences of the white and non-white populations in the U.S. (86)

Perhaps what this analysis suggests is that the categories of difference are still considerably bound by discursive formations and the tropes of difference as well as by histories.

Almaguer's final argument ends with an analysis of Cherríe Moraga's *Loving in the War Years* (1983). In his essay, Almaguer finds that Moraga depicts and reconstructs the family as the natural site of social unity based on her understandings of racially mixed categories and "realities." Ironically, what Almaguer originally began as a cartography of the Chicano male homosexual has now turned into a feminist analysis and reading of a Chicana lesbian, Cherríe Moraga. His analysis develops from the perspective that male homosexual desire in a modern state as it Oedipalizes the family, the lesbian, and its own relative social constructs. Almaguer comments on the obvious male privilege constructed within state and family but does not connect the process of modern hegemony and female subjugation to the family itself. His influential and important essay consolidates and replicates the unstated repressive unity rooted in the terminologies "cultural nationalist Chicano" and "gay" or "straight." The terms become unstable when placed alongside other traditional categories that mark sexuality for men but signal constraints for women. Almaguer may be arguing for a queer identity as one that is marked according to the precepts assembled in Anglo-American culture but instead remains within the Chicano studies paradigm of cultural differentiation. Implicit in his claim is the nationalist alliance that situates Chicanos with Mexican men and other Latino men, in homosocial environments that normally prevent any Latina female sexuality from emerging freely except within the confines of familial space.[16]

Despite the trend toward cultural and textual interpretations, Escoffier's claims that a continuing practice of theory and the use of it "may produce an unbridgeable gap between gay academics and the community" (1990, 47) are important to recall for another reason. This is perhaps one of the liabilities of difference. Post-structuralist theories and methodologies rely on the embeddedness of differences. Ki Namaste, in "Deconstruction, Lesbian and Gay Studies, and Interdisciplinary Work" (1993), employs the use of deconstruction to set up an alternative project for gays and lesbians. Namaste cites a closed textual reading related to the concept of "border" and how borders are monitored or policed. Namaste offers an alternate practice that utilizes deconstruction as a "methodology for intervention" and one that, if sustained, will lead to a queer discourse (57).

Namaste's approach engages interdisciplinarity as a new direction in the development of a gay and lesbian studies program:

> The development of interdisciplinary lesbian and gay studies could possibly mean a radically different understanding of the lives and experiences and realities of lesbians and gay men. Perhaps most radically, it has the potential to even mean an utter abandonment of "lesbian" and "gay" as labels used to signify ontological essence. (59)

Academic practices such as these have lent LGBTQI studies legitimacy with respect to other disciplines, despite the critical nature of the practice. Readings of gay and lesbian outside the boundaries of traditional or universal representation invite unprecedented possibilities and perhaps even propel a view for the future. In fact, difference within a direct social imperative reconciles the grievances of the past with a strong desire for the future. A social and critical impetus is one case for the advancement of gay and lesbian scholarship. In calling for a different analysis, unspecified, unregulated acts, perhaps even undisclosed events, hail in a new direction for gay and lesbian studies. After the liberation movements of the 1960s and 1970s, policy and social transformation had to address the persistence of difference and the subsequent formation of nontraditional and coalitional alliances. While the tone of "rediscovery" fashioned earlier scholarship, the newest approaches in academic and community discourse will more than likely borrow from each other's innovative qualities (Eaklor 1997, Nardi 2001).

The intellectual representatives of community formation influence policy decisions, decide educational objectives, promote political issues, administer goals within the institution, and ultimately restructure social progress. Presence, however, does not translate into well-supported programming or true institutionalized change. Like other minority efforts, LGBTQI studies in the academic institution today are in a precarious situation. Because of its relatively recent appearance in academia and a poor understanding of queer communities in general, a minority studies approach is restricted by the general devaluation of such scholarship in the United States until it has been "proven" (Collins 1992). Because of the tremendous influence liberation movements have had on queer sociocultural formation, proponents of a lesbian and gay initiative regard community advancement as an important development for its critical discourse, one which is currently in operation across the various neighborhoods of study (Namaste 1993).

Efforts to secure protection from discrimination through federal legislation and Supreme Court decisions have not been extended to gays and lesbians in the larger constitutional legacy or as civil rights (Cruikshank 1990, 87). If anything, current health care and military policies illustrate the narrowest acknowledgment of queer culture and sexuality by the federal government (Vandeveyer 1992). Without the proper implementation of policies that guarantee protection to groups of people based on same-sex desires or relationships, the cultural discourse provided by civil rights, educational curricula, political initiatives, and institutional practices seems inadequate.

A few additional critical questions need to be raised: Why construct a gay and lesbian studies program? Should gay and lesbian studies function separately from other programs of study within the institution? How are gay and lesbian studies going to claim difference within the dynamics of queer discourse? Are future investments in gay and lesbian studies going to develop according to the conventional terms of "difference," which claims exclusion within the traditional disciplines, or will they presume solidarity in the interdisciplinary models such as women's studies and ethnic studies? What is the future of gay and lesbian studies? These questions resuscitate one feature endemic to modern society and minority scholarship—the social construction of difference and where the separation has led us in the early period of the new century. How the trope of difference marks categories—defies, separates, or explains them—has been a concern for minority scholars. The idea of difference within a gay and lesbian location carries one other charge, however, and that is intentionally designed to elicit another type of response. By reconstructing difference, we might imagine the world much more divergent than previously imagined, a world much more malleable and less restrictive than the ideological ordinances that shape and construct communities.

Gay and lesbian studies programs can afford other guarantees: in the most immediate case, to create a model of study that challenges the development of the "discipline" as a representative icon of the institution. As a long-term investment, queer methodology and practice should incorporate creative logics in cultural studies and community formation, as models for social unity. Creating the terms and space relevant to current cultural discourse is also warranted. An enabling theoretical model, such as the term "queer" for gay and lesbian studies, allows the reconfiguration of difference to occur while maintaining the subject of difference. To some extent, the model unites the two. The analysis created from a queer dynamic will surely enable "different" readings to unfold and will model interdisciplinarity in practice.

These seemingly clear or admirable assumptions already offered in traditional disciplines tend to repress specific delineations of gender and sexuality by dividing or deciding the boundaries and limitations in theoretical practices. The category of "difference" read as a mere oppositional construct renders the problematic of queer subjectivity a benign process lacking agency or political motivation. In this context, difference becomes just one of a lineup of choices or decisions. Which type of difference can we select? There is also a sense of hopefulness in community deliberation and cultural discourse so that the effort to create an enabling practice in queer theory might procure a future as well as allow exploring its past.[17] Next I explore another, final possibility in Chicana lesbian feminist writing to demonstrate this example of how queer theory pushes analyses beyond previously established borders or boundaries.

QUEERNESS AND CULTURAL HYBRIDITY

The very act of naming oneself Chicana is a strategic position when one is faced with national and ethnic hegemonies that seek to categorize identity according to exclusive binary paradigms. Paula Moya explains:

> A Chicana, according to the usage of women who identify that way, is a politically aware woman of Mexican heritage who is at least partially descended from the indigenous people of Mesoamerica and who was born and/or raised in the United States. What distinguishes a Chicana from a Mexican-American, a Hispanic, or an American of Mexican descent is her political awareness; her recognition of her disadvantaged position in a hierarchically organized society arranged according to categories of class, race, gender, and sexuality; and her propensity to engage in political struggle aimed at subverting and changing those structures. (1997, 139)

Through their ethnic and national hybridity, Chicanas are most threatening to the established phallogocentric nationalist order. Elsewhere, Alfred Arteaga emphasizes the hybrid element of Chicano/a identity to be necessary to counter dominant discourses by transcending unitary concepts. Hybridity is a fundamental physical reality of Chicanismo. A consequence of essential hybridity, as examined earlier, is subjective ambiguity. The mestizo, the mixed-race European-American and native-indigenous person, can therefore be both *indio* or Indian and *hispano* or Hispanic. The ambiguity is most significant within the either/or racial binarism, as Arteaga says:

> Hybridization, or cultural mestizaje, differs from both autocolonialism and nationalism in that it is inherently polyglot. Hybridized discourse rejects the principle of monologue and composes itself by selecting from competing discourses . . . Hybridization asserts dialogue by articulating an alternate discourse and by organizing itself in internal dialogue. (1994, 18)

Ramón Saldívar argues that this process permeates Chicano literature. By applying Theodore Adorno's theory of the incessant presence of otherness within the self and the presence of the self within the other to the analysis of Chicano identity, Saldívar emphasizes the deconstruction of binary paradigms found in expressions of Chicano cultural identity:

> Chicano narrative and the constructed identity of the Chicano subject is a function of the deconstructed "difference" of various binary oppositions. (1990a, 159)

Such binary oppositions are included in the designations "self" and "other," or Spanish and Indian, American and Mexican, masculine and feminine, colonizer and colonized. When Chicanas represent an identity as one that decenters hierarchical binary paradigms, the idea of otherness itself is problematized. This, in turn, is a powerful tool against oppression because through the representation of a hybrid identity Chicanas subvert manipulation of a heterogeneous identity within a hegemonic discourse that would appropriate them as "Other" (Saldívar 1990a, 174). The subversion is located especially in Chicana literature because, as Saldívar asserts, the decentered notion of subjectivity resists hegemonic manipulation, as identity is decentralized (ibid.). Therefore, there can be no territorializing gaze upon a feminized body or other for the sake of the patriarchal or national interest. Due to their ethnic and cultural hybridity, as well as the complex nature of their liminal identities between and outside the imagined communities of not one but two nations, it is understandable that Chicana feminists are motivated and taking risks while promoting social change and justice, confronting equity issues, and countering homophobia.

Lesbianism marks Anzaldúa's deviance from the heterosexual imperative of Anglo, Mexican, and Chicano cultures as well as her identification with liminal subjects of different cultural backgrounds:

> Being the supreme crossers of cultures, homosexuals have strong bonds with the queer white, Black, Asian, Native American, Latino, and with the queer in Italy, Australia and the rest of the planet. We come from all colors, all classes, all races, all time periods. Our role is to link people with each other. (1987, 84)

This formulation may risk essentializing the lesbian of color as a necessarily revolutionary class—a problem to which I return below. Anzaldúa, however, insists that life in the borderlands is a practice, not an essence. Her mestizaje puts history through a sieve, winnows out the lies, looks at the forces that we as a "race" or "tribe," as women, have been. Anzaldúa says, *Luego bota lo que no vale*—a Chicana tosses out what is useless (82). In the construction of the mestiza consciousness she addresses, this step is a conscious rupture against all the oppressive traditions of any culture. Chicanas, she continues, communicate ruptures, "document examples of the struggles." They "reinterpret history and, using new symbols . . . begin shaping new myths." In the process, she concludes, Chicanas "surrender . . . all notions of safety, of the familiar. Deconstruct, construct" (82).

Finally, Anzaldúa's association of psychic unrest, writing, and the borderlands, together with the heterogeneity of her implied audience and her explicit invitations in her preface to *Borderlands/La Frontera* to non-Chicanas to meet her at the border, suggests that few of us escape the pain of the borderlands, and she calls us to participate actively in the work ahead to heal the wound caused by historical division, cultural misunderstanding, and the twin legacies of racism and sexism. A line in a poem in the same work states, "To live in the Borderlands means one insists we recognize the multiple communities to which we belong and examine the conflicts, as well as the connections among them" (195). The poem ends with this encouragement:

> *To survive the Borderlands*
> *you must live sin fronteras*
> *become a crossroads. (Ibid.)*

Anzaldúa thus transforms the borderlands from a space in which she is caught among conflicting loyalties and overlapping oppressions into a space in which she remaps and revises her cultural identity. In what is one of the most quoted and recognizable parts of the book, the fifth chapter, "How to Tame a Wild Tongue," Anzaldúa describes the evolution of Chicano Spanish in the borderlands. She consistently differentiates between Chicanas and Latinas, a difference that begins with language itself:

> Their language was not outlawed in their countries. They had
> a whole lifetime of being immersed in their native tongue;
> generations, centuries in which Spanish was a first language,
> taught in school, heard on radio and TV, and read in the
> newspaper. (58)

In contrast, she describes Chicanas as speaking as many as eight languages. Calling language a "homeland," she insists upon the validity of each one, insisting, "I am my language" (59). In a later passage, she again insists upon the specificity of her Chicana identity, describing people who use other labels, such as Spanish, Hispanic, Spanish-American, Mexican-American, Latin American, and Latin, as "copping out"—acculturating and thus denying the particularity of their Chicano identity (62). Although Anzaldúa does state that the "Latinoist movement is good" (89), she also insists that it is not enough, focusing instead on the historical and cultural specificity of Chicanos in her new, inclusive theory of Aztlán.

In her work, the idea of Aztlán moves away from Chicana/o nationalism directly to a feminist model without losing its emphasis on the values of home and family so sacred to early Chicana/o movement activists; it enlarges its own definition to address the issues of global migration, transnational capital, and shifting identities, insisting always on the fluidity and impermeability of categorizations and definitions. This Aztlán is not the same Aztlán presented by *la causa* co-founder Rodolfo "Corky" Gonzáles at the Chicano National Liberation Youth Conference in Denver in 1969 (Mariscal 2005). Instead, it is a vision of Aztlán inclusive of linguistic, cultural, and spiritual border crossers. As a metaphorical palimpsest, Aztlán will continue to change and be redefined by succeeding generations of Chicana/o scholars, never completely erasing its earlier definitions (Alarcón 1997).

Whether Anzaldúa can be considered the basic and best example of Chicana/o postnationalism has been debated, if not under the term "postnational," certainly in the implication of moving beyond the confines of a narrowly defined cultural nationalist perspective that continues to dominate some Chicana/o studies works and discussions. To end with them would be lending too much credence to the idea that they were "foundational" and "enduring." Their contributions and focus on labor, on justice, and on equality were and are important; but clearly, in the example of Anzaldúa, so much more transpired during the Chicano/a civil rights movement and so much has followed it that to focus only on the patriarchical and male legacy would be a disservice. Anzaldúa, now deceased, issued theorizations that stood up to such narrow legacy-creation mythologies and worked toward inclusivity, a brave and necessary act. In that, her text also makes a statement about the future direction of postnationalist understandings for Chicanos and Chicanas.

CONCLUSION

The postnational was an adjustment phase, a period of immense progress and growth. Despite the different political elements and issues with the advancement of capitalism, it has not diminished the need for Chicanas/os' scholarly and creative work. On the contrary, the "postnationality" framing of this book is a way to account for the previous nationalist aspects of the Chicana/o movement that occurred as a result of the advancement of global capital disruptions. Chicanas/os' traversal of the national, global, and transnational fields of study affords an initial examination and even more study. Such intense movements of people and commerce at the border have all but eliminated the need for geographical boundaries, and the sudden shift from a nationalistic mode suggests changing social conditions.

From an anecdotal standpoint, back in the 1980s imagining different, complex circumstances outside the realm of labor, class struggles, or resistance was inconceivable. Now the sense of the global and transnational is necessary, and the only true way that Chicanas/os have been able to develop a different strategy was to appeal to a heterogeneous arrangement of the social and political spheres. In this book, however, I have aimed to explain Chicana/o cultural nationalism's shift in perspective, assessing it as a philosophical and rhetorical composition that came to rely upon national codings. The formation of Chicana/o cultural production initially marked an exchange between Mexico and the United States to a limited extent but also encouraged U.S. national "minorities" to teach others about Mexican and Chicano cultures.

Postnationality has been configured as a series of sentiments, dispositions that are vital for situating the direction in Chicana/o transnational culture and its emergence. One of the successes of the changes is the way Chicana/o cultural interpretations have grown. For one, the intense focus on defining the authentic experience of Chicana/o political and class subjectivity has shifted to include cultural as well as social means of representation. My original formulation for this book was oriented toward the structuring of nationalism as a subjugated knowledge such that despite its expediency in capitalism, the sense of participation in the discourse of globalism was lacking.

Emerging into a global era has not been easy; anticolonial resistance movements have struggled to reorganize the historical experience of conquest and colonization, while many theorists view the liberation struggles of U.S. minorities as fundamentally tied to global anti-imperialist resistance. But because the ideology of nationalism appeals to the dispossessed, a framework for reinterpreting the experience of racial, ethnic, cultural domination within the United States has to be present in the discourse. Modified and reasserted as cultural nationalism, "Chicanismo" became a guiding principle to affirm cultural identity and organize collectively the historically persistent denial of social, political, and economic equality within U.S. society. But the question of how to make history and culture, when the sense of time and place no longer have the same significance as it did in the past, still remains to be answered.

In one of the few moments when Michel Foucault writes about identity in *The Archeology of Knowledge* (1972), he wanders into a historical discussion about the nature of identity. Ironically, as Foucault rarely discusses the place of identity, this particular passage seems to confront the same critical dilemmas in "minority" scholarship today. Foucault describes this tension between the genealogist and the historian in this way:

> The historian offers this confused and anonymous European, who no longer knows himself or what name he should adopt, the possibility of alternative identities, more individualized and substantial than his own. But the man with historical sense will see this substitution is simply a disguise. . . . The new historian, the genealogist, will know what to make of this masquerade. He will not be too serious to enjoy it; on the contrary, he will push the masquerade to its limit and prepare the great carnival of time where masks are constantly appearing. (Foucault 2004, 83)

The masks in this "carnival of time" characterize a performance of historical identities. Two views are posited: those of the historian and the genealogist. The former's serious demeanor offers this figurative "lost European" an identity "more individualized than his own." The latter, "the man with historical sense," the genealogist, is able to witness the carnival as a masquerade in which these figurative "masks are constantly appearing." Foucault's characterization is an appropriate way to close this discussion about the many ways Chicanas/os have created a national cultural identity. Removing the colonial tropes, one finds the hidden subterfuge of "forsaken" identity; in cultural nationalism lay an opportunity for renewal, for reestablishing the lost time that had been demolished under colonial displacements and global entanglements. Even as the provisional self determines her identification with a fabrication of historical fiction, we find in Chicana/o cultural nationalism a framework for contradictions in an identity that was neither national nor yet global. Chicanas/os' sense of displacement relied upon the deconstruction of American history. Foucault's remarks belie the fact that we have exhausted Marxist dialectical currency in our examinations of culture, nationalism, and sexuality as historical subjects. It is one thing, however, to accept the theory that most identities are performed and exhibited in myriad patterns with their own integrated logic. It is another to attribute this effect to Marxist readings of race and culture under capitalism and the evolution of American minority discourses.

As a theoretical explanation for the thematic tensions and concerns for different narrative foci in looking at the formation of the Chicana/o subject from a cultural studies perspective, I have argued that Marxist criticism in Chicana/o studies has influenced our understanding of power relations between the dominant society and the construction of a given "minority" subject. One of the most extensive analyses of this can be summarily reviewed in Ramón Saldívar's *The Chicano Narrative: Dialectics of Difference* (1990). Saldívar's study of Chicana/o literary subjectivity represents a classic Chicana/o Marxist literary approach that reads class and race as cultural differences and as the basis for marginalization or, as he states, as the "dialectics of difference." Naturally, this view places much emphasis on literary forms, publishing, canon formation, and textual analysis, practices that have long been criticized for a consideration of subjects involved in their own self-production.

In the chapter "Narrative, Ideology, and the Reconstruction of American Literary History," Saldívar proposes "a method of interpretation that will provide a ground for the development of reading Chicano literary works that intentionally exploit their peripheral status to, and exclusion from, the body of works that we might call majority literature" (11). Implicit in this essay is the foregone conclusion that "exclusion" is the basis for Chicana/o narrative study that exploits the peripheral status and is therefore productive of a given minority voice in culture (ibid.). The dialectics of difference that José Saldívar describes in *The Dialects of Our America* (1991) frames the "minority" in direct opposition to a majority form. This was perhaps the most common assumption made in Chicana/o Marxist criticism throughout the 1980s. The assumption could not quite predict that California would have the nation's largest population of people of Mexican descent; in other words, the word or status of "minority" was qualified by the sweeping demographics.

If readings of Chicana/o literature are intentionally produced in opposition to majoritarian ideals, then a cultural studies view would be more concerned with the intentional exploitation of the peripheral status because such a concern certainly indicates a different, but conscious, relationship with literary production. While Saldívar does not emphasize the latter assumption, the assumption does signal a move beyond the excluded minority subject and the more deliberate sense of agency we might confer upon someone who intentionally exploits his or her peripheral status.

One of the harshest lessons learned from this assumption is that we need to break away from the assumption that minorities are always formed in direct opposition to majoritarian-created ideals. This view can be challenged from minority criticisms of race and higher education. During the 1980s and 1990s, figures including Dinesh D'Souza, Shelby Steele, Clarence Thomas, and Ward Connerly adamantly challenged the role and value of ethnic identification in academic study and public policy. My study has been based on the explicit assumption that Chicana/o nationalism is a contradictory, ambiguous, and conflicted project that possessed emancipatory moments leading beyond it. While cultural nationalism initially provided a powerful discourse for Chicanas/os, I suggest that this discourse eventually manifested its limits. The notion of a collective Chicana/o identity was contested by alternative narratives of self, in Rodriguez as well as others, in a complex process in which various narratives about nationalism fought against one another, some with more success than others.

The development of a Chicana feminist movement bears witness to the historical political possibilities that arise from this "openness"—a strategic site of engagement, contestation, and rearticulation that calls upon existing identities even as it transforms them. Such a deconstruction of identity does not constitute a deconstruction of politics; "rather it establishes as political the very terms through which identity is articulated" (Butler 1990, 148).

It is not sufficient to simply label individuals as servants of a hegemonic new world order. It is necessary to understand the conservative issues individuals bring to the transformation of conservatism in an age of postmodernism. I therefore sought to transform the view of early Chicana/o literary criticism by looking at the post-Marxist readings of subject formation. I consider this book an attempt to respond to some of the contradictions of Chicana/o formation under a more deliberate and conscious evocation of marginal ideals. Worked into this analysis is the presumption that the identities once thought to be clear within the articulations of nationhood often mask their radical potential between what is permissible within representations of culture and what is reprehensible in dominant ideologies. Chicanas/os, like queers and feminists, exceeded boundaries of what is permissible and reprehensible. Thus, one must be able to conclude Chicano subject formation across a historical scheme by citing various strategies for articulating Chicana/o discourses that are also necessary for a postnational critique.

Aside from Saldívar's dialectics of difference, the formation of the Chicana/o subject has led to an impossible set of circumstances, what I term an "irreconcilable history." It can be displayed in plays and on the radio.[1] The end point of Marxist strategies and the beginning of new stylized performance of historical subjectivity as genealogy is "a self-conscious exploitation of the peripheral status." The citation of irreconcilability is a self-conscious choice of words that draws upon the trope of marriage to characterize Marxist criticism within contemporary critical practices.

I elaborate this point by drawing comparisons from feminist criticism of Marxism in social practices and the claims made by feminist scholars in their disenchantment with Marxist socialist thought. Heidi Hartmann, in "The Unhappy Marriage of Marxism and Feminism: Towards a More Progressive Union" (1981), made certain qualifications about the divergent goals and interests between class and gender analysis. What I find even more compelling in Hartmann's trope of marriage is the implied unrequited interest of gender and Marxism in contemporary gender and class analysis. The trope of marriage is useful for discovering the tension in race and gender in Chicana/o critical studies as well as between Mexico and the United States.[2]

The disenchantment with which Hartmann notes the relations between gender and class is a conspicuous separation of the divided interests. One of the underlying concerns about this shift toward theory appears related to the influences of post-structuralist deconstruction in the academy, that is, the questioning of metaphysical origins to rethink the colonized and subjugated body from an antifoundationalist model. Unlike Marxist criticisms in feminist thought and in American class analysis, cultural studies and post-structuralist criticism have, in my view, led to the inclusion of gender readings and to the inclusion of Chicana/o gays and lesbians as well as to an ongoing interest in spirituality and metaphysics. Challenging the nature of origins has ultimately loosened up the space for gender criticism and for gay and lesbian studies.

It should be made clear that postnationalism does not state that an antinationalist position is even necessary to enter into transnationalism. Especially during the 1990s, the question of identity indicated problems with minority studies to radically conceptualize contemporary postmodern conservatism and to link traditional historical locations with the intensification of global corporate culture.

These critiques of identity have been articulated by activists and academics coming from a wide range of perspectives. Activist women of color, conservative pundits, postmodernist theorists, and feminists of all colors and theoretical perspectives have noted the very real challenges posed by the concept of identity. The answers to the question of how to respond to these challenges, however, have varied widely. Some critics have retained an allegiance to the concept of identity and have attempted to reformulate or complicate their understandings of it. Ethnic studies scholars and members of various student groups, for example, continue to deploy identity as an organizing principle in their scholarly, political, and activist endeavors. Such scholars and activists have insisted that identity categories do not devolve into essentialist programs. Instead, identity categories provide modes of examining significant correlations between lived experience and social location. Other critics have advocated the abandonment of the whole enterprise of determining who belongs to what group or what that belonging might mean to the lives of social group members. Traditional Marxist critics and scholars would want to attribute this change in radical perspective to Michel Foucault's reworking of the modern historical subjectivity and especially to criticism against Marxist models of oppression so often cited in postcolonial and minority critical terms. However, the dialectics of change, as witnessed in the twenty-first century, also means structuring the nation to include the marginalized.

Critics still believe that a Marxist strategy is already implied in and perhaps overlapping critical race studies and cultural studies. A debate among leftist antifoundationalists at a UC Santa Cruz conference in 1998 suggested that the specter of conservatism has taken root among traditional Marxists.[3] The term "left conservatism," was coined to mark the Marxists who characterize the differences in leftist criticism between old-style and new-style Marxist strategies.[4]

These same problems plaguing leftist criticism have slowly made their way into Chicana/o studies. The debate between the antifoundationalists and traditional Marxists makes apparent the historical materialist problems that inform the debates among factions. Divisions can be seen to mirror the same ideological grids that I find in Chicana/o critical thinking and what I think is a place where an irreconcilability of terms has seeped into our critical discussions about the role of identity and that of politics.

Via postnationalism, I have suggested the different ways Chicana/o like other minority currents are caught in a historical contradiction. The discontinuities of representation occur because of our irresolute situation as cultural national subjects within a complex global system of divergent power and political interests, of ideology, of shifting hegemonic relations, and most of all, of the anti-inclusive nature of leftist and/or progressive programs. This assumption rests on the view Marxist criticism and especially Chicana/o scholars have already engaged about the limitations of race, gender, and even sexuality as categories that can influence each other. Again, our postnationalism underwrites many of the tenets established in Chicanas/os' use of material criticism. But contemporary cultural projects have to move beyond binary terms because the material circumstances within a critique driven by global, transnational, postmodern, queer, gender, and sexuality interests necessitate it.

Feminist scholar Ella Shohat located a specific discontinuity in her analysis of Third World women's films. Noting that her views represent a departure rather than an extension of European narrative development, she writes that while "hegemonic Europe may clearly have begun to deplete its strategic repertoire of stories, Third World people, First World minoritarian communities, women and gays and lesbians have only begun to tell and deconstruct theirs" (2006, 290). If, according to Shohat, we are just beginning to narrate and deconstruct some of "our" stories, are we also encountering critical problems along the way that alert us to the complications of identification? Much of what we already understand about national subjectivity, at least in its modern incarnation, that is, from "nation," is that there are no precise boundaries that can fully explain the various dislocations that comprise all people's experiences.

The Chicana/o movement inspired a unique intellectual reworking of the political and emotional affects that compose the shame of the colonized and the pride of the nationalist; most Mexican-Americans and other marginal groups faced active, full discrimination prior to the 1960s and 1970s. This moment of renewal, of change and insurgent locution, inspired a language and representation of liberation, of social amelioration as well as a performance-oriented project. Pride as a source of transformation became an even greater source of strength because the transvaluation of consciousness also became central to feminist and Chicana/o gay and lesbian criticisms.

This break in conventional thinking about Chicanas/os as a dissimulated body in a cultural national project created an irreconcilable history between the materialist and the idealist. In reconciling the linguistic, political, and cultural rules of citizenship, the movement toward liberation also may have altered the course of the intellectual problems we now have to consider *against* the colonial memory. The impetus for change under "culture" and "nationalism" would later be seen as a dubious and yet ironic passage of emergence, a recalcitrant and anti-intellectual posture when LGBTQI ideas were presented. While in this book I lay out a basis for exploring new Chicana/o subject formations within the spaces of transnational culture, I also have located the specific problems that confound expectation and rouse ideological support beyond the point of "just" identity or simply "of" nationalism.

NOTES

CHAPTER I

1. In "The Politics of Postnational American Studies" (2001), Donald Pease examines the debate over the reorientation of American studies along postnationalist coordinates within the context of the responses to Janice Radway's 1998 address to the American Studies Association as its president. "Postnational American studies" describes an interdisciplinary formation that would change the epistemological objects and introduce an alternative politics of power and knowledge for the field. But the postnational does not operate on its own; it is a construction that is internally differentiated out of its intersection with other unfolding relations. In his article Pease describes a contest between on the one hand the postnational state that serves the transnational corporations and accommodates their demand for exploitable labor and on the other hand the transnational social movements and subnational collective practices that seek to reorganize gendered and racialized capitalist relations around more equitable social and economic standards.

The concept of transnationalism focuses on the heightened interconnectivity among people all around the world and the loosening of boundaries between countries. The nature of transnationalism has social, political, and economic impacts that affect people all around the globe. The concept of transnationalism has facilitated the flow of people, ideas, and goods between regions. It has been greatly affected by the Internet, telecommunications, immigration, and, most importantly, globalization.

2. See Carnegie 2002, Pease 2001, Rowe 1998.

3. Muñoz' book is a unique exploration of the origins and development of Chicano radicalism in America. Carlos Muñoz Jr., himself a leader of the Chicana/o movement of the 1960s, places the movement in the wider context of the political development of Mexicans and their descendants in the United States. The 1989 revised edition of *Youth, Identity, and Power* filled a significant gap in the history of political protest in the United States and made a major contribution to the history of the cultural development of the Chicana/o population as a whole.

4. Many publications filtered through the National Association of Chicano and Chicana Studies (NACCS) explained the difference; Elenas 1999.

5. See Lisa Disch's 1999 interview with Judith Butler on the subject of Butler's 1997 book *Excitable Speech and the Politics of the Performative*.

6. Several important Chicana lesbian authors influenced this moment and helped illustrate the varied concerns of many gays and lesbians; see Cherríe Moraga's *Last Generation* (1993), Emma Pérez' "Sexuality and Discourse" (1991) and *Decolonial Imaginary* (1999), Gloria Anzaldúa's *Borderlands/La Frontera* (1987), and Deena J. González' "Speaking Secrets" (1998).

7. Simon and Schuster published explorations of some issues women confronted in the late 1960s. Later black feminism took on race as part of the feminist discourse, for example in Patricia Hill Collins' "Toward an Afrocentric Feminist Epistemology" from her *Black Feminist Thought* (1990), Barbara Christian's "The Race for Theory" (1987), and Antonia Castañeda's "Women of Color and Writing of Western History" (1992) and "'Que Se Pudieran Defender'" (2000).

8. See also Chatterjee 1986, 1993.

9. In her essay Rebolledo addresses the concern raised also by Alvina Quintana about misreadings of Chicana text, signaling the danger that "the critic, immersed in pursuing some essential point, will become overly enthusiastic and confuse the authorial voice with that of the narrative or poetic voice. As critics we must be careful not to confuse author with speaker" (Quintana 1996, 351).

10. Ybarra-Frausto (1977) and Sommers (1978) make valid contributions to the theoretical influences that have shaped feminist cultural studies and those of Chicana/o gays and lesbians.

11. Cynthia Orozco's numerous essays have shed light on the issue of history and Chicana scholarship. They include "Chicana Labor History" (1984), "Sexism in Chicano Studies and the Community" (1986), "Getting Started in Chicana Studies" (1990), and "Beyond Machismo, La Familia, and Ladies Auxiliaries" (1995).

12. Oscar Lewis' work on the "culture of poverty" shed light on the significance of acculturation, and Oscar Handlin's work legitimized the study of immigrant history with the publication of *Race and Nationality in American Life* (1957). See Zinn 1975a,b; Pierce and Segura 1993.

13. Numerous Chicana/o studies conferences have been held across Europe. Germany, Spain, and Turkey have hosted major international conferences in which the study of Chicanas/os as an ethnic minority has been the subject and focus.

14. One the most obvious examples of this is the massive recovery project initiated by Arte Público and the University of Houston in their effort to recover lost works. Ramón A. Gutiérrez provides a further illustration in his "Nationalism and Literary Production: The Hispanic and Chicano Experiences" (1993).

CHAPTER 2

1. Throughout the 1960s and 1970s several attempts were made to form a Chicana feminist movement. See Cotera 1983, 1984; Hardy-Fanta 1993; Sierra 1984.

2. Maxine Baca Zinn's "Family, Feminism, and Race in America" (1996) and Irene I. Blea's *La Chicana and the Intersection of Race, Class, and Gender* (1992) take up conventional notions of Chicana feminist issues.

3. Suzanne Tessler, "Compulsory Sterilization Practices" (1976). See also Elena Gutiérrez' *Fertile Matters* (2008) and Virginia Espino's "Women Sterilized as they Give Birth: Forced Sterilization and Chicana Resistance in the 1970s" (2000).

4. See Emma Pérez' reflections on this dynamic and problem in *The Decolonial Imaginary* (1999, 38). The same thread can be followed in specific articles detailing women's concerns all along; for example see Marisela R. Chávez, "We Lived and Breathed and Worked the Movement" (2000).

5. Marta Cotera's essay "Chicana Feminism" (1977) defined the work that Chicana feminists had undertaken. Alma García, in *Chicana Feminist Thought: The Basic Historical Writings* (1997), defines some of the preliminary foundational work by Chicanas. Later Dionne Espinoza in her dissertation, "Pedagogies of Nationalism and Gender" (2001), organized one of the first revisions of Chicana feminist practice, detailing the strategies of resistance by early Chicana feminists. Maylei Blackwell's work with feminist organization takes it to the next level when she expands on the analysis to include activists excluded from the Chicano movement. Among the essays in the collection edited by Chandra Mohanty, Ann Russo, and Lourdes Torres, *Third World Women and the Politics of Feminism* (1991), I draw particular attention to Nayereh Tohidi's "Gender and Islamic Fundamentalism," in which Tohidi documents the ubiquity of fundamentalism as a counterweight to American imperialism. This is an excellent example of the ways revolutionary projects undertake reactionary overtones.

6. Among the more than thirty titles published by Third Woman Press, several have had commercial success; these include *My Wicked, Wicked Ways* (1992), a book of poetry by MacArthur Award–winner Sandra Cisneros, and *Sexuality of Latinas* (1989), edited by Alarcón, Castillo, and Moraga and reprinted several times. A popular anthology frequently used as a college text, Moraga and Anzaldúa's *This Bridge Called My Back*, was republished in 2001. *Chicana Critical Issues: The Journal of Mujeres Activas en Letras y Cambio Social* is an interdisciplinary, peer-reviewed, biannual publication of MALCS. This feminist Chicana/Latina/Native academic organization is dedicated to building bridges between community and university settings, to transforming higher education, and to promoting new paradigms and methods.

7. Vicki L. Ruiz published the first historical secondary monograph on the subject of cannery women in 1987, the same year Anzaldúa published her monumentally influential *Borderlands/La Frontera*. Ruiz has sustained her intent in Chicana labor and initiated a series of encyclopedic works appealing to a Latina audience. That disciplinary breadth is shaped by the growing number of publications in the field of Latina studies.

8. "Images of La Chicana" (n.d., n.p.). The archival document is kept under Commission Board Appointments, 1983, UCLA Comisión Femenil papers. This ma-

terial can be found in the early papers and pamphlets describing the group's work and political trajectory. I thank Yolanda Redder, director of the Chicana/o studies archives, for discussion about special circumstances of the Comisión collection.

9. Ibid.

10. The 1983 MALCS declaration is kept in UCLA's Chicana/o studies archives.

11. See González, "Speaks Secrets: Living Chicana Theory" (1998), on the types of controversies specifically involving sexuality.

12. A copy of the original MALCS bylaws can be found in the UCLA Chicana/o Studies Library Special Collection. For further discussion of the institutional issues see González 1998.

13. The dynamic element of Chicana feminism also can be seen in newer projects undertaken by Rosa Linda Fregoso, Angie Chabram-Dernersesian, Maylei Blackwell, Dionne Espinoza, Deborah Vargas, Emma Pérez, and Elena Gutiérrez.

14. Emma Pérez offers yet another look at the compromises of liberalism and Chicana intellectual consciousness in *The Decolonial Imaginary* (1999).

15. In Ester Hernández' 1990 *La Ofrenda* (The Offering), she reinscribes the traditional sixteenth-century image of the apparition of the Virgen de Guadalupe, an iconic figure for both Mexicanas/os and Chicanas/os. In her rendering, the Virgin reveals herself on the back of a thoroughly modern, high-tech Chicana of indigenous ancestry, illustrating symbolically how Latinas literally bear their cultural identities with them as they face the contemporary world.

16. Segura and Pesquera 1990, Sosa Riddell 1974.

17. Mirandé 1979, Pierce and Segura 1993.

18. Prominently exemplifying Chicana feminism's possibilities to effect policy changes, in this case through electoral politics, is California state Senator Gloria Romero's move from academe to the state assembly and then to the state Senate, where she is majority leader; see http://dist24.casen.govoffice.com.

19. Gloria Anzaldúa recounted the story about the way she was denied admission into the History of Consciousness Program despite the fact that her book *Borderlands* was a major part of the curriculum at UC Santa Cruz. She noted that her denial into "His Con" was based upon her writing style and her concern for the voices of women of color. The Literature Board at UC Santa Cruz later accepted her into its program and awarded her Ph.D. posthumously in 2005.

20. Anzaldúa and Moraga 1981, Beneria 2003.

21. St. Mary's University sponsored Gender on the Borderlands, a two-day history conference July 12–14, 2001, to examine gender in the geographic Mexican-U.S. borderlands. The conference addressed gender-centered subjects in the history of this region, from studies of gender in Native American societies before contact with Europeans to research and studies of gender in the contemporary postmodern era of transnationalism and globalization.

22. *Stanford Encyclopedia of Philosophy*, http://plato.stanford.edu/entries/identity-politics/.

23. Sandoval calls this "differential consciousness," an acquired skill to convert binary forms of opposition into "ideological and tactical weaponry" (1991).

CHAPTER 3

1. Antonio Gramsci theorized the concept of "cultural hegemony" during fascist Italy under Benito Mussolini. In most of his writing he drew heavily from Marxist theory to examine the plight of the worker in Italy and formulate a critique of bourgeois culture. Gramsci was imprisoned for his work with the Communist Party; *Selections from the Prison Notebooks of Antonio Gramsci* (1971) popularized the study of U.S. people of color and postcolonial studies to extend the analysis of class to include ideas and intellectual productions.

2. Mary Rowlandson's short book on her captivity, originally published in 1682, is considered a seminal work in American literary studies. In the story, Rowlandson depicts her life among the natives, but the structure of the story also details her experience as an "encounter" with the frontier. This tale, like Hawthorne's *Scarlet Letter* (1812), James Fenimore Cooper's Natty Bumppo in *Last of Mohicans* (1826), and Hermann Melville's *Moby Dick* (1851) set forth ethnic confrontations as metaphors for their frontier experiences. The taming of the land and elements represents an expansion as a necessary facet of the frontier narrative.

3. Frederick Jackson Turner's original essay (1883) was reprinted as "The Significance of the Frontier in American History" in *The Frontier in American History* (1947).

4. De Leon and Griswold del Castillo's *North to Aztlán* (1996) has segments on the early period of the borderland region. Also see Baaken and Farrington's *The Gendered West* (2001), a collection of essays including some on the Southwest and California of the Spanish and Mexican periods.

5. See Martínez' *U.S.-Mexico Borderlands* (1996) for a general cross-disciplinary analysis of the problems, theoretical and material, regarding the border.

6. See Judith Haberstam's "Butch/FTM Border Wars" in *Female Masculinity* (1999) for a discussion of the relation of identity, embodiment, and gender. I was especially struck by the way Haberstam discusses the issues surrounding transexuality with what she calls a "border war." The implication of a border war suggests that the history of the border itself serves as a metaphor for other contested boundaries outside of a national discourse.

7. Examples of seductionism, whether as workers, queers, or "illegal aliens," abound in right-wing discourse. Reiterative media attention to "immigration reform" makes the point about where the topic figures in the national imaginary.

8. See Timothy J. Dunn's examination of what he calls "low-intensity conflict" in *Militarization of the U.S.-Mexico Border* (1996). His study of the justification for the U.S. war on drugs and the passage of specific legislation confirms the "militarization" of domestic land.

9. I have found David Harvey's "From Fordism to Flexible Accumulation" in *The Condition of Postmodernity* (1990) useful for looking at the economic transformation taking place in some border regions.

10. Dirik Raat argues in *Mexico and the United States* (1996) that the United States benefited from its colonial legacy while Mexico floundered. Raat identifies two types of colonialism. The United States experienced British rule, while Mexico experienced colonialism under Spain and France. Raat asserts that Spain's colonizing history shaped modern Mexico through strict adherence to hierarchy in its social organization. He notes that Spain's military initiative depended on the notion of *reconquista*.

11. See Lawrence Herzog's "Urban Space in Cross Cultural Perspective" in his *Where North Meets South* (1990).

12. See Alarcón's "Traductora, Traidora" (1989) for an extended discussion of the female icon in the historical narrative of conquest. It is important to recognize the ways in which Alarcón problematizes the female's dual role of virginal, goddess-like figure who can, as cultural translator, also be attributed with the role of intellectual "translator/betrayer."

13. My translation. This song is from the *Dreaming of You* album released posthumously (1996) by EMI Televisa Music.

14. See José Saldívar's *Border Matters* (1997) for analysis of the corrido as a model of resistance against the threat of an abusive law; often though not necessarily Anglo in form, the corrido consistently assumes a paternalistic and threatening tone.

15. Both David Montejano's *Anglos and Mexicans in the Making of Texas* (1987) and Armando Trujillo's *Tejano Legacy* (1998) offer insights into relations between Anglo and Mexican cultures.

16. The Mexican-American immigrant experience has a long history in relation to U.S. policy. For a discussion on the complexity of the immigrant experience see Alejandro Portes and Rubén Rumbaut's *Immigrant America: A Portrait* (1990). One of the most astounding social phenomena Portes and Rumbaut describe is that the most ardent call for more restrictions comes from the children of immigrants. It is an observation the authors find ironic (26–27).

17. See the collection edited by Juan Perea, *Immigrants Out* (1997). Perea's compilation of essays documents anti-immigration sentiments associated with the rise of nativist beliefs that are part of the American response to the global economic crisis and flexible labor trends in these global markets.

18. Among Bourdieu's works on "cultural production" are *Language and Symbolic Power* (1991) and *The Rule of Art* (1996). These works allow for a microtheoretical understanding of the way citizenship is constructed. Something as ordinary as one's own position as a citizen overlooks the immensity of the proposition.

19. According to Bourdieu (1991), a habitus is a series of dispositions that motivate and instruct agents to act in accordance with the dispositions. Examining the disposition of citizenship, or its habitus, one can begin to see the unnatural

yet naturalized aspects of citizenship in ordinary behavior through the cultural practice.

20. Mounted agents of U.S. immigration services patrolled the border in an effort to prevent illegal crossings as early as 1904, but their efforts were irregular and undertaken only when resources permitted. The inspectors, usually called mounted guards, operated out of El Paso, Texas. Though they never totaled more than seventy-five, they patrolled as far west as California trying to restrict the flow of illegal Chinese immigration. See also Nuñez-Neto 2006.

21. Bustamante focuses (1977) on three aspects of undocumented immigration from Mexico to the United States: the status of empirical research on this phenomenon; known characteristics of the migration and preliminary findings from Bustamante's survey of newly deported workers in nine Mexican border cities; and past attempts and proposed means to solve the problems related to undocumented immigration.

22. I like Sonia Saldívar-Hull's *Feminism on the Border* (2000) because it makes visible how narratives by and about women shape the pervading hegemonic relations.

23. For a discussion on the relationship between the body and power see Michel Foucault's *Power/Knowledge* (1980, 55–78).

CHAPTER 4

1. As ethnic, gender, and class exclusions were removed through the nineteenth and twentieth centuries and the public sphere approached its ideal more closely, Habermas identified (1991) a concurrent deformation of the public sphere through the advance of social welfare, the growth of culture industries, and the evolution of large private interests. Also see Hebdige 1979, Kondo 1997, Root 2005.

2. See Calefato 2004; González 2000, chapter 2; Parkins 2002.

3. Building on the experience of New York as a "culture capital," Sharon Zukin shows (1996) how three notions of culture, ethnicity, aesthetic, and marketing tool are reshaping urban places.

4. The rumor spread that Hilfiger had made disdainful remarks on *The Oprah Winfrey Show*. Winfrey said she had never met him and he had not appeared on her show before. She then invited Hilfiger to her program on January 11, 1999, and there he attempted to set the record straight and emphasized his enterprise's non-discriminatory policies.

CHAPTER 5

1. D. R. Godine, Boston, first published *Hunger of Memory* in 1982; citations here are from the 1983 Bantam edition. The surname Rodríguez is accented in its

original Spanish spelling; it is unclear whether Richard Rodriguez and/or his parents dropped the accent to facilitate assimilation into majority Anglo culture.

2. Rodriguez was a graduate student at UC Berkeley's English department but did not complete a dissertation, thus joining the ranks of "ABD" (all but dissertation) doctoral students who leave graduate school short of acquiring doctorates or hang on, working as instructors and lecturers. Many say the pressure to complete a dissertation stymied their other intellectual ambitions; ergo, they dropped out. The dropout rate for minority graduate and professional school students is high. Also see Juana María Rodríguez 2003, 174.

3. See Casas 2007, Chavez 2004, Deverell 2005, and Haas 1995 for discussions of the development of racial discourses and of anti-immigrant sentiment in nineteenth-century California.

4. The more frequently cited of these autobiographical accounts include Antonio Villareal's *Pocho*, Tomás Rivera's *Y no se lo tragó la tierra*, Rodolfo "Corky" González', *I Am Joaquin*, Ernesto Galarza's *Barrio Boy*, and Rudolfo Anaya's *Bless Me Ultima*. Most of these autobiographies build upon the "heroic model" as a counternarrative of resistance. The centrality of such "triumph" must be seen to coexist between Mexican colonial history as a fact of diasaporic formation of Chicanas/os as exiles and among the more obvious social prejudices in U.S. history.

5. Folkenflik's essay "The Self as Other" in *The Culture of Autobiography* (1993), which he edited, captures the rhetorical basis for describing some of the inclinations within ethnic autobiography. Folkenflik clearly draws from French poststructuralism, while I would like to consider some of his remarks as a critique of classical representations of the self.

6. See *The Ethnic Canon* (1995), edited by David Palumbo Liu. As a collection, Liu's book combines the processes of national subject formation and the simultaneous construction of an ethnic voice. I can say that most of the essays in this collection draw from that very problem of having to construct an individual identity within the limited demands of citizenship.

7. See Henry Staten's essay "Authenticity, Class, and Autobiography: The Case of *Hunger of Memory*" (1998). Staten's argument hinges on the tacit understanding that *Hunger of Memory* is based on Rodriguez', family narrative of Mexican identity and class distinctions and therefore should not fall under the category and scrutiny of Chicana/o critical investigation.

8. See Payne 1992. In particular, I was drawn to Payne's introduction, in which he explains the need to publish and establish an organized venture that recognizes the variety of cultural responses in shaping American consciousness.

9. More notably, as a means of decolonizing the subjugated identity, minorities in the 1960s and 1970s transformed the designation of one's own racialization into a favorable source of self-identification through slogans that activate a sense of social contestation against the often disparaging imprints on the racialized body— Black Is Beautiful, Gay Pride, and so forth. The renaming of the Chicana/o within

the cultural nationalist period did precisely that—the "transvaluation" of a demeaning stereotype that had in effect produced a network of related designations.

CHAPTER 6

1. Recent work on gay and lesbian migrations between the United States and
Latin America are but one example; see Gutmann 2003. Earlier critiques of exclusionary tendencies in U.S. gay and lesbian movements are found in the significant Chicana lesbian texts by Moraga and Anzaldúa.

2. Examples would be U.S. Latino organizations in the 1970s including GALA
(Gay and Lesbian Latino Alliance, San Francisco); in the 1970s and 1980s, Ellas en
Acción (She/Them, San Antonio); and later, LLEGO (Latino/a Lesbian and Gay Organization, national). These organizations criticized exclusion and discrimination
within other gay and lesbian organizations.

3. Examples include *Ugly Betty* recently but also, earlier, *Queer Eye for the
Straight Guy, The Ellen DeGeneres Show,* and *Queer as Folk.* All play along the
theme that gays and lesbians share similar goals, even if "of color." Few appear
in *Ugly Betty,* save for the 'tween younger nephew who demonstrates a penchant
for things that mark him as "gay." The other shows are remarkably bland in color
constructions.

4. Falwell was speaking on Pat Robertson's *700 Club* TV program on Septem-
ber 13, 2001.

5. CNN.com, "Falwell Apologizes to Gays, Feminists, and Lesbians," Septem-
ber 14, 2001.

6. "On the Mexican side of the border, the emergence of manufacturing plants
known as 'maquiladoras'—defined as Mexican assembly plants that manufacture
finished goods for export to the United States—has played a major role in border
economies. The term is derived from the word 'maquila,' which in colonial Mexico
was the fee that grain mills would charge to process farmers' grain. The U.S. Government Accountability Office estimated that 26,000 American-based companies
supply Mexican maquiladoras with raw materials and components, and their Mexican counterparts enlist cheap but productive labor. It is estimated that more than
1 million Mexicans are employed in more than 3,000 maquiladoras along the border" (Hereford 2006, citing Matt Rosenberg, "Maquiladoras in Mexico," About.
com, June 6, 2004).

7. See Arrizón 2007. Richard T. Rodriguez (2007) and Horacio Roque (2005)
explore different epochs in queer masculinity and the social space to conclude that
the element of looking like a U.S. citizen but discernible still as "queer" is important within the social and political spaces U.S. queer people of color have created.

8. This is not to say that U.S. feminism historically all but ignored race and
ethnicity. As many feminist historians have uncovered, racial and ethnic solidarity

occurred in, for example, the abolition movement, suffrage movement, and labor and union movements. See Pascoe 1993; Ruiz 1987, 19.

9. The movements and communities that have organized against social oppression are particularly directed at the formation of the modern state and its institutionalized practices. See Foucault's *Power/Knowledge* (1980).

10. Audre Lorde's *Zami: A New Spelling of My Name* (1982), to which she refers as a "biomythography," sustains this point. See Lyotard 1984, Phelan 1992.

11. Sue Ellen Case argues differently in "Tracking the Vampire" (1991). Although the term "queer" functions to reconcile ontological precepts of difference in gender, I extend "queer" to work as a means of cultural production outside of Western metaphysics and perhaps interrogate the marking of difference onto Third World spaces and communities.

12. The following institutions have programs: Yale, City University of New York (CUNY), Massachusetts Institute of Technology (MIT), City College of San Francisco, Duke University, and the University of Toronto.

13. Boswell 1980, Collins 1992, Escoffier 1990.

14. What is important is to look at the distinction in Escoffier's paradigm of queer intellectuals. The first wave, the "Stonewall" generation, includes Dennis Altman, John D'Emilio, Martin Duberman, Karla Jay, Jonathan Katz, and Esther Newton. The second wave, the "post-Stonewall" generation, includes John Boswell, Lee Edelman, David Halperin, and Eve Sedgwick. In his 1992 essay, however, Escoffier does not seem to know where to place Teresa de Lauretis, I imagine because the feminist trajectory in her work seems difficult to place.

15. Escoffier fails to recognize minority scholarship in more general terms and the contributions by scholars who incorporate theoretical and critical writings. See Norma Alarcón's "The Theoretical Subjects of *This Bridge Called My Back*" (1993).

16. Almaguer has been one of the important voices in early Chicano studies working with historical materialism within his sociological training and in his teaching. When his interests shifted to sexuality, it seems clear that the focus also shifted away from straightforward historical materialism. He says as much in the introduction to his book *Racial Fault Lines* (1994).

17. Queer readings have supported an understanding of religions across the world in texts like the Bible. What would happen if literature courses regularly taught authors as queer rather than neglecting their sexuality?

CONCLUSION

1. Southern California radio host and *Orange County Weekly* staff writer Gustavo Arellano also writes the nationally syndicated column *¡Ask a Mexican!*, in which he answers questions about Mexican culture; see *La Bloga* bloguero Daniel Olivas' "Interview with Gustavo Arellano" at http://labloga.blogspot.com/2007/04/interview-with-gustavo-arellano.html.

2. In a roundtable discussion in 2000, Deena González said, "The U.S. and Mexico married in 1877; divorce is impossible as the economy of one or the other folds with any true separation!" (Chicano History: The 1980s, Western History Association roundtable, San Antonio, Texas).

3. Left Conservatism: A Workshop, January 8, 1998, sponsored by UC Santa Cruz Center for Cultural Studies.

4. For a more detailed reading of Alan Sokal's parody of postmodern criticism originally published in *Social Text* see the introduction to Sokal and Jean Bricmont's *Fashionable Nonsense: Postmodern Intellectual Abuse of Science* (1998).

BIBLIOGRAPHY

Alarcón, Norma. 1981. "Chicana Feminist Literature: A Re-Vision Through Malintzin/or Malintzin: Putting Flesh Back on the Object." In *This Bridge Called My Back: Writings by Radical Women of Color*, ed. Cherríe Moraga and Gloria Anzaldúa. Watertown, MA: Persephone.

———. 1989. "Traductora, Traidora: A Paradigmatic Figure of Chicana Feminism." *Cultural Critique* 13 (Fall): 57–87.

———. 1990a. "Chicana Feminism: In the Tracks of 'the' Native Woman." *Critical Studies* 4, no. 3:248–256.

———. 1990b. "The Theoretical Subject(s) in *This Bridge Called My Back* and Anglo-American Feminism." In *Making Face, Making Soul/Haciendo Caras*, ed. Gloria Anzaldúa. San Francisco: Aunt Lute.

———. 1993. "The Theoretical Subjects of *This Bridge Called My Back*." In *Haciendo Caras: Critical Writing by Radical Women of Color*, ed. Gloria Anzaldúa. San Francisco: Aunt Lute.

———. 1994a. "Anzaldúa's Fronteras: Inscribing Gynetics." In *Displacement, Diaspora, and Geographics of Identity*. Durham, NC: Duke University Press.

———. 1994b. "Conjugating Subjects: The Heteroglossia of Essence and Resistance." In *An Other Tongue: Nation and Ethnicity in the Linguistic Borderlands*, ed. Alfred Arteaga. Durham, NC: Duke University Press.

———. 1995. "Cognitive Desires: An Allegory of/for Chicana Critics." In *Chicana (W)rites: On Word and Film*, ed. Maria Herrera-Sobek and Helena Maria Viramontes. Berkeley, CA: Third Woman.

———. 1997. "Conjugating Subjects in the Age of Multiculturalism." In *Mapping Multiculturalism*, ed. Avery Gordon and Chris Newfield. Minneapolis: University of Minnesota Press.

———. 1998. "Tropology of Hunger: The Miseducation of Richard Rodriguez." In *Ethnic Canon: Histories, Institutions, and Interventions*, ed. David Palumbo Liu. Minneapolis: University of Minnesota Press.

Alarcón, Norma, Ana Castillo, and Cherríe Moraga, eds. 1989. *The Sexuality of Latinas*. Berkeley, CA: Third Woman.

Alarcón, Norma, Rafael Castro, Deena González, Margarita Melville, Emma Pérez, Tey Diana Rebolledo, Christine Sierra, and Adaljiza Sosa Ridell, eds. 1993. *Chicana Critical Issues: Mujeres Activas en Letras y Cambio Social*. Chicana/Latina Studies. Berkeley, CA: Third Woman.

Aldama, Arturo J., and Naomi H. Quiñonez. 2002. *Decolonial Voices: Chicana and Chicano Cultural Studies in the 21st Century*. Bloomington: Indiana University Press.

Allen, Paula Gunn. 1988. "Who Is Your Mother? Red Roots of White Feminism." In *Multicultural Literacy: Graywolf Annual Five*, ed. Rick Simonson and Scott Walker. Saint Paul, MN: Graywolf.

Allenby, Greg M., Lichung Jen, and Robert P. Leone. 1996. "Economic Trends and Being Trendy: The Influence of Consumer Confidence on Retail Fashion Sales." *Journal of Business and Economic Statistics* 14, no. 1:103–111.

Almaguer, Tomás. 1991. "Chicano Men: A Cartography of Homosexual Identity and Behavior. *Differences* 3, no. 2:75–100.

———. 1994. *Racial Fault Lines: The Historical Origins of White Supremacy in California*. Berkeley: University of California Press.

Alvarez, Luis Alberto. 2006. "The Power of the Zoot: Race, Community, and Resistance in American Youth Culture." Ph.D. diss., University of Texas.

Anaya, Rudolfo. 1994. *Bless Me Ultima*. New York: Warner.

Anaya, Rudolfo A., and Francisco Lomelí, eds. 1989. *Aztlán: Essays on the Chicano Homeland*. Albuquerque, NM: Academia El Norte.

Andersen, Benedict. 1983. *Imagined Communities: Reflections on the Origins and Spread of Nationalism*. London: Verso.

Anthias, Floya, and Nira Yuval-Davis, eds. 1992. *Racialized Boundaries: Race, Nation, Gender, Colour, and Class and the Anti-Racist Struggle*. London: Routledge.

Anzaldúa, Gloria. 1987. *Borderlands/Frontera: The New Mestiza*. San Francisco: Aunt Lute.

———, ed. 1990. *Making Face, Making Soul: Haciendo Caras, Creative and Critical Perspectives by Women of Color*. San Francisco: Aunt Lute.

———, ed. 1993 *Haciendo Caras: Critical Writing by Radical Women of Color*. San Francisco: Aunt Lute.

Arrizón, Alicia. 2007. *Queering Mestizaje: Transculturation and Performance*. Ann Arbor: University of Michigan Press.

Arteaga, Alfred. 1994. "An Other Tongue." In *An Other Tongue: Nation and Ethnicity in the Linguistic Borderlands*, ed. Alfred Arteaga. Durham, NC: Duke University Press.

Austin, J. L. 1980. *How to Do Things with Words*. Cambridge: Harvard University Press.

Baaken, Gordon Morris, and Brenda Farrington, eds. 2000. *The Gendered West*. New York: Garland.

Barthes, Roland. 1974. *S/Z*. New York: Hill and Wang.

———. 1990. *The Fashion System*. Trans. Matthew Ward and Richard Howard. Berkeley: University of California Press.

Baudrillard, Jean. 1990. *Fatal Strategies*. Trans. Philip Breitchman and W. J. G. Niesluchoski; ed. Jim Fleming. New York: Semiotext(e).

Bauer, Dale M., and Priscilla Wald. 2000. "Complaining, Conversing, and Co-alescing." *Signs: Journal of Women in Culture and Society* 25, no. 4:1299–1303.

Beneria, Lourdes. 2003. *Gender, Development, and Globalization: Economics as If All People Mattered*. New York: Routledge.

Benstock, Shari, and Suzanne Ferris. 1994. *On Fashion*. New Brunswick, NJ: Rutgers University Press.

Berlant, Lauren. 2002. *The Queen of America Goes to Washington City: Essays on Sex and Citizenship*. Durham, NC: Duke University Press.

Berubé, Michael. 1999. "That's Not What I Said." *Chronicle of Higher Education*, May 21, B4.

Bhabha, Homi K. 1990. *Nation and Narration*. London: Routledge.

———. 1994. *The Location of Culture*. New York: Routledge.

Blackwell, Maylei. 2003. "Contested Histories: Las Hijas de Cuauhtemoc, Chicana Feminisms, and Print Culture in the Chicano Movement, 1968–1973." In *Chicana Feminisms: A Critical Reader*, ed. Gabriela Arredondo, Aida Hurtado, Norma Klaln, Olga Najera Ramírez, and Patricia Zavella. Durham, NC: Duke University Press.

Blea, Irene I. 1992. *La Chicana and the Intersection of Race, Class, and Gender*. Westport, CT: Praeger.

Bork, Robert. 1996. *Slouching Toward Gomorrah: Modern Liberalism and American Decline*. New York: Reagan Books, HarperCollins.

Boswell, John. 1980. *Christianity, Social Tolerance, and Homosexuality: Gay People in Western Europe*. Chicago: University of Chicago Press.

Bourdieu, Pierre. 1991. *Language and Symbolic Power*. Trans. Gino Raymond and Matthew Adamson; ed. John B. Thompson. Cambridge: Harvard University Press.

———. 1996. *The Rule of Art: Genesis of the Literary Field*. Stanford, CA: Stanford University Press.

Brennan, Timothy. 1990. "The National Longing for Form." In *Nation and Narration*, ed. Homi K. Bhabha. New York: Routledge.

Brown, Wendy. 1995. *States of Injury: Power and Freedom in Late Modernity*. Princeton, NJ: Princeton University.

Broyles-Gonzalez, Yolanda. 1986. "Women in El Teatro Campesino: '¿Apoca Estaba Molacha la Virgen de Guadalupe?'" In *Chicana Voices: Intersections of Class Race and Gender*, ed. Teresa Córdova, Norma Cantú, Gilberto Cardenas, Juan Falgá, and Christine Sierra. Albuquerque: University of New Mexico Press.

———. 1990a. "The Living Legacy of Chicana Performers: Preserving History Through Oral Tradition." In *Frontiers: A Journal of Women's Studies* 11, no. 1:46–52.

————. 1990b. "What Price 'Mainstream'? Luis Valdez' Corridos on Stage and Film." In *Cultural Studies* 4, no. 3 (October): 281–293.

————. 1994. *El Teatro Campesino: Theater in the Chicano Movement*. Austin: University of Texas Press.

Bruhn, Kathleen. 2006. *Mexico: The Struggle for Democratic Development*. Berkeley: University of California Press.

Bryndon, Anne, and Sandra Nissen. 1998. *Consuming Fashion: Adorning the Transnational Body*. New York: Berg.

Buell, Frederick. 1998. "Nationalist Postnationlism: Globalist Discourse in Contemporary American Culture." *American Quarterly* 50, no. 3:548–591.

Bustamante, Jorge A. 1977. "Undocumented Immigration from Mexico: Research Report." *International Migration Review* 11, no. 2:149–177.

Butler, Judith. 1990. *Gender Trouble: Feminism and the Subversion of Identity*. New York: Routledge.

————. 1993. *Bodies That Matter: On the Discursive Limits of "Sex"*. New York: Routledge.

————. 1997a. *Excitable Speech and the Politics of the Performative*. New York: Routledge.

————. 1997b. *The Psychic Life of Power: Theories in Subjection*. Palo Alto, CA: Stanford University Press.

Bystydzienski, Jill M., and Steven P. Schacht, eds. 2001. *Forging Radical Alliances Across Difference: Coalition Politics for the New Millennium*. New York: Rowman and Littlefield.

Calderón, Hector, and José David Saldívar. 1991. *Criticism in the Borderlands: Studies in Chicano Literature, Culture and Ideology*. Durham, NC: Duke University Press.

Calefato, Patrizia. 2004. *The Clothed Body*. New York: Berg.

Campos Carr, Irene. 1989. "Proyecto La Mujer: Latina Women Shaping Consciousness." In *Women's Studies International Forum* 12, no. 1:45–49.

Candelaria, Cordelia. 1980. "La Malinche, Feminist Prototype." *Frontiers: A Journal of Women's Studies* 5, no. 2:1–6.

Cantú, Norma. 1986. "Women Then and Now: An Analysis of the Adelita Image vs. the Chicana as Political Writer and Philosopher." In *Chicana Voices*, ed. Córdova et al.

————. 1997. *Canicula: Snapshots of Girlhood en La Frontera*. Albuquerque: University of New Mexico Press.

Carby, Hazel. 1982. "White Women Listen! Black Feminism and the Boundaries of Sisterhood." In *The Empire Writes Back*, ed. Bill Ashcroft, Gareth Griffiths, and Helen Tiffin. Centre for Contemporary Cultural Studies, University of Birmingham. London: Hutchinson.

————. 1987. *Reconstructing Womanhood: The Emergence of the Afro-American Woman Novelist*. New York: Oxford University Press.

Cardenas de Dwyer, Carlota. 1975. "Chicano Literature: An Introduction." *Caracol* 1, no. 10:6–7.

Carmichael, Stokely. 1967. *Black Power: the Politics of Liberation in America*. New York: Random House.

Carnegie, Charles. 2002. *Postnationalism Prefigured: Caribbean Borderlands*. New Brunswick. NJ: Rutgers University Press.

Casas, Raquel. 2007. *Married to a Daughter of the Land: Interethnic Marriages in California, 1820–1880*. Las Vegas: University of Nevada Press.

Case, Sue Ellen. 1991. "Tracking the Vampire." *Differences. Lesbian and Gay Sexualities* 3 (Summer): 1–20.

Castañeda, Antonia I. 1990a. "Gender, Race, and Culture: Spanish-Mexican Women in the Historiography of Frontier California." In *Frontiers: A Journal of Women Studies* 11, no. 1:8–20.

———. 1990b. "Oppression, Power, Privilege, Complicity, Denial, Silence, and Autonomy: Issues in Chicana Feminism." Paper presented at MALCS Summer Institute, Berkeley, CA, August.

———. 1992. "Women of Color and Writing of Western History." *Pacific Historical Review* 61, no. 4:501–533.

———. 2000. "'Que Se Pudieran Defender (So You Could Defend Yourselves)': Chicanas, Regional History, and National Discourses." *Frontiers: A Journal of Women Studies* 22, no. 3:116–142.

Castillo, Ana. 1991. "La Macha: Toward a Beautiful Whole Self." In *Chicana Lesbians: The Girls Our Mothers Warned Us About*, ed. Carla Trujillo. Berkeley, CA: Third Woman.

Chabram, Angie. 1990. "Chicana/o Studies as Oppositional Ethnography." *Cultural Studies* 4, no. 3:228–247.

Chabram, Angie, and Rosa Linda Fregoso. 1990. "Chicana/o Cultural Representations: Reframing Alternative Critical Discourses." *Cultural Studies* 4, no. 3:203–212.

Chabram-Dernersesian, Angie. 1992. "I Throw Punches for My Race, but I Don't Want to Be a Man: Writing Us—Chica-Nos/Chicanas—into the Movement Script." In *Cultural Studies*, ed. Lawrence Grossberg, Cary Nelson, and Paula Treichler. London: Routledge.

———. 1993. "And Yes . . . The Earth Did Part: On the Splitting of Chicana/o Subjectivity." In *Building with Our Hands: New Directions in Chicana Studies*, ed. Adela de la Torre and Beatriz Pesquera. Berkeley: University of California Press.

Chatterjee, Partha. 1986. *Nationalist Thought and the Colonial World: A Derivative Discourse?* London: Zed.

———. 1993. *The Nation and Its Fragments: Colonial and Postcolonial Histories*. Princeton, NJ: Princeton University Press.

Chavez, Ernesto. 2002. *¡Mi Raza Primero!: Nationalism, Identity, and Insurgency in the Chicano Movement*. Berkeley: University of California Press.

Chávez, Marisela R. 2000. "We Lived and Breathed and Worked the Movement." In *Las Obreras: Chicana Politics of Work and Family*, ed. Vicki L. Ruiz. Vol. 1. Los Angeles: Aztlán Anthology Series.

Chavez, Miroslava. 2004. *Negotiating Conquest: Gender and Power in California, 1770–1880*. Tucson: University of Arizona Press.

Chow, Rey. 1991. "Violence in the Other Country: China as Crisis, Spectacle, and Woman." In *Third World Women and the Politics of Feminism*, ed. Chandra Talpade Mohanty, Ann Russo, and Lourdes Torres. Bloomington: Indiana University Press.

———. 1993. *Writing Diaspora: Tactics of Intervention in Contemporary Cultural Studies*. Bloomington: Indiana University Press.

Christian, Barbara. 1987. "The Race for Theory." In *Feminisms*, ed. Sandra Kemp and Judith Butler. New York: Oxford University Press.

Cisneros, Sandra. 1992. *My Wicked, Wicked Ways*. Berkeley, CA: Third Woman.

Cocks, Joan. 1989. *The Oppositional Imagination*. London: Routledge.

Cohen, Ed. 1992. "Who Are 'We'? Gay 'Identity' as Poetical (E)motion (A) theoretical Rumination." *Inside/Out: Lesbian Theories, Gay Theories*, ed. Diana Fuss. London: Routledge.

Collins, Jack. 1992. "Matters of Fact: Establishing a Gay and Lesbian Studies Department." *Journal of Homosexuality* 24:109–123.

Collins, Patricia Hill. 1990. *Black Feminist Thought: Knowledge, Consciousness, and the Politics of Empowerment*. London: HarperCollins Academic.

Connell, R. W. 1987. *Gender and Power*. Stanford, CA: Stanford University Press.

Córdova, Teresa, Norma Cantú, Gilberto Cardenas, Juan Falgá, and Christine Sierra, eds. 1986. *Chicana Voices: Intersection of Class, Race, and Gender*. Austin: Center for Mexican American Studies.

Cotera, Marta P. 1973. "La Mujer Mexicana: Mexicano Feminism." *Magazin* 1, no. 9:30–32.

———. 1976. *Diosa y Hembra: The History and Heritage of Chicanas in the US*. Austin, TX: Information Systems Development.

———. 1977. "Chicana Feminism." Essay. Austin, TX: Information Systems Development.

———. 1980. "Feminism: The Chicana and Anglo Versions, a Historical Analysis." In *Twice a Minority: Mexican American Women*, ed. Margarita B. Melville. St. Louis, MO: Mosby.

———. 1983. "Brief Analysis of the Political Role of Hispanas in the United States." Prepared for Women of Color Institute, Washington, DC. November. Benson Latin American Collection, University of Texas, Austin.

———. 1984. "Hispanic Political Tradition." *Intercambios Feminiles* 2/3:1, 24.

Cox, Kevin R., ed. 1997. *Spaces of Globalization: Reasserting the Power of the Local*. New York: Guildford.

Cruikshank, Margaret. 1990. *The Gay/Lesbian Liberation Movement*. New York: Routledge.

Davis, Angela. 1992. "Black Nationalism: The Sixties and the Nineties." In *Black Popular Culture*, ed. Gina Dent. Seattle, WA: Bay.

Davis, Angela Y. 1994. "Afro Images: Politics, Fashion, and Nostalgia." In *Critical Inquiry* 21, no. 1:37–45.

Davis, Kathy, and Sue Fisher. 1993. "Power and the Female Subject." In *Negotiating at the Margins: The Gendered Discourses of Power and Resistance*, ed. Sue Fisher and Kathy Davis. New Brunswick, NJ: Rutgers University Press.

Decker, Jeffrey Louis. 1993. "Mr. Secrets: Days of Obligation: An Argument with My Mexican Father Richard Rodriguez." *Transition* 61:124–133.

de la Haye, Amy, and Elizabeth Wilson. 1999. *Defining Dress: Dress as Object, Meaning, and Identity*. Manchester, England: University of Manchester Press.

de la Torre, Adela, and Beatriz M. Pesquera. 1993. *Building with Our Hands: New Directions in Chicana Studies*. Berkeley: University of California Press.

de Lauretis, Teresa, ed. 1986. *Feminist Studies/Critical Studies*. Bloomington: Indiana University Press.

———. 1987. *Technologies of Gender: Essays on Theory, Film, and Fiction*. Bloomington: Indiana University Press

De Leon, Arnoldo, and Richard Griswold del Castillo. 1996. *North to Aztlán: A History of Mexican Americans in the United States*. New York: Twayne.

del Castillo, Adelaida R., ed. 1989. *Between Borders: Essays on Mexicana/Chicana History*. Encino, CA: Floricanto.

D'Emilio, John. 1983. *Sexual Politics, Sexual Communities in the United States 1940–1970*. Chicago: University of Chicago Press.

D'Emilio, John, and Estelle B. Freedman. 1988. *Intimate Matters: History of Sexuality in America*. New York: Harper and Row.

Deverell, William. 2005. *Whitewashed Adobe: The Rise of Los Angeles and Its Mexican Past*. Berkeley: University of California Press.

Díaz-Cotto, Juanita. 2001. "Lesbian Feminist Activism and Latin American Feminist Encuentros." In *Sexual Identities/Queer Politics*, ed. Mark Blasius. Princeton, NJ: Princeton University Press.

Disch, Lisa. 1999. "Judith Butler and the Politics of the Performative." *Political Theory* 27, no. 4 (August): 545–559.

D'Souza, Dinesh. 1991. *Illiberal Education: The Politics of Race and Sex on Campus*. New York: Free Press.

Duara, Prasenjit. 1995. *Rescuing History from the Nation*. Chicago: University of Chicago Press.

Dunn, Timothy J. 1996. *Militarization of the U.S.-Mexican Border 1978–1992*. Austin: University of Texas Press.

Eagleton, Terry. 1991. *Ideology: An Introduction*. London: Verso.

———. 1996. *The Illusion of Postmodernism*. Cambridge: Blackwell.

Eaklor, Vicki L. 1997. "Where Are We Now, Where Are We Going, and Who Gets to Say?" *The Gay '90s: Disciplinary and Interdisciplinary Formations in*

Queer Studies, ed. Thomas Foster, Carol Siegel, and Ellen E. Berry. New York: NYU Press.

Eisenstein, Zillah. 1988. *The Female Body and the Law*. Berkeley: University of California Press.

Elenas, C. Alejandra. 1999. "Toward the Construction of a Chicana/o Identity: Borderlands and the Educational Discourse." In *Selected Proceedings from the 22nd NACS Conference*, ed. Ada Sosa Riddell. National Association of Chicano Studies.

Enloe, Cynthia. 1989. *Bananas, Beaches, and Bases. Making Feminist Sense of International Politics*. Berkeley: University of California Press.

Escobar, Eduardo. 1999. *Race, Police, and the Making of a Political Identity*. Berkeley: University of California Press.

Escoffier, Jeffrey. 1990. "The Ivory Closet." *Outlook* 3, no. 2 (Fall): 40–48.

———. 1992. "Generations and Paradigms: Mainstreams in Lesbian and Gay Studies." *Journal of Homosexuality* 24, no. 1/2:7–26.

Espino, Virginia. 2000. "Women Sterilized as Give Birth: Forced Sterilization and Chicana Resistance in the 1970's." In *Las Obreras*, ed. Ruiz.

Espinoza, Dionne. 2001a. "Pedagogies of Nationalism and Gender: Cultural Resistance in Selected Representational Practices of Chicana/o Movement Activists, 1967–1972." Ph.D. diss., Cornell University.

———. 2001b. "Revolutionary Sisters: Women's Solidarity and Collective Identification Among Chicana Brown Berets in East Los Angeles, 1967–1970." *Aztlán* 26, no. 1 (Spring): 15–58.

Espinoza, Dionne, and Lorena Oropeza, eds. 2006. *Enriqueta Vasquez and the Chicano Movement: Writings from El Grito del Norte*. Houston: Arte Público.

Ewen, Stuart. 1991. "All Consuming Images: The Politics of Style in Contemporary Culture." *Journal of Marketing* 55, no. 3:88–90.

Fallis, Guadalupe Valdes. 1974. "The Liberated Chicana—A Struggle Against Tradition." *Women: A Journal of Liberation* 3:20.

Fanon, Frantz. 1967. *Black Skin, White Masks*. New York: Grove.

Fernandez-Kelly, Maria Patricia. 1983. "Mexican Border Industrialization, Female Labor Force Participation, and Migration." In *Women, Men, and the International Division of Labor*, ed. June Nash and Maria Patricia Fernandez-Kelly. Albany, NY: SUNY Press.

Flores, Francisco. 1971. "Conference of Mexican American Women: Un Remolino." *Regeneración* 1 no. 1 (January): 1–5.

Florida, Richard, and Gary Gates, 2002. "Technology and Tolerance: The Importance of Diversity to High Technology Growth." Center for Urban and Metropolitan Policy. *Brookings Institute Policy Study* 20, no. 1 (Winter): 1–5.

Folkenflik, Robert. 1993. "The Self as Other." In *The Culture of Autobiography: Constructions of self-Representation*, ed. Robert Folkenflik. Stanford, CA: Stanford University Press.

Foucault, Michel. 1970a. *Madness and Civilization*. New York: Pantheon.

———. 1970b. *The Order of Things: The Archeology of Human Sciences*. New York: Random House.

———. 1972. *The Archeology of Knowledge*. New York: Pantheon.

———. 1978. *The History of Sexuality*. Vol. 1. New York: Pantheon.

———. 1980. *Power/Knowledge: Selected Interviews and Other Writings 1972–1977*. New York: Pantheon.

———. 1985. *The Use of Pleasure: The History of Sexuality*, vol. 2. Trans. Robert Hurley. New York: Vintage.

———. 1995. *Discipline and Punish: The Birth of the Prison*. Originally published in 1979. Reprint, New York: Vintage.

———. 2004. "Nietzsche, Genealogy, and History." In *The Postmodern Reader: Foundational Texts*, ed. Michael Drolet. New York: Routledge.

Franco, Jean. 1988. "Beyond Ethnocentrism: Gender, Power, and the Third World Intelligentsia." In *Marxism and the Interpretation of Culture*, ed. Cary Nelson and Lawrence Grossberg. Urbana: University of Illinois Press.

Fraser, Nancy. 1991. *Unruly Practices*. Minneapolis: University of Minnesota Press.

———. 1992. "Rethinking the Public Sphere." In *Habermas and the Public Sphere*, ed. Craig Calhoun. Cambridge: MIT Press.

Fregoso, Rosa Linda. 1990. "*Born in East LA* and the Politics of Representation." *Cultural Studies* 4, no. 3:264–280.

———. 1992. "Chicana Film Practices: Confronting the Many Headed Demon of Oppression." In *Chicanos and Film: Representation and Resistance*, ed. Chon Noriega. Minneapolis: University of Minnesota Press.

———. 1993. *The Bronze Screen: Chicana and Chicano Film Culture*. Minneapolis: University of Minnesota Press.

———. 2003. *Mexican Encounters: The Making of Social Identities on the Borderlands*. Berkeley: University of California Press.

Fregoso, Rosa Linda, and Angie Chabram. 1990. "Chicana/o Cultural Representations: Reframing Alternative and Critical Discourses." *Cultural Studies* 4 no. 3:203–341.

Fuss, Diana. 1989. *Essentially Speaking: Feminism, Nature, and Difference*. Routledge: New York.

———. 1992. "Fashion and the Homospectatorial Look." *Critical Inquiry* 18, no. 4:713–737.

Galindo, Leticia D., and Maria Dolores Gonzales, eds. 1999. *Speaking Chicana: Voice, Power, and Identity*. Tucson: University of Arizona Press.

García, Alma. 1990. "The Development of Chicana Feminist Discourse, 1970–1980." In *Unequal Sisters: A Multi-Cultural Reader in U.S. Women's History*, ed. Ellen DuBois and Vicki Ruiz. New York: Routledge.

———, ed. 1997. *Chicana Feminist Thought: The Basic Historical Writings*. New York: Routledge.

García, Mario T. 1989. *Mexican Americans: Leadership, Ideology, and Identity, 1930–1960*. New Haven, CT: Yale University Press.

García, Richard. 1978. "The Chicano Movement and the Mexican American Community, 1972–1978: An Interpretive Essay." *Socialist Review* 8, nos. 4–5 (July–October): 117–141.

Gil Gomez, Ellen M. 2002. "Marketing Latin/America: Latinos as Consumers in the US Marketplace." *American Quarterly* 54, no. 3:537–542.

Gilroy, Paul. 1987. *There Ain't No Black in the Union Jack: The Cultural Politics of Race and Nation*. London: Hutchinson.

———. 1992a. "It's a Family Affair." In *Black Popular Culture*, ed. Gina Dent. Seattle, WA: Bay.

———. 1992b. "Cultural Studies and Ethnic Absolutism." In *Cultural Studies*, ed. Grossberg, Nelson, and Treichler.

———. 1992c. "The End of Antiracism." In *Race, Culture and Difference*, ed. James Donald and Ali Rattansi. London: Sage and Open University.

Goldman, Shifra M. 1990. "The Iconography of Chicano Self-Determination: Race, Ethnicity, and Class." *Art Journal* 49, no. 2:167–173.

Gómez, Alma, Cherríe Moraga, and Mariana Romo-Carmona, eds. 1983. *Cuentos: Stories by Latinas*. New York: Kitchen Table, Women of Color.

Gómez-Peña, Guillermo. 1996. *The New World Border: Prophecies, Poems and Loquerias for the End of the Century*. San Francisco: City Lights.

Gómez Quiñones, Juan. 1978. *Mexican Students por la Raza: The Chicano Student Movement in Southern California: 1967–1977*. Santa Barbara, CA: Editorial La Causa.

———. 1986. "Studying Chicanas: Bringing Women into the Frame of Chicano Studies." In *Chicana Voices*, ed. Córdova et al.

———. 1990. *Chicano Politics: Reality and Promise, 1940–1990*. Albuquerque: University of New Mexico Press.

Gonzáles, Sylvia. 1980. "Towards a Feminist Pedagogy for Chicana Self-Actualization," *Frontiers: A Journal of Women Studies* 5:48–51.

González, Deena J. 1998. "Speaking Secrets: Living Chicana Theory." In *Living Chicana Theory*, ed. Carla Trujillo. Berkeley, CA: Third Woman.

———. 2000. *Refusing the Favor*. Oxford, England: Oxford University Press.

Gramsci, Antonio. 1971. *Selections from the Prison Notebooks of Antonio Gramsci*. Trans. and ed. Quintan Hoare and Geoffrey Nowell Smith. New York: International Publishers.

Grewal, Inderpal. 1994. "Autobiographic Subjects and Diasporic Locations: Meatless Days and Borderlands." In *Scattered Hegemonies: Postmodernity and Transnational Feminist Practices*, ed. Inderpal Grewal and Caren Kaplan. Minneapolis: University of Minnesota Press.

———. 1996. *Home and Harem: Nationalism, Imperialism, and the Culture of Travel*. Durham: NC: Duke University Press.

Grewal, Inderpal, and Caren Kaplan, eds. 1994. *Scattered Hegemonies: Postmodernity and Transnational Feminist Practices*. Minneapolis: University of Minnesota Press.

Griswold del Castillo, Richard, Teresa McKenna, and Yvonne Yarbro-Bejarano, eds. 1990. *Chicano Art: Resistance and Affirmation: 1965–1985*. Los Angeles: Wight Art Gallery, University of California.

Gutierrez, Elena. 2008. *Fertile Matters: The Racial Politics of Mexican-Origin Women's Reproduction*. Austin: University of Texas Press.

Gutiérrez, Ramón A. 1993. "Nationalism and Literary Production: The Hispanic and Chicano Experiences." In *Recovering the U.S. Hispanic Literary Heritage*, ed. Ramón Gutiérrez and Genaro Padilla. Houston: Arte Público.

——. 1996. "The Erotic Zone: The Sexual Transgression on the US Mexican Border." In *Mapping Multiculturalism*, ed. Avery Gordon and Christopher Newfield. Minneapolis: University of Minnesota Press.

Gutiérrez-Jones, Carl. 1995. *Rethinking the Borderlands: Between Chicano Culture and Legal Discourse*. Berkeley: University of California Press.

——. 1998. "Injury by Design." Special issue, "The Future of American Studies," *Cultural Critique* 40 (Autumn): 73–102.

Gutmann, Matthew, ed. 2003. *Changing Men and Masculinities in Latin America*. Durham, NC: Duke University Press.

Haas, Lizbeth. 1995. *Conquest and Historical Identities in California 1769–1836*. Berkeley: University of California Press.

Habermas, Jürgens. 1991. *The Structural Transformation of the Public Sphere: An Inquiry into a Category of Bourgeois Society*, trans. Thomas Burger with Frederick Lawrence. Cambridge, MA: MIT Press.

——. 1992. *Postmetaphysical Thinking*. Cambridge, MA: MIT Press.

Haberstam, Judith. 1999. "Butch/FTM Border Wars." In *Female Masculinity*, Durham, NC: Duke University Press.

Haggis, Jane. 1990. "The Feminist Research Process—Defining a Topic." In *Feminist Praxis: Research, Theory, and Epistemology in Feminist Sociology*, ed. Liz Stanley. New York: Routledge.

Hall, Jacquelyn Dowd. 2005. "The Long Civil Rights Movement and the Political Uses of the Past." *Journal of American History* 91, no. 4:1233–1263.

Hall, Stuart. 1986. "Gramsci's Relevance for the Study of Race and Ethnicity." *Journal of Communication Theory* 10, no. 2:5–27.

——. 1989. "Cultural Identity and Cinematic Representation." In *Framework* 36:68–81.

——. 1990. "Cultural Identity and Diaspora." In *Identity: Community, Culture, Difference*, ed. Jonathon Rutherford. London: Lawrence and Wishart.

——. 1992. "What Is the 'Black' in Black Pop Culture?" In *Black Popular Culture*, ed. Gina Dent. Seattle: Bay.

Handlin, Oscar. 1957. *Race and Nationality in American Life*. New York: Doubleday.

Hardy-Fanta, Carol. 1993. *Latina Politics, Latino Politics, Gender, Culture, and Political Participation in Boston*. Philadelphia: Temple University.

Hartmann, Heidi. 1981. "The Unhappy Marriage of Marxism and Feminism." In *Politics, Patriarchy, and Practice*, ed. Roger Dale, Geoff Esland, Ross Fergusson, and Madeleine MacDonald. Vol. 2 of *Education and the State*. Sussex, England: Open University, Falmer.

Hartsock, Nancy. 1990. "Foucault on Power: A Theory for Women." In *Feminism/Postmodernism*, ed. Linda J. Nicholson. New York: Routledge.

Harvey, David. 1990. *The Condition of Postmodernity: An Enquiry into the Origins of Cultural Change*. Cambridge, MA: Blackwell.

Hassan, Ihab. 1987. *The Postmodern Turn: Essays in Postmodern Theory and Culture*. Columbus: Ohio State University Press.

Hebdige, Dick. 1979. *Subculture: The Meaning of Style*. London: Metheun.

Heller, Celia S. 1968. *Mexican American Youth: Forgotten Youth at the Crossroads*. New York: Random House.

Hennesey, Rosemary "Queer Theory, Left Politics." In *Rethinking Marxism* 7, no. 1 (Fall): 48–61.

Hereford, Jesse. 2006. "The U.S.-Mexico Border: Integrated Economies." *Economic Development America* (Spring): 2. http://www.iedconline.org/EDAmerica/Spring2006/integration.html.

Herrera-Sobek, Maria, ed. 1985. *Beyond Stereotypes: The Critical Analysis of Chicana Literature*. Binghamton, NY: Bilingual Press/Editorial Bilingue.

———. 1990. *The Mexican Corrido: A Feminist Analysis*. Bloomington: Indiana University Press.

Herrera-Sobek, Maria, and Helena Maria Viramontes, eds. 1988. *Chicana Creativity and Criticism: Charting New Frontiers in American Literature*. Houston: Arte Público.

Herzog, Lawrence. 1990. *Where North Meets South: City Spaces and Politics on the Us Mexican Border*. Austin: Center for Mexican American Studies, University of Texas.

Hobsbawn, Eric J. 1990. *Nations and Nationalism Since 1789*. Cambridge, England: Cambridge University Press.

Holguin Cuadraz, Gloria. 1996. "Experiences of Multiple Marginality: A Case Study of Chicana 'Scholarship Women.'" In *Racial and Ethnic Diversity in Higher Education*, ed. M. Garcia, A. Nora, L. Rendon, C. Sotello, and V. Turner. Needham Heights, MA: Simon and Schuster.

Hollenshead, Carol, and Gloria D. Thomas. 2001. "Resisting from the Margins: The Coping Strategies of Black Women and Other Women of Color Faculty Members at a Research University." *Journal of Negro Education* 70, no. 3:166–175.

Holub, Renate. 1992. *Antonio Gramsci: Beyond Marxism and Postmodernism*. London: Routledge.

Homo-Delgado, Asuncion, Diana Ortega, Nina M. Scott, and Nancy Sternbach, eds. 1989. *Breaking Boundaries: Latina Writing and Critical Readings*. Amherst: University of Massachusetts Press.

hooks, bell. 1981. *Ain't I a Woman: Black Women and Feminism*. Boston: South End.

―――. 1984. *Feminist Theory: From Margin to Center*. Boston: South End.

―――. 1989. *Talking Back: Thinking Feminist, Thinking Black*. Boston: South End.

―――. 1990. *Yearning: Race, Gender, and Cultural Politics*. Boston: South End.

Hurtado, Aida. 1981. "Relating to Privilege: Seduction and Rejection in the Subordination of White Women and Women of Color." In *Signs: Journal of Women in Culture and Society* 14, no. 4:833–855.

―――. 2003. *Voicing Chicana Feminisms: Young Women Speak Out on Sexuality and Identity*. New York: NYU Press.

Jaggar, Alison M. 2000. "Globalizing Feminist Ethics." In *Decentering the Center*, ed. Uma Narayan and Sandra Harding. Bloomington: Indiana University Press.

Jameson, Fredric. 1998. Preface, *The Cultures of Globalization*, ed. Fredric Jameson and Masao Miyoshi. Durham, NC: Duke University Press.

Jardin, Alice. 1985. *Gynesis: Configurations of Woman and Modernity*. Ithaca, NY: Cornell University Press.

Jargose, Ana Marie 1996. *Queer Theory: An Introduction*. New York: NYU Press.

Jones, Kathleen. 1988. "On Authority: Or Why Women Are Not Entitled to Speak." In *Feminism and Foucault: Reflections on Resistance*, ed. Irene Diamond and Lee Quinby. Boston: Northeastern University Press.

Joseph, Nathan. 1986. *Uniforms and Nonuniforms: Communication Through Clothing*. New York: Greenwood.

Juergensmeyer, Mark. 2002. "Paradox of Nationalism in a Global World." In *Postnationalism Self: Belonging and Identity*, ed. Ulf Hedetoft and Metter Hjort. Minneapolis: University of Minnesota Press.

Kaplan, Caren, Norma Alarcón, and Minoo Moallem, eds. 1999. *Between Woman and Nation: Nationalism, Transnational Feminisms, and the State*. Durham, NC: Duke University Press.

Kirsch, Max H. 2000. "Capitalism and Its Transgressors." In *Queer Theory and Social Change*. New York: Routledge.

Kondo, Dorinne K. 1990. *Crafting Selves: Power, Gender, and Discourse of Identity in a Japanese Workplace*. Chicago: University of Chicago Press.

―――. 1997. *About Face: Performing Race in Fashion and Theatre*. New York: Routledge.

Laclau, Ernesto, and Chantal Mouffe. 1985. *Hegemony and Socialist Strategy: Toward a Radical Democratic Politics*. London: Verso.

Lamas, Marta. 1991. "Identity as Women?: The Dilemma of Latin American

Feminism." In *Being America: Essays on Art, Literature, and Identity from Latin America*, ed. Rachel Weiss and Alan West. New York: White Pine.

Leal, Luis. 1979. "The Problem of Identifying Chicano Literature." In *The Identification and Analysis of Chicano Literature*, ed. Francisco Jiménez. New York: Bilingual.

Lewis, Reina. 1997. "Looking Good: The Lesbian Gaze and Fashion Imagery." Special issue, "Consuming Cultures," *Feminist Review* 55 (Spring): 92–109.

Lipsitz, George. 1986–1987. "Cruising Around the Historical Bloc: Postmodernism and Popular Music in East Los Angeles." *Cultural Critique* 5 (Winter): 157–177.

Liu, David Palumbo, ed. *Ethnic Canon: Histories, Institutions, and Interventions*. Minneapolis: University of Minnesota Press.

Liu, Lydia. 1994. "The Female Body and Nationalist Discourse: The Field of Life and Death Revisited." In *Scattered Hegemonies: Postmodernity and Transnational Feminist Practices*. Minnesota: University of Minnesota Press.

Lloyd, David. 1993. *Anomalous States: Irish Writing and the Postcolonial Moment*. Durham, NC: Duke University Press.

Lomas, Clara. 1989. "Mexican Precursors of Chicana Feminist Writing." In *Multiethnic Literature in the US: Critical Introductions and Classroom Resources*, ed. Cordelia Candelaria. Boulder: University of Colorado Press.

Longeaux y Vásquez, Eriqueta. 1969. "The Women of La Raza." *El Grito del Norte* 2 (July): 8–9.

———. 1970. "The Mexican American Woman." In *Sisterhood Is Powerful*, ed. Robin Morgan. New York: Vintage.

———. 1971. "Soy Chicana Primero." *El Grito del Norte* 4 (April): 11.

Lopez, Sonia A. 1977. "The Role of the Chicana in the Student Movement." In *Essays on La Mujer*, ed. Rosaura Sanchez and Rosa Martinez Cruz. Los Angeles: Chicano Studies Center Publications, University of California.

Lorde, Audre. 1982. *Zami: A New Spelling of My Name*. Trumansburg, NY: Crossing.

———. 1984. *Sister/Outsider*. Trumansburg, NY: Crossing.

Lowe, Lisa. 1996. *Immigrant Acts: On Asian American Cultural Politics*. Durham, NC: Duke University Press.

Lugones, Maria, and Elizabeth Spelman. 1986. "Have We Got a Theory for You! Feminist Theory, Cultural Imperialism, and the Demand for 'The Woman's Voice.'" In *Women and Values: Readings in Recent Feminist Philosophy*, ed. Marilyn Pearsall. Belmont, CA: Wadsworth.

———. 1990. "Playfulness, 'World' Traveling, and Loving Perception." In *Making Face, Making Soul*, ed. Anzaldúa.

Lyotard, Jean-François. 1984. *The Postmodern Condition: A Report on Knowledge*. Minneapolis: University of Minnesota Press.

Macias, Anna. 1982. *Against All Odds: The Feminist Movement in Mexico to 1940*. Westport, CT: Greenwood.

Maffesoli, Michel. 1993. "Identification or The Pluralisation of the Person." *Journal of Homosexuality* 25, no. 1:31–40.

Mani, Lata. 1990. "Multiple Mediations: Feminist Scholarship in the Age of Multinational Reception." In *Feminist Review* 35 (Summer): 24–41.

Marcus, George E., and Michael M. J. Fisher. 1986. *Anthropology as Cultural Critique: An Experimental Moment in the Human Sciences*. Chicago: University of Chicago Press.

Marin, Marguerite. 1980. "Protest in an Urban Barrio: A Study of the Chicano Movement." Ph.D. diss., University of California, Santa Barbara.

Mariscal, Jorge. 2005. *Brown-Eyed Children of the Sun: Lessons from the Chicano Movement: 1965–1975*. Albuquerque: University of New Mexico Press.

Marquez, Evelina, and Margarita Ramirez. 1977. "Women's Task Is to Gain Liberation." In *Essays on La Mujer*, ed. Sanchez and Martinez Cruz.

Martin, Biddy, and Chandra Talpade Mohanty. 1986. "Feminist Politics: What's Home Got to Do With It?" In *Feminist Studies/Critical Studies*, ed. de Lauretis.

Martínez, Elizabeth. 1972. "The Chicana." *Ideal* 44:1–3.

———. 1990. "Chingon Politics Die Hard: Reflections on the First Chicano Activist Reunion." *Z Magazine*, April, 46–50.

———. 1992. *500 Años del Pueblo Chicano/500 Years of Chicano History in Pictures*. Albuquerque, NM: Southwest Organizing Project.

———. 1997. "Viva la Chicana and All Brave Women of La Causa." In *Chicana Feminist Thought. The Basic Historical Writings*, ed. Alma García. New York: Routledge. Originally printed in *El Grito del Norte*, 1971.

Martinez, Oscar J., ed. 1996. *U.S.-Mexico Borderlands: Historical and Contemporary Perspectives*. Wilmington, DE: Jaguar.

Mazón, Mauricio. 1984. *The Zoot-Suit Riots: The Psychology of Symbolic Annihilation*. Berkeley: University of California Press.

McClintock, Anne. 1995. *Imperial Leather: Race, Gender, and Sexuality in the Colonial Contest*. New York: Routledge.

McKenna, Teresa. 1990. "Intersections of Race, Class, and Gender: The Feminist Pedagogical Challenge." *Pacific Coast Philology* 25, no. 1/2:31–38.

Melville, Margarita, ed. 1980. *Twice a Minority: Mexican American Women*. St. Louis, MO: C. V. Mosby.

Mendoza, Breny. 2002. "Transnational Feminisms in Question." *Feminist Theory* 3, no. 3:295–314.

Mignolo, Walter. 2000. *Local Histories/Global Designs: Coloniality, Subaltern Knowledges, and Border Thinking*. Princeton, NJ: Princeton University Press.

Millett, Kate. 1978. *Sexual Politics*. New York: Ballantine.

Mirandé, Alfredo. 1979. "A Reinterpretation of Male Dominance in the Chicano Family." *Family Coordinator* 28, no. 4:473–479.

Mirandé, Alfredo, and Evangelina Enríquez. 1979. *La Chicana. The Mexican American Woman*. Chicago and London: Chicago University Press.

Mixon, J. Wilson, and Noel D. Uri. 1991. "Effects of US Affirmative Action Programs in Women's Employment." *Journal of Policy Modeling* 13:367–382.

Miyoshi, Masao. 1993. "Borderless World? From Colonialism to Transnationalism and the Decline of the Nation-State." *Critical Inquiry* 20, no. 4 (Summer): 726–751.

Moallem, Minoo. 1999. "Transnationalism, Feminism, and Fundamentalism." In *Between Woman and Nation*, ed. Kaplan, Alarcón, and Moallem.

Mohanty, Chandra Talpade. 1991. "Cartographies and Struggle: Third World Women and the Politics of Feminism." In *Third World Women and the Politics of Feminism*, ed. Mohanty, Russo, and Torres.

Mohanty, Chandra Talpade, Ann Russo, and Lourdes Torres, eds. 1991. *Third World Women and the Politics of Feminism*. Bloomington: Indiana University Press.

Montejano, David. 1987. *Anglos and Mexicans in the Making of Texas 1836–1986*. Austin: University of Texas Press.

Mora, Magdalena, and Adelaida del Castillo, eds. 1980. *Mexican Women in the United States: Struggles Past and Present*. Los Angeles: Chicano Studies Center, University of California.

Moraga, Cherríe. 1983. *Loving in the War Years: Lo Que Nunca Pasó por Sus Labios*. Boston: South End.

———. 1986. "From a Long Line of Vendidas: Chicanas and Feminism." In *Feminist Studies, Critical Studies*, ed. de Lauretis.

———. 1987. *Giving Up the Ghost*. Los Angeles: West End.

———. 1993. *The Last Generation*. Boston: South End.

Moraga, Cherríe, and Gloria Anzaldúa, eds. 1981. *This Bridge Called My Back: Writings by Radical Women of Color*. Watertown, MA: Persephone.

Moya, Paula. 1997. "Postmodernism, 'Realism' and the Politics of Identity." In *Feminist Genealogies*, ed. Jacqui Alexander and Chandra Talpade Mohanty. New York: Routledge.

Muñoz, Carlos Jr. 1989. *Youth, Identity, and Power: The Chicano Movement*. London: Verso.

Muñoz, José Esteban. 1999. *Disidentifications: Queers of Color and the Performance of Politics*. Minneapolis: University of Minnesota Press.

Namaste, Ki. 1993. "Deconstruction, Lesbian and Gay Studies, and Interdisciplinary Work: Theoretical, Political, and Institutional Strategies." *Journal of Homosexuality* 24, no. 1/2:50–63.

Nardi, Peter M. 2001. "The Mainstream of Lesbian and Gay Studies?" *Handbook of Lesbian and Gay Studies*, ed. Diane Richardson and Steven Seidman. Thousand Oaks, CA: Sage.

Nathan, Debbie. 1991. *Women and Other Aliens: Essays from the U.S.-Mexican Border*. El Paso, TX: Cinco Puntos.

National Association for Chicano Studies (NACS). *Voces de la mujer*. 1986. Austin: Mexican American Studies Center, University of Texas.

Nestle, Joan. 1992. *Persistent Desire: A Femme Butch Reader.* Boston: Alyson.

Nicholson, Linda J., ed. 1997. *The Second Wave: A Reader in Feminist Theory.* New York: Routledge.

Nieto Gómez, Anna. 1971. "Hijas de Cuauhtemoc." *Regeneración* 1, no. 10.

———. 1973. "Las Feminists." In *Encuentro Feminil* 1:34–37.

Nieto Gómez, Anna, and Elma Barrera. 1975. "Chicana Encounter." *Regeneración* 2, no. 4.

Nietzsche, Friedrich Wilhelm. 1968. *The Will to Power.* New York: Vintage.

———. 1996. *On the Genealogy of Morals: A Polemic.* Trans. Douglas Smith. Oxford, England: Oxford University Press. Originally published in 1887.

Noriega, Chon, ed. 1992. *Chicanos and Film: Representation and Resistance.* Minneapolis: University of Minnesota Press.

Nuñez-Neto, Blas. 2006. *Border Security: The Role of the U.S. Border Patrol.* Washington, DC: Congressional Research Service.

Ogbar, Jeffrey O. G. 2004. *Black Power and African American Identity.* Baltimore, MD: Johns Hopkins University Press.

Olivarez, Elizabeth. 1975. "Women's Rights and the Mexican American Woman" In *Regeneración* 2, no. 4:40–42.

Oliver, Lawrence J. 1991. "Deconstruction or Affirmative Action: The Literary-Political Debate over the 'Ethnic' Question." *American Literary History* 3, no. 4:792–808.

Omi, Michael, and Howard Winant. 1994. *Racial Formation in the United States: From the 1960's to the 1990's.* New York: Routledge.

Orendain, Melanie. 1974. "Sexual Taboo y La Cultura" In *Imágenes de la mujer,* ed. Rita Sanchez. Menlo Park, CA: Nowels.

Orozco, Cynthia. 1984. "Chicana Labor History: A Critique of Male Consciousness in Historical Writing." *La Red/The Net,* no. 77:2–5.

———. 1986. "Sexism in Chicano Studies and the Community." In *Chicana Voices,* ed. Córdova et al.

———. 1990. "Getting Started in Chicana Studies." *Women's Studies Quarterly* 18, nos. 1–2:46–69.

———. 1995. "Beyond Machismo, La Familia, and Ladies Auxiliaries: A Historiography of Mexican-Origin Women's Participation in the United States, 1870–1990." In *Mexican American Women Changing Images,* ed. Juan R. Garcia. Tucson: Mexican American Studies and Research Center, University of Arizona.

Orozco, Yolanda. 1976. "La Chicana and 'Women's Liberation.'" *Voz Fronteriza,* January 6, 12.

Ortíz, Ricardo L. 1999. "Revolution's Other Histories: The Sexual, Cultural, and Critical Legacies of Roberto Fernandez Retamar's 'Caliban,'" *Social Text* 58 (Spring): 33–58.

Page, Donna. 1971. "Chicanos Meet Indo-Chinese." *El Grito del Norte* 4, no. 4/5: K.

Pardo, Mary. 1998. *Mexican American Women Activists: Identity and Resistance in Two Los Angeles Communities.* Philadelphia: Temple University Press.

Paredes, Américo. 1978. "On Ethnographic Work Among Minority Groups: A Folklorist's Perspective." In *New Directions in Chicano Scholarship,* ed. Ricardo Romo and Raymond Paredes. San Diego: University of California.

Paredes, Raymond. 1992. "Autobiography and Ethnic Politics: Richard Rodriguez' *Hunger of Memory.*" In *Multicultural Autobiography: American Lives,* ed. James Robert Payne. Knoxville: University of Tennessee Press.

Parker, Andrew, Mary Russo, Doris Sommer, and Patricia Yeager, eds. 1992. *Nationalism and Sexualities.* New York: Routledge.

Parkins, Wendy. 2002. *Fashioning the Body Politic: Dress, Gender, and Citizenship.* New York: Berg.

Pascoe, Peggy. 1993. *Relations of Rescue: The Search for Female Moral Authority in the American West 1874–1939.* New York: Oxford University Press.

Pateman, Carole. 1988. *The Sexual Contract.* Stanford, CA: Stanford University Press.

Payne, James Robert. 1992. *Multicultural Autobiography: American Lives.* Knoxville: University of Tennessee Press.

Pease, Donald. 2001. "The Politics of Postnational American Studies." *European Journal of American Studies* 20, no. 2:78–90.

Perea, Juan, ed. 1997. *Immigrants Out: The New Nativism and the Anti-Immigrant Sentiment Impulse in the United States.* New York: NYU Press.

Pérez, Emma. 1991. "Sexuality and Discourse: Notes from a Chicana Survivor." In *Chicana Lesbians,* ed. Trujillo.

———. 1993. "'She Has Served Others in More Intimate Ways': The Domestic Service Reform in Yucatan, 1915–18." *Aztlán* 20, nos. 1–2:11-33.

———. 1999. *The Decolonial Imaginary: Writing Chicanas into History.* Bloomington: Indiana University Press.

Pérez-Torres, Rafael. 1995. *Movements in Chicano Poetry: Against Myths, Against Margins.* New York: Cambridge University Press.

Pesquera, Beatriz, and Denise Segura. 1990. "Beyond Indifference and Antipathy: The Chicana Movement and Chicana Feminist Discourse." *Aztlán* 19, no. 2:69–92.

Phelan, Shane. 1992. *Identity Politics: Lesbian Feminism and the Limits of Community.* Philadelphia: Temple University Press.

———. 1993. "Becoming Out: Lesbian Identity and Politics," *Signs: Journal of Women in Culture and Society* 18, no. 4 (Summer): 765–814.

———. 2001. *Sexual Strangers: Gays, Lesbians, and the Dilemmas of Citizenship.* Philadelphia: Temple University Press.

Pierce, Jennifer L., and Denise A. Segura. 1993. "Chicana/o Family Structure and Gender Personality: Chodorow, Familism, and Psychoanalytic Sociology Revisited." *Signs: Journal of Women in Culture and Society* 19, no. 1:62–91.

Porter, Carolyn. 1988. "Are We Being Historical Yet?" *South Atlantic Quarterly* 21, no. 2:743–786.

Portes, Alejandro, and Rubén Rumbaut. 1990. *Immigrant America: A Portrait.* Berkeley: University of California Press.

Quintana, Alvina. 1987. "Challenge and Counter Challenge: Chicana Literary Motifs." *Against the Current* 2, no. 2:25–32.

———. 1996. *Home Girls: Chicana Literary Voices.* Philadelphia: Temple University Press.

Raat, Dirik. 1996. *Mexico and the United States: Ambivalent Vistas.* Athens: University of Georgia Press.

Reagon, Bernice Johnson. 1983. "Coalition Politics: Turning the Century." In *Home Girls: A Black Feminist Anthology*, ed. Barbara Smith. New York: Kitchen Table.

Rebolledo, Tey Diana. 1990. "The Politics of Poetics: Or, What Am I, a Critic, Doing in This Text Anyhow?" In *Making Face, Making Soul*, ed. Anzaldúa.

Rendon, Armando B. 1972. *Chicano Manifesto.* New York: Collier Macmillan.

Rich, Adrienne. 1995. "Compulsory Heterosexuality and Lesbian Existence." In *Professions of Desire: Lesbian and Gay Studies in Literature*, ed. George Haggerty and Bonnie Zimmerman. New York: Modern Language Association.

Rincón, Bernice. 1971. "La Chicana: Her Role in the Past and Her Search for a New Role in the Future." *Regeneración* 1, no. 10:15–17.

Rivera, Tomás. 1990. *Y no se lo tragó la tierra/And the Earth Did Not Part.* Houston: Arte Público.

Rocco, Raymond. 1990. "The Theoretical Construction of the 'Other' in Postmodernist Thought: Latinos in the New Urban Political Economy." *Cultural Studies* 4, no. 3:321–331.

Rodríguez, Juana María. 2003. *Queer Latinidad: Identity Practices, Discursive Spaces.* New York: NYU Press.

Rodriguez, Richard. 1983. *Hunger of Memory: The Education of Richard Rodríguez.* New York: Bantam.

Rodriguez, Richard T. 2007. "Imagine a Brown Queer: Inscribing Sexuality in Chicano/a-Latino/a Literary and Cultural Studies." *American Quarterly* 59, no. 2 (June): 493–501.

Root, Regina. 2005. "Tailoring the Nation: Fashion Writing in 19th Century Argentina." In *Fashioning the Body Politic: Dress, Gender and Citizenship*, ed. Wendy Perkins. New York: Oxford University Press.

Roque, Horacio. 2005. "A Living Archive of Desire: Teresita la Campesina and the Embodiment of Queer Latino Community Histories." In *Archive Stories: Facts, Fictions, and the Writing of History.* Durham, NC: Duke University Press.

Rosaldo, Renato. 1986. "When Natives Talk Back: Chicano Anthropology Since the Late 60's." In *Renato Rosaldo Lecture Series Monograph* 2:3–20. Tucson, AZ: Mexican-American Studies and Research Center.

————. 1993. "Notes Toward a Critique of Patriarchy from a Male Position." *Anthropological Quarterly* 66, no. 2:81–86.

Rose, Tricia. 1991. "Fear of a Black Planet: Rap Music and Black Cultural Politics in the 1990's." Special issue, "Socialization Forces Affecting the Education of African American Youth in the 1990s," *Journal of Negro Education* 60, no. 3:276–290.

Rowe, John Carlos. 1998. "Post-Nationalism, Globalism, and the New American Studies." Special issue, "The Futures of American Studies," *Cultural Critique*, no. 40 (Autumn): 11–28.

Rowlandson, Mary. 1682. *Sovereignty and Goodness of God: Together with the Faithfulness of Promises Displayed: Being of a Narrative of the Captivity and Restoration of Mrs. Mary Rowlandson.* Reprint c1997, Boston: Bedford.

Rubenstein, Ruth P. 2001. *Dress Codes: Meaning and Messages in American Culture.* New York: Westview.

Rueda, Catriona. 2006. *With Her Machete in Her Hand.* Austin: University of Texas Press.

Ruiz, Vicki L. 1987. *Cannery Women, Cannery Lives: Mexican Women, Unionization, and the California Food Processing Industry, 1930–1950.* Albuquerque: University of New Mexico Press.

————, ed. 2000. *Las Obreras: Chicana Politics of Work and Family.* Los Angeles: Aztlán Anthology Series. Vol. 1.

Ruiz, Vicki L., and Susan Tiano, eds. 1987. *Women on the U.S.-Mexican Border: Responses to Change.* Winchester, MA: Allen and Unwin.

Saenz, Lionila Lopez. 1972. "Machismo ¡No! Igualdad ¡Sí!" *La Luz* 1, no. 2 (May).

Said Edward. 1978. *Orientalism.* New York: Pantheon.

————. 1983. *The World, the Text, and the Critic.* Cambridge: Harvard University Press.

————. 1985. *Beginnings: Intention and Method.* New York: Columbia University Press.

————. 1993. *Culture and Imperialism.* New York: Knopf.

Saldaña-Portillo, María Josefina. 2003. *The Revolutionary Imagination in the Americas and the Age of Globalization.* Durham, NC: Duke University Press.

Saldívar, José David. 1991. *The Dialectics of Our America.* Durham, NC: Duke University Press.

————. 1997. *Border Matters: Remapping American Cultural Studies.* Berkeley: University of California Press.

Saldívar, Ramón. 1990a. *Chicano Narrative: The Dialectics of Difference.* Madison: University of Wisconsin Press.

————. 1990b. "Narrative, Ideology, and the Reconstruction of the American Literary History." In *Criticism in the Borderlands,* ed. Calderón and Saldívar.

Saldívar-Hull, Sonia. 1991. "Feminism on the Border: From Gender Politics to Geopolitics." In *Criticism in the Borderlands,* ed. Calderón and Saldívar.

————. 2000. *Feminism on the Border: Chicana Gender Politics and Literature.* Berkeley: University of California Press.

Sanchez, Corrine. 1973. "Higher Education y la Chicana?" *Encuentro Femenil* 1.

Sanchez, Marta Ester. 1985. "The Birthing of the Poetic 'I' in Alma Villanueva's 'Mother May I?': The Search for a Feminine Identity." In *Beyond Stereotypes*, ed. Herrera-Sobek.

Sanchez, Rosaura. 1987. "Postmodernism and Chicano Literature." *Aztlán* 18, no. 2:1–14.

————. 1990. "Ethnicity, Ideology, and Academia." In *Cultural Studies* 4, no. 3 (October): 294–302.

Sanchez, Rosaura, and Rosa Martinez Cruz, eds. 1977. *Essays on La Mujer.* Los Angeles: Chicano Studies Center, University of California.

Sandoval, Chela. 1990. "Feminism and Racism: A Report on the 1981 National Women's Studies Association Conference." In *Making Face, Making Soul*, ed. Anzaldúa.

————. 1991. "U.S. Third World Feminism: The Theory and Method of Oppositional Consciousness in the Postmodern World." In *Genders* 10:1–23.

————. 2000. *Methodology of the Oppressed.* Minneapolis: University of Minnesota Press.

————. 2002. "Dissident Globalizations, Emancipatory Methods, Social-Erotics." In *Queer Globalizations*, ed. Cruz Malave and Martin Manalansan IV. New York: NYU Press.

Sassen, Saskia. 2001. *Global City.* New York: Princeton University Press.

Schacht, Richard, ed. 1994. *Essays on Nietzsche's* On the Genealogy of Morals. Berkeley: University of California Press.

Scott, Joan W. 1988. *Gender and the Politics of History.* New York: Columbia University Press.

————. 1992. "Multiculturalism and the Politics of Identity." *October* 61 (Summer): 12–19.

Scranton, Phillip. 2001. *Beauty and Business: Commerce, Gender, and Culture in Modern America.* New York: Routledge.

Sedgwick, Eve Kosovsky. 1990. *Epistemology of the Closet.* Berkeley: University of California Press.

Segura, Denise, and Beatriz Pesquera. 1990. "Beyond Indifference and Antipathy: The Chicana Movement and Chicana Feminist Discourse." *Aztlán* 19, no. 2:69–92.

Sharpe, Jenny. 2000. "Is the United States Postcolonial? Transnationalism, Immigration, and Race." In *Postcolonial America*, ed. C. Richard King. Urbana: University of Illinois.

Shohat, Ella. 1997. "Post Third Worldist Culture: Gender, Nation, and the Cinema." In *Feminist Genealogies, Colonial Legacies, Democratic Futures*, ed. Jacqui Alexander and Chandra Mohanty. New York: Routledge.

————. 2006. *Taboo Memories, Diasporic Voices.* Durham, NC: Duke University Press.

Sierra, Christine Marie. 1984. "Surveying the Latina Political Landscape." *Intercambios Femeniles* 2, no. 3:1–24.

Simon, David. 2004. "Men as Success Objects and Women as Sex Objects." In *Empirical Approaches to Sociology: A Collection of Classic and Contemporary Readings*, ed. Gregg Lee Carter. Boston: Pearson Education.

Smitherman, Geneva. 1997. "The Chain Remains the Same: Communicative Practices in the Hip Hop Nation." *Journal of Black Studies* 28, no. 1:3–25.

Sokal, Alan, and Jean Bricmont. 1998. *Fashionable Nonsense: Postmodern Intellectual Abuse of Science.* New York: Picador.

Somerville, Siobahn. 1994. "Scientific Racism and the Emergence of the Homosexual Body." *Journal of the History of Sexuality* 5, no. 2:243–266.

Sommers, Joseph. 1978. "From the Critical Premise to the Product: Critical Modes and Their Applications to a Chicano Literary Text." In *New Directions in Chicano Scholarship*, ed. Ricardo Romo and Raymond Paredes. La Jolla: Chicano Studies Program, University of California, San Diego.

Sosa Riddell, Adaljiza. 1974. "Chicanas and El Movimiento." *Aztlán: Chicano Journal of the Social Sciences and the Arts* 5, nos. 1–2 (Spring–Fall): 155–165.

Sotello, Caroline, and Viernes Turner. 2002. "Women of Color in Academe: Living with Multiple Marginality." Special issue, "The Faculty in the Millennium," *Journal of Higher Education* 73, no. 1:74–93.

Spellman, Elizabeth. 1988. *Inessential Woman: Problems of Exclusion in Feminist Thought.* Boston: Beacon.

Spivak, Gayatri Chakravorty. 1987. *In Other Worlds: Essays in Cultural Politics.* New York: Methuen.

————. 1988. "Can the Subaltern Speak?" In *Marxism and the Interpretation of Culture*, ed. Cary Nelson and Lawrence Grossberg. Chicago: University of Illinois Press.

————. 1990. *The Post-Colonial Critic: Interviews, Strategies, Dialogues.* New York: Routledge.

————. 1993. *Outside in the Teaching Machine.* London: Routledge.

Springer, Kimberley 2001. "Black Feminist Organizations and the Emergence of Interstitial Politics." In *Modern American Queer History*, ed. Allida M. Black. Philadelphia: Temple University Press.

Staten, Henry. 1998. "Authenticity, Class, and Autobiography: The Case of *Hunger of Memory*." Special Series on Ethnicity. *PMLA* 113, no. 1 (January): 103–116.

Steiner, Stan. 1970. *La Raza: The Mexican Americans.* New York: Harper and Row.

Streeby, Shelly. 2002. *American Sensations: Class, Empire, and the Production of Popular Culture.* Berkeley: University of California Press.

Suarez, Cecilia. 1973. "Sexual Stereotype—Psychological and Cultural Survival." *Regeneración* 2, no. 3.

Surace, Samuel J., and Ralph H. Turner. 1956. "Zoot-Suiters and Mexicans: Symbols in Crowd Behavior." *American Journal of Sociology* 62, no. 1:14–20.

Tafolla, Carmen. 1985b. *To Split a Human: Mitos, Machos y la Mujer Chicana*. San Antonio, TX: Mexican American Cultural Center.

Terry, Jennifer. 1991. "Theorizing Deviant Historiography." Special issue, "Queer Theory," *Differences: A Journal of Feminist Cultural Studies* 3, no. 2 (Summer): 55–74.

Tessler, Suzanne. 1976. "Compulsatory Sterilization Practices." In *Frontiers: A Journal of Women Studies* 1, no. 2:52–66.

Tohidi, Nayereh. 1991. "Gender and Islamic Fundamentalism." In *Third World Women*, ed. Mohanty, Russo, and Torres.

Torres, Eden. 2003. *Chicana Without Apology: Chicana Sin Verguenza*. New York: Routledge.

Trinh, Minh-ha T. 1989. *Woman, Native, Other: Writing Postcoloniality and Feminism*. Bloomington: Indiana University Press.

Trujillo, Armando. 1998. *Tejano Legacy: Ranchers and Settlers in South Texas, 1734–1900*. Albuquerque: University of New Mexico Press.

Trujillo, Carla, ed. 1991. *Chicana Lesbians: The Girls Our Mothers Warned Us About*. Berkeley, CA: Third Woman.

———. 1998a. "La Virgen de Guadalupe and Her Reconstruction in Chicana Lesbian Desire." In *Living Chicana Theory*, ed. Trujillo.

———, ed. 1998b. *Living Chicana Theory*. Berkeley, CA: Third Woman.

Turner, Frederick Jackson. 1883. Essay. Reprinted 1947 as "The Significance of the Frontier in American History" in *The Frontier in American History*, New York: Henry Holt.

Vaid, Urvashi. 1995. *Virtual Equality: The Mainstreaming of American Gay and Lesbian Liberation*. New York: Anchor.

Vandeveyer, Claude. 1992. "Homosexuals and AIDS: New Approaches to the Illness." *Journal of Homosexuality* 25, no. 3:319–327.

Vasconcelos, José. 1979. *La raza cósmica*. Trans. Didier T. Jaen. Pensamiento Mexicano 1. Los Angeles: Centro de Publicaciones.

Vigota, Mara Viveros. 2003. "Contemporary Latin American Perspectives on Masculinity." In *Changing Men and Masculinities in Latin America*, ed. Gutmann.

Villareal, Antonio. 1958. *Pocho*. Garden City, NY: Doubleday.

Visweswaran, Kamala. 1994a. "Betrayal: An Analysis in Three Acts." In *Scattered Hegemonies*, ed. Grewal and Kaplan.

———. 1994b. *Fictions of Feminist Ethnography*. Minneapolis: University of Minnesota Press.

Warnock, John. 1995. *The Other Mexico: The North American Triangle Completed*. New York: Black Rose.

Weeks, Jeffrey. 1981. *Sex Politics and Society. The Regulation of Sexuality since 1800*. 2nd edition. London: Longman.

Wiegman, Robyn. 2002. "The Progress of Gender: Whither 'Women.'" In *Women's Studies on Its Own*, ed. Wiegman. Durham, NC: Duke University.

———. 2005. "The Possibility of Women's Studies." In *The Future of Women's Studies: Foundation, Interrogations, Politics*, ed. Liz Lapovsky Kennedy and Agatha Beins. Piscataway, NJ: Rutgers University Press.

West, Cornel. 1993a. *Beyond Eurocentrism and Multiculturalism*. Monroe, ME: Common Courage.

———. 1993b. *Race Matters*. Boston: Beacon.

Williams, Raymond. 1976. *Keywords: A Vocabulary of Culture and Society*. Oxford, England: Oxford University Press.

———. 1989. *The Politics of Modernism*. London: Verso.

Wing, Adrienne Katherine, ed. 2000. *Global Feminism: An International Reader*. New York: NYU Press.

Woodhill, Winifred. 1993. *Transfigurations of the Maghreb: Feminism, Decolonization and Literatures*. Minneapolis: University of Minnesota Press.

Yarbro-Bejarano, Yvonne. 1986a. "Cherríe Moraga's Giving up the Ghost: The Representation of Female Desire." *Third Woman* 3, no. 1/2:113–120.

———. 1986b. "The Female Subject in Chicano Theatre: Sexuality, Race and Class." *Theatre Journal* 38, no. 4 (December): 389–407.

———. 1988. "Chicana Literature From a Chicana Feminist Perspective." In *Chicana Creativity and Criticism*, ed. Herrera-Sobek and Viramontes.

———. 1995a. "The Lesbian Body in Latina Cultural Production." In *Entiendes? Queer Readings, Hispanic Writings*, ed. Emilie L. Bergmann and Paul Julian Smith. Durham, NC: Duke University Press.

———. 1995b. "Expanding the Categories of Race and Sexuality in Lesbian and Gay Studies." In *Professions of Desire: Lesbian and Gay Studies in Literature*, ed. George Haggerty and Bonnie Zimmermann. New York: Modern Language Association.

Ybarra-Frausto, Tomás. 1977. "The Chicano Movement and the Emergence of a Chicano Poetic Consciousness." *New Scholar* 6:81–109.

———. 1990. "Rasquachismo: A Chicano Sensibility." In *Chicano Art*, ed. Griswold del Castillo, McKenna, and Yarbro-Bejarano.

Yuval-Davis, Nira, and Floya Anthias, eds. 1989. *Woman-Nation-State*. New York: St. Martin's.

Zavella, Patricia. 1987. *Women's Work and Chicano Families: Cannery Workers of the Santa Clara Valley*. Ithaca, NY: Cornell University Press.

———. 1988. "The Politics of Race, Class, and Gender: Organizing Chicana Cannery Workers in Northern California." In *Women and the Politics of Empowerment*, ed. Anna Bookman and Sandra Morgen. Philadelphia: Temple University Press.

———. 1989. "The Problematic Relationship of Feminism and Chicana Studies." *Women's Studies* 17:25–36.

Zinn, Maxine Baca. 1975a. "Chicanas: Power and Control in the Domestic Sphere." *De Colores* 2/3:19–31.

———. 1975b. "Political Familism: Toward Sex Role Equality in Chicano Families." *Aztlán* 6:13–27.

———. 1982. "Mexican American Women in the Social Sciences." *Signs: Journal of Women in Culture and Society* 8:259–272.

———. 1996. "Family, Feminism, and Race in America." In *Race, Class, and Gender: Common Bonds, Different Voices*, E. N. Altan, D. Wilkinson, and M. B. Zinn. Thousand Oaks, CA: Sage.

Zukin, Sharon. 1996. *The Culture of Cities*. New York: Blackwell.

INDEX